Praise for *The S[...]*

"Read this book at your own peril [...]
the way you think about money an[...]
everyone's birthright. A masterwor[...] [...]heart."

     —William Ury, founder of Harvard's
Program on Negotiation and coauthor of *Getting to Yes*

"Eloquently and passionately written, *The Soul of Money* describes how money can be a vehicle to fulfill our highest ideals of life and love and to discover new meanings in our lives. I recommend it highly."

 —Dean Ornish, M.D., Preventive Medicine Research Institute,
University of California, San Francisco

"Lynne Twist has a remarkable ability to cast spiritual light on the subject of money. This book is a rare gift."

          —Marianne Williamson,
author of *A Return to Love* and *Healing the Soul of America*

"Lynne Twist reveals how money can either plague or liberate our hearts. We used to think that nature was competitive and cruel. Due to recent brilliant science, we now see life as generous, mutualistic, and symbiotic. The same transformation of perception awaits us with regards to money. We made it up. What do we want it to be in our life? Lynne's own transformation guides us here to be fully present to unimaginable abundance in every sense of the word."

        —Paul Hawken, founder and
executive director of Project Drawdown;
author of *Blessed Unrest*

"Lynne Twist holds grandmother wisdom about a right relationship with money. Your soul will recognize the truths between these covers."   —Vicki Robin, coauthor of the
international bestseller *Your Money or Your Life*

"*The Soul of Money* helped me understand money not as good or evil, but rather as a resource for expressing our humanity into the world. For anyone who wants to improve their relationship with money, I could not recommend this book more highly."

       —Sam Polk, former hedge-fund trader and
founder of the nonprofit Groceryships

"*The Soul of Money* will completely shift how you view, talk about, earn, spend, give, invest, and relate to money. . . . As a financial advisor, I am certain that the path to real financial ease and success starts with mastering Lynne's ideas of sufficiency, generosity, and our connection to all human beings."
—Spencer Sherman, founder of Abacus Wealth Partners and author of *The Cure for Money Madness*

"*The Soul of Money* is a groundbreaking book that will reshape your relationship with money in a way that is unique, visionary, and consistent with the new future we all dream of. . . . [This] book is for any businessperson who is awake enough to see how important business can be to create a powerful future."
—Heidi Roizen, venture capitalist, technology spokesperson, and cofounder of T/Maker

"[A] must read book for those who regard asset accumulation as a necessary evil, and philanthropy merely an easy way to reduce taxes. Written by a professional who understands how to make philanthropy more enjoyable, this book will greatly benefit investors, fundraisers, philanthropists, and successful laymen who want to make the world a better place."
—Alan B. Slifka, Halcyon/Alan B Slifka Management Funds, The Abraham Fund Initiatives, The Coexistence Initiative

"*The Soul of Money* shows with exquisite sensitivity that the way we treat ourselves and the way we treat our money are two sides of the same coin. Lynne Twist puts the magic back in money by understanding that it is a form of energy with which we can perform miracles."
—James Garrison, president, State of the World Forum

"Lynne Twist is a creative artist, who generously shows us how to give the gift of giving and through this process, realize our deepest dreams. *The Soul of Money* is a *must* read for anyone who wants to make a difference."
—Michael Toms, New Dimensions World Broadcasting Network and author of *A Time for Choices: Deep Dialogues for Deep Democracy*

"This is a beautiful, surprising book, rich with practical advice, inspiring stories and wisdom. *The Soul of Money* will transform your relationship to money and heal and delight your soul."
—James S. Gordon, M.D., Center for Mind-Body Medicine; author of *Manifesto for a New Medicine*; President's Commission on Complementary Medicine

"Lynne Twist's eloquent book, *The Soul of Money*, is an indispensable resource for all those interested in transforming their relationship with money and its influence in their lives. It sheds much light on this critically important subject at just the right time." —Charles A. Garfield, Ph.D., author of *Peak Performers*; University of California Medical School, San Francisco

"*The Soul of Money* is a long overdue wake-up call for the transformation of ourselves and our world to peace, harmony, and abundance for all."
—Robert Muller, former UN Assistant Secretary General and cofounder of the UN University for Peace in Costa Rica

"I want to warn you, your life will not be the same after you pick up this book. *The Soul of Money* delivers a message that will move, inspire, and touch your soul so deeply that you will not be able to live your life in the same way." —Paul Dolan, president, Fetzer Vineyards, Hopland, California

"What a truly great book! Profound, passionate, and practical. If sanity around money were a virtue, Lynne Twist would be a saint."
—John Robbins, author of *The Food Revolution* and *Diet for a New America*; founder of EarthSave International

"Lynne's journey into the soul of money can teach us all how to reclaim the sacred with our money."
—Theodore J. Mallon, businessman, philanthropist, and author of *The Journey Toward Masterful Philanthropy*

"Lynne has taken the topic that occupies us most—money—and turned it into a profound spiritual teaching of enormous practicality."
—Margaret Wheatley, author of *Leadership and the New Science* and *Turning to One Another*

THE SOUL OF MONEY

THE SOUL OF MONEY

Reclaiming the Wealth of Our Inner Resources

Lynne Twist

with Teresa Barker

Foreword by Jack Canfield

W. W. Norton & Company
Independent Publishers Since 1923
New York   London

Copyright © 2017, 2003 by Lynne Twist
Foreword copyright © 2017 by Jack Canfield

For information about permission to reproduce selections from this book, write to
Permissions, W. W. Norton & Company, Inc., 500 Fifth Avenue, New York, NY 10110

For information about special discounts for bulk purchases, please contact
W. W. Norton Special Sales at specialsales@wwnorton.com or 800-233-4830

Manufacturing by LSC Harrisonburg
Book design by Brooke Koven
Production manager: Amanda Morrison

The Library of Congress has cataloged an earlier edition as follows:

Twist, Lynne.
The soul of money : transforming your relationship with money and life /
by Lynne Twist with Teresa Barker.—1st ed.
p. cm.
Includes bibliographical references.
ISBN 0-393-05097-1 (hardcover)
1. Money—Psychological aspects. 2. Money. 3. Conduct of life.
I. Barker, Teresa. II. Title.
HG222.3.T855 2003
332.4'01'9—dc21

2003008423

ISBN: 978-0-393-35397-6 pbk.

W. W. Norton & Company, Inc., 500 Fifth Avenue, New York, N.Y. 10110
www.wwnorton.com

W. W. Norton & Company Ltd., 15 Carlisle Street, London W1D 3BS

8 9 0

This book is dedicated to my grandchildren,
Ayah, Isa, and Ibrahim,
who embody the beauty, love, and possibility
I see for the world.

—LYNNE TWIST

CONTENTS

ACKNOWLEDGMENTS

It took a village to write this book and its reissue. It would not have been possible without the support, participation, collaboration, and generosity of many, many people.

I want to acknowledge my brilliant collaborative writer, Teresa Barker. Her keen intelligence, deep partnership, and sturdy professionalism made what you are about to read possible.

My remarkable literary agent, Gail Ross, encouraged me years ago in a way that transformed the idea of writing this book into a reality. She has stayed with me and supported me every step of the way.

My editors at W. W. Norton, Angela von der Lippe and Amy Cherry, brought wisdom, graceful intelligence, and years of experience to each page. They managed the complex process of turning a manuscript into a book of which both W. W. Norton and I could be proud.

More than twenty years of experience with The Hunger Project were the platform for much of what I have written here. My teacher and mentor during those years and for most of my adult life has been and will continue to be Joan Holmes, the former president of The Hunger Project. Her example, her brilliance, her integrity, and her unyielding commitment have in many ways forged and shaped who I am.

Other colleagues during my Hunger Project years were vital contributors to my understanding of money and how it relates to the deepest issues we face as a human community. John Coonrod, Carol Coonrod, Mike Wick, Franc Sloan, Tom Driscoll, Ted Howard, Dick Bishop, Jay Greenspan, Sherry Pettus, Catherine Parrish, Bill Parrish, Kendra Goldenway, Ronn Landsman, Mike Cook, Les Traband, Lee Traband, Larry Flynn, Raul Julia, Merel Julia, Janet Schreiber, Fay Freed, Joe Friedman, Dana Carman, Jane Shaw, Michael Frye, Tom Henrich, Gunnar Nilsson, Scott Paseltiner, Lalita Banavali, Naji Loynmoon, Fitigu Tadesse, Badiul Majumdar, Tazima Majumdar, Shingo Nomura, Mikio Uekusa, Hiroshi Ohuchi, Ian Watson, Peter Bourne, John Denver, Robert Chester, Annetta Chester, Valerie Harper, Gordon Starr, Dianne Morrison, and countless others are all colleagues who have left a deep and profound imprint on my life and helped shape my perception of the world. The thousands of Hunger Project volunteers, activists, fund-raisers, and investors with whom I have worked over many years were both the laboratory and the inspiration for this message and to them I am deeply grateful.

I particularly want to acknowledge Faith Strong, who, as a woman, as a philanthropist, and as a partner in my work in the world, has taught me more than she will ever know.

My friend Tom Burt was my full partner in this endeavor, always encouraging me, inspiring me, and pushing me lovingly into the next space to have the vision of this book realized.

Neal Rogin, longtime friend and colleague, has always helped me find words for the inexpressible. Wink Franklin, president emeritus of the Institute of Noetic Sciences, helped me name this book and the work that it represents, as well as providing wise counsel for many years of my life. The encouragement of

Michael and Justine Toms to write this book was steadfast throughout the process. Michael's seminal interview with me on the Soul of Money was the launching pad for the book.

Years of partnership at the State of the World Forum with its president, Jim Garrison, gave me deep dimensions of global wisdom and access that have expanded my experience of the world.

Dave Ellis has been a wise and steady coach and counselor for two decades. Terry Axelrod has helped me sharpen my focus and deepen my understanding of the sacred work of fund-raising. Kristi Nelson provided incredible insight and wisdom for this book and co-founded the Soul of Money Institute with me. She embodies this message fully in every breath she takes. Brother David Steindl-Rast has been one of my most beloved teachers this lifetime and his example of grateful living continues to shape everything I am.

Midstream, in one of the most difficult parts of the writing process, my dear friend and fellow writer, Vicki Robin, encouraged me to apply to the Mesa Refuge writer's retreat and I was gifted with two precious weeks there by the founder and owner, Peter Barnes. Being at Point Reyes at that time was a vital turning point in making this book a reality. Thank you Vicki and Peter.

My friend and soul sister, Tracy Howard, has stood by me and for me since the day we met. The process of this book was no exception in our lifelong partnership.

To my colleagues on the boards of the Institute of Noetic Sciences, the Fetzer Institute, and the Pachamama Alliance, I owe a debt of gratitude for all that I have learned, all that I have been given, and for the grace and blessing of your wise counsel and friendship. Much of it is reflected in these pages.

To the members of the Turning Tide Coalition, this book is a tribute to each of you and the profound conversations we have shared.

Deep gratitude is due to the members of The Transformational Leadership Council (TLC), who have supported me and helped to spread this message and my work in the world far and wide to hundreds of thousands of people.

My Achuar brothers and sisters in the Ecuadorian Amazon and all the indigenous partners I have worked with in the Pachamama Alliance have become a part of who I am. The staff, members, and investors of the Pachamama Alliance are beacons of light in our world that embody the principles of what is written here.

Werner Erhard has been and continues to be one of the most brilliant teachers I have ever known. The programs and courses he created and the programs of Landmark Education have provided insights, distinctions, and the very context from which I live and see the world. For this and so much more, I am deeply grateful.

My dear friend, Jack Canfield, provided the perfect foreword for this message and has been a mentor and teacher to me since the day we met.

My sisters, Holly Madigan and Wendy Sadler, and my brother, Griff Williams, supported the process of this book completely and are a constant inspiration to me.

In this and in all things, my beloved colleagues at the Soul of Money Institute, Sara Vetter, Tammy White, Cait Steiner, Haley Hansel, and Torie White have been my allies and partners in the project to reissue this book. They bless my life and work with their capacity to serve and provide whatever is needed to fulfill our common vision.

Finally, I want to acknowledge my family: my mother and father, who were both brilliant examples of the best that a man and woman can be. My amazing adult children, Basil, Summer, and Zachary, who have allowed me the space to be myself their entire lives and continue to provide me with the inspiration to be the best person I can be. My daughter-in-law, Halima Nalo Afi, is a total blessing and my adopted "angel" daughter, Hafsat Abiola-Costello inspires me to my core. My five incredible and beautiful grandchildren—Ayah, Isa, Ibrahim, Jacqueline Joy, and Ivory Rose—absolutely light up my life every single day. The unconditional love we all share as a family is the pool from which I draw everything that is meaningful to me.

Last but most important of all, I am grateful to Bill Twist, my husband, soul mate, lifelong partner, and best friend, whose strength, stability, integrity, humor, and love is the source of everything precious in my life. His love and our extraordinary partnership of more than 50 years make anything and everything possible.

The many people around the world with whom I have had the privilege of working over the years are too numerous to mention by name, but are woven into the fabric of this book and its message. They know who they are and this book is intended to make available the love, wisdom, and sense of wonder that they have contributed to me.

—LT

In addition to the village Lynne describes, I want to express my gratitude to my husband, Steve, and our children, Aaron, Rachel, and Rebecca, and Dolly Joern, my beloved mother-in-law, for their generosity and enthusiasm in support of this work, and for the contribution of their own wisdom. As for Lynne, I will borrow from Maya Angelou to express my appreciation for our partnership and friendship: "When we give cheerfully and accept gratefully, everyone is blessed." And I am.

—THB

FOREWORD

I heard Lynne Twist share the message of *The Soul of Money* for the very first time in 2005 at a meeting of the Transformational Leadership Council (TLC) in Victoria, British Columbia. It was a stunning and life-altering experience for me.

I started the TLC years ago to gather together trainers, workshop leaders, coaches, authors, filmmakers, and others who were engaged in facilitating transformation so we could all learn from each other and keep our minds open and our hearts engaged in our own transformation.

Lynne, a global activist, fund-raiser, speaker, consultant, and author, had already dedicated decades of her life to global humanitarian and environmental initiatives, and it would have been easy for her to talk about all she'd seen that was wrong with the world. But she didn't. When Lynne spoke, and as she had written in *The Soul of Money*, it wasn't in opposition to anything. It was to share a way of understanding the world and our vast potential in it that was grounded in righting our relationship with money and life.

In her talk that day, and in the book you hold in your hands,

Lynne described the mindset of scarcity—the sense that we never have enough—and the Three Toxic Myths that keep us scrambling so desperately for more, when the real prosperity and satisfaction in life comes from the outlook and experience of sufficiency. When we align our relationship with money and our relationship with life through an experience of sufficiency, we invest every aspect of that relationship—how we earn, save, spend, or invest money—with soul, with a higher purpose that carries everything and everybody forward. Her message was truly a stunner for the audience that day at the TLC meeting. They had come to hone their professional skills and strategies for commercial success, and, before Lynne spoke, they had worked with some of the best leaders in the transformational business world that day. Lynne, however, provided an entirely different set of tools and a different foundation on which to live in a meaningful, truly satisfying relationship with money and life.

She talked about this experience of sufficiency, the sense of appreciation and "enoughness" that gives our lives meaning no matter what our circumstances. She talked about how, when we align our relationship with life and our relationship with money, we are empowered in unimaginable ways. I knew at a personal level that this was true; I had made my way from a painful, impoverished childhood to phenomenal success with the inspirational *Chicken Soup for the Soul* books, followed by the international bestseller *The Success Principles: How to Get from Where You Are to Where You Want to Be* and a new focus on the capacity for inspired leadership and success that is innate in each of us. Mine was a purpose-driven life and career, to be sure. But even so, Lynne's *Soul of Money* stories and principles opened up a new way of seeing everything I knew from my own experience, but from a deeper, more profound, and more authentic place than I had ever seen before.

This idea that our relationship with money so profoundly defines us—limits us or empowers us—really turned my head around. The entire conference audience was spellbound as well, many of them moved to tears. Participants told me afterward that Lynne's message was nothing short of transformational for them as they prepared to return to their work and lives.

Several years later I invited Lynne to speak at a business conference. This was an audience of CEOs and other senior leadership from about fifty large- and medium-sized American companies, ranging from financial services to consumer products. Lynne was something of an anomaly. She wasn't an executive—wasn't even a businessperson—and, as she would tell me later, felt she had no real reason to be there except that we had invited her. She was slated for a half-hour talk, but as she began to share her *Soul of Money* stories and principles, this audience of corporate executives was also spellbound. They clearly didn't want the session to end. So we extended her time, postponing lunch at everyone's request so these corporate leaders could ask Lynne questions and be in conversation with her. She responded to each question with a story from her travels and work alongside the so-called poorest and richest people on earth—from Mother Teresa to multibillionaires—transforming our understanding of their true assets and vulnerabilities, and the power each of us has to align money and soul for the greatest return on investment. Lynne concluded the conversation about scarcity and sufficiency to a standing ovation, unusual for this crowd. Again, it had been a revelation to the people there.

Lynne's ongoing commitment to bring together the global communities of business and of activists, nonprofits and others in what she calls the "social profit" sector, and have them work collaboratively, is something I admire, embrace, and support. As her book, her talks, and her vision of this rich, expansive partnership strikes that chord in the heart of who we are, I see anew how powerful her message is. Her message is the ready seed of transformation that, once planted in our hearts and souls, nourishes our essential relationship with money and our money culture.

Lynne has been a friend since our first encounter. And I have since partnered with her as a change-maker for a sustainable economic and environmental future for our planet. My wife and I have traveled to Ecuador with Lynne and her husband, Bill, to join in the work of the Pachamama Alliance, which they cofounded with indigenous partners to protect the Amazon rainforest. There in the rainforest I saw how deeply the natural world holds lessons to teach us about our relationship with money and our relationship with one another, and those themes are beautifully presented in this book.

For most of my life as a trainer and success coach I had defined success as *being able to produce whatever results you wanted in the world*. After meeting and working with Lynne, I changed my definition of success to *fulfilling your soul's purpose*. My soul's purpose, as I now understand it, is *to inspire and empower people to live their highest vision in a context of love and joy in harmony with the highest good of all concerned*. I added "in harmony with the highest good of all concerned" after the financial meltdown in 2009, because I believe if the people on Wall Street had been concerned with the highest good of all concerned rather than strictly their own personal greed based on fear and the mindset of scarcity, they never would have engaged in the actions that almost brought the whole world economy to its knees.

Because of Lynne's brilliant book and her broader work, my wife, Inga, and I have changed our relationship with money. We have become much more conscious of how we earn, spend, invest, donate, and steward our money. We are grateful to Lynne for the deeper sense of purpose and fulfillment we experience in all areas of our life.

The book you hold in your hands brings Lynne's unique and powerful message forward at a time when it is desperately needed. *The Soul of Money* is a timeless inspiration, blending unforgettable stories and soul-sourced principles from Lynne's decades of work in the trenches of activism to advance human rights, environmental protection, and a sustainable future for our children and generations to come. Whatever your circumstances may be today, the lessons Lynne shares in these pages will be a catalyst for greater wealth, greater contribution, greater meaning, and greater satisfaction in your life.

Jack Canfield is coauthor of the *Chicken Soup for the Soul*® series and *The Success Principles: How to Get from Where You Are to Where You Want to Be.*

INTRODUCTION
TO THE 2017 EDITION

I am pleased and grateful to welcome you to this 2017 edition of *The Soul of Money*. When the book was first published, in September 2003, my aim was to share a powerful philosophy and practice in our relationship with money. As the message has spread around the world, the response has been overwhelming, humbling really.

This book is entitled *The Soul of Money*, but it is really about our own soul and how and why we often eclipse it, dismiss it, or compromise it in our relationship with money: the way we get money, use money, give money, or sometimes just try to avoid thinking about money. This book is about finding a new freedom, truth, and joy in our relationship with money, whatever our circumstances. And it is about awakening and using the unexamined portal of our relationship with money to deliver a widespread transformation in all aspects of our life. Ultimately, this book is a pathway to personal and financial freedom.

I am not an economist or a banker or an investment advisor. I have no degrees in finance or business. I do, however, have a deep and special knowledge, experience, and understanding of money.

My education in money has come through direct and intimate experiences in five decades of work in philanthropy, raising hundreds of millions of dollars and providing leadership in major global initiatives: to end world hunger; to protect the Amazon rainforest; to empower indigenous peoples; to improve health, economic, and political conditions for women; and to advance the scientific understanding of human consciousness.

Each of these commitments has brought me into partnership with wise, inspiring individuals working at the intersection where the lives of those with money—often great fortunes—meet the lives of those who have little or no money. Together, we have worked to direct money effectively toward resolving some of the planet's most pressing issues.

Immersed in this collaborative world of philanthropy, human enterprise, and environmental stewardship, I have traveled into remote areas and worked with ancient cultures where the concept of money has just recently arrived on the scene. As a foundation trustee and adviser, I have worked with some of today's leading activists and thinkers to develop strategies to create a just, thriving, and sustainable way of life for all. In service of these commitments, I have had the privilege of working side by side and in partnership with some of the poorest people on earth. By that I mean "resource-poor" people in places like the Sahel Desert of northern Senegal, the villages of India, the Rift Valley of Ethiopia, countries in Central and South America, and in portions of the United States, where, regardless of their rich cultural gifts or even valued natural resources, people live in harsh conditions in which hunger, poverty, and oppression are the environment of everyday life. I've also been privileged to work side by side and in partnership with some of the wealthiest or "resource-rich" people on the planet, including billionaire families, in affluent countries such as Sweden, France, Germany, Japan, Canada, the United Kingdom, Australia, and, of course, the United States.

In this context of money, I have been deeply engaged in many cultures in a way that has enabled me to see the differences, but also the striking commonalities, in our basic human relationship with money and the way that relationship governs, dominates, and stresses our lives. I've became aware of powerful unexamined assumptions about money and life that hold us back, wear us out, or distort our most basic perception of the world and of one another. But I've also witnessed the immense healing power of even the smallest amount of money when we use it to express our humanity—our highest ideals and our most soulful commitments and values. *The Soul of Money* shows how we can right our relationship with money, realign it to transform the world around us and create conditions for unparalleled, sustainable prosperity and well-being.

When *The Soul of Money* was first published in that autumn of 2003, we were unaware as a global community that we were headed toward a catastrophic global financial breakdown and prolonged economic crisis. The apparent prosperity of 2005–2007 masked the increasingly reckless practices that built the U.S. housing bubble and the subsequent collapse of related derivative markets from Wall Street to Main Street. At the time, some people felt that something just wasn't right, but the forces in play—the momentum of big money and the insatiable drive for *more*—seemed unstoppable. Four years later, almost to the day, came the collapse of the U.S. housing and mortgage industry, and the ensuing months led to a global financial meltdown and one of the most devastating economic crises in modern history.

In that utter failure of the economic system and the tenets on which it had grown so voracious and destructive, the *Soul of Money* core principles of scarcity and sufficiency struck home with a special urgency. The financial crisis dramatically exposed the dangers of what I call the lie of scarcity: the mindset that tells us we can never have enough and drives us to strive above all and against all for more and more.

In contrast, what I call the surprising truth of sufficiency takes us to a different place. It heightens our awareness and appreciation of "enough"—a state of mind in which our experience of who we are, what we have, and our full wealth of inner resources deepens, expands and flourishes. In the context of sufficiency we reconnect with our inner resources—creativity, collaboration, commitment, courage. When we bring these resources to our relationship with money, we generate authentic prosperity for ourselves and others.

Since first writing this book, my work with the indigenous peoples in the Amazon has deepened and broadened. My husband, Bill, and I cofounded The Pachamama Alliance to empower them to navigate their relationship with the modern world in a way that both protects and preserves these vital forests, the heart and lungs of the planet. This partnership also gives us access in the modern world to indigenous traditions and deep wisdom.

Our indigenous partners live in balance and harmony with the natural world and with one another, which is the source of their prosperity and well-being. As the consumer society has monetized and commoditized nearly everything—water, air, land, and food—it becomes ever more clear how dysfunctional our culture is and how it leads us in the direction that will be our demise if we don't turn the tide.

In continuing conversations with scientists and scholars, economists, political leaders and policymakers, spiritual leaders and activists, a new truth has emerged about our relationship with money and life. Actually, it is quite an old truth, but increasing pressures for profit above all else have brought it more vividly into view: we must think and talk about money as part of a true ecosystem—a single system in which we view the *economy* and the *ecology* as fundamentally bound together.

For too long the economy has been viewed as separate from ecology, but nature has showed us that the two are inextricably joined. In fact, the economy is a subset of the ecology. Every single thing—food, clothing, electronics, homes and office buildings, cars and the fuel to run them, even this book you hold in your hands—is made from resources that come from the earth.

Scientists who calculate the footprint of our species on the earth—the measure of resources we consume versus the capacity of the earth to replenish those resources—say that we passed the point of a sustainable balance about thirty years ago. We now take vastly more from the earth than she can regenerate. In financial terms, we're living off an ecological credit card that we can never pay back. We are over our heads in ecological debt and we are passing that burden on to generations to come. We must find ways to replenish and conserve those resources, find a way to live within our ecological means, or we will go from crisis to deepening crisis in a downward spiral. The economic crisis is an accurate reflection of an ecological crisis, and we'll never actually resolve it until we learn how to live within our ecological means.

I feel that the wisdom which has emerged from these diverse and many-layered experiences is not mine, but a gift that has been given to me so that it can be passed on to others. Over the years, readers have told me how dramatically the stories and principles presented in *The Soul of Money* changed their lives, even saved their lives. I've been delighted to know that many of those who have attended *Soul of Money* seminars and Pachamama workshops have gone forward as philanthropists, fund-raisers and activists to raise awareness and channel resources to bring forth an environmentally sustainable, spiritually fulfilling, socially just, human presence on this planet.

The book's reach into the world of finance and economics has been heartening as well. *The Soul of Money* has been required and recommended reading at universities and colleges, in finance courses and graduate schools of business, including Harvard, Stanford, and MIT, as a unique way of looking at our relationship with money. The principles have been used in training and professional development programs in sectors of the financial services industry, including wealth management.

I am humbled to hear from so many corners how the book has been the catalyst for conversation in book clubs, community organizations, and online forums, and has been the subject of spiritual study and sermons in diverse congregations. Translated into Chinese, French, German, Japanese, Korean, Spanish, and Vietnamese, *The Soul of Money* continues to awaken entrepreneurs, business people, students, activists, philanthropists, and countless other people in countries and cultures all over the world.

There are hundreds of spiritual practices. Many paths lead

people to wholeness and peace of mind. Exploring your relationship with money can lead you to that place. It might seem strange to think that money could be such a path, but I have seen it and traveled it myself, and I've seen many others do the same.

This book is not about turning away from money or simplifying expenditures, or doing budgets or financial planning, although the wisdom gained will be relevant to all those activities. This book is about living consciously, fully, and joyfully in our relationship with money, and learning to understand and embrace its flow. This is your opportunity to embark on a remarkable and rare journey, one that aligns money and soul, to transform your life.

THE SOUL OF MONEY

Part One

LOVE, LIES, AND
A GREAT AWAKENING

1

Money and Me,
Money and Us

Money is like an iron ring we put through our nose. It is now
leading us around wherever it wants. We just forgot that we are
the ones who designed it.

—MARK KINNEY

In a thriving village deep in the Amazon rain forest, a ten-
day hike from any form of civilization as we know it,
Chumpi Washikiat and his people are engaged in a bold,
brave, risky, and unprecedented venture. They are learning how
to use money.

Although he is twenty-six years old, Chumpi had had very
few interactions with money until a few years ago. His indigenous group, the Achuar, had lived without money for thousands
of years. For all that time, generations of Achuar people grew
up, worked to raise families, built homes, and maintained communities, all without money. These indigenous people were and
are highly attuned to the most significant influences in their

life—the forces of nature and their relationships with one another and the forest—but they had no relationship with money. Reciprocity was the social currency. It was understood that everyone shared with everyone else and everyone took care of everyone else. If Tantu's daughter married Natem's son, then their friends and neighbors came together to build them a house. When a hunter killed a wild boar, the whole village feasted. Life's ups and downs were determined mostly by forces of nature. Any battles were fought over matters of honor. Money had nothing to do with any of it.

Chumpi grew up in this environment, but it was his destiny to be part of the generation that would change all that. In the early 1970s the Achuar had their first contact with the modern world through missionaries. Within two decades their ancestral land became the target of oil companies and other commercial interests threatening to strip the rain forest for hardwoods and the oil that lay below. In 1995, my husband, Bill, and I were invited by the Achuar leaders to become partners in their effort to protect the land and the indigenous peoples' way of life. This is how I met Chumpi, a skilled young Achuar man and warrior.

A few years after that first meeting, Chumpi was chosen by the elders and leaders of the Achuar to come to America to study. He was to be the first Achuar person to learn English, essential if the Achuar were to be effective with outsiders in any conservation efforts or commercial enterprises. At the same time, Chumpi also set about learning the other language of contemporary Western life: the language of money. This would be required vocabulary for survival in a world where, quite different from their own, nearly everyone and everything is driven consistently, and sometimes exclusively, by money.

Chumpi lived with us in our home, attended classes at a nearby college, and studied hard to learn English. His education about money was more on the level of inhaling. Everywhere he went, the language and meaning of money filled the air, from billboards, advertisements, and commercials, to price cards on the muffins at the local bakery. In conversations with other students he learned about their hopes, dreams, and prospects for life after graduation, or as they put it, "life in the real world"—the money world. He began to see how it is in America: that virtually everything in our lives and every choice we make—the food we eat, the clothes we wear, the houses we live in, the schools we attend, the work we do, the futures we dream, whether we marry or not, or have children or not, even matters of love—everything is influenced by this thing called money.

It didn't take long before Chumpi saw that he and his people now had a relationship with money. Money had meaning. If the Achuar wanted to save their rain-forest homeland, they would have to work with the fact that it was valuable to others for its moneymaking potential. Some other indigenous groups from the region had learned about money the hard way. They had traded the rights to their land for money that was gone as quickly as it had come, and in the end they had lost their land, their homes, their way of life, and the heritage that had been theirs for all time before.

The Achuar heeded the lesson. They recognized that their particular challenge would be to use the power of money clearly and consistently to serve their highest goal: to protect the rain forest and manage its resources to support a sustainable future for themselves and all life. They understood that their new and historically unprecedented relationship with money must be grounded firmly in their own core values and their highest commitments to life and land, or, as it had for their neighbors, money would bring their ruin. This challenge continues for them today—testing the fabric of their relationships and the ancient communal principles of their culture.

When the Achuar are in their rain forest home they are prosperous and have everything they need, and have been so for centuries, even millennia. One step out of the rain forest into our world and they can't eat, find shelter, or live for any length of time without money. Money is not an option; it is a requirement. Bill and I, fortunate to witness and participate with the Achuar in their first significant engagement with the world of money, have felt called by it to reexamine our own relationship with money, and our culture's relationship with money.

Like Chumpi and the Achuar, we all have an identifiable, though largely unconscious and unexamined, relationship with money that shapes our experience of life and our deepest feelings about ourselves and others. Whether you count your change in dollars, yen, rupees, or drachmas, money is one of the central, linchpin issues in all our lives. It is in mine, and it is a central issue for everyone I've ever met, no matter how much or how little money they have.

Everyone is interested in money, and almost all of us feel a chronic concern, or even fear, that we will never really have enough or be able to keep enough of it. Many of us pretend that money isn't important to us, or think it shouldn't be. Many of us live openly with the accumulation of money as our primary goal. No matter how much money we have, or don't have, the worry that we don't or won't have enough of it quickens our heart around money issues. The harder we try to get it, or even try to ignore it or rise above it, the tighter money's grip on us grows.

Money has become a playing field where we measure our competence and worth as people. We worry that if we stop striving for more, we'll somehow lose our place on the team, or lose our advantage. If we're not gaining ground, we feel that we're losing it. If we're not ahead of others financially, or at least even with them, we feel we're falling behind and need to catch up. The game can be exciting at times, scary at other times, but always the stakes are high because on the playing field of money, if we're not winners, we're losers.

Even when the game is going our way, we often feel a nagging disconnect, the gap between the way we imagine life should be and the way we are living it, under the day-to-day pressure to earn more, buy more, save more, get more, have more, and to be more. Not even the wealthy find the peace and freedom with their money that you would think comes with having so much; it doesn't. It takes more to play the game in those circles, but the game is the same. You can be a CEO who earned $7 million last year, but if your golfing partner just turned a deal for $10 million, and you didn't, that puts you behind in the money game. As the financial stakes get higher, the more there is to lose, and the more demanding the game becomes to stay ahead. No one escapes the powerful push and pull of money. Everyone reacts to the ups and downs of money in their life.

Whether we look at money in the context of our personal or family lives, the workplace, or in the health and welfare of nations, the same picture emerges: Money is the most universally motivating, mischievous, miraculous, maligned, and misunderstood part of contemporary life.

THIS THING WE CALL MONEY

If we peel back thousands of years of cultural conditioning and assumptions to take a fresh look at money, we can begin with some very basic observations. Money is not a product of nature. Money doesn't grow on trees. Pennies don't rain from heaven. Money is an invention, a distinctly human invention. It is a total fabrication of our genius. We made it up and we manufacture it. It is an inanimate object that has appeared in many different forms in its more than 2,500-to-3,500-year history, whether we're talking about shells or stones or ingots of precious metals, a paper bill or a blip on the computer screen. From the very beginning, money was invented to facilitate the sharing and exchanging of goods and services among individuals and groups of people. Money still facilitates the sharing and exchange of goods and services, but somewhere along the way the power we gave money outstripped its original utilitarian role.

Now, rather than relating to money as a tool we created and control, we have come to relate to money as if it is a fact of nature, a force to be reckoned with. This stuff called money, mass-produced tokens or paper bills with no more inherent power than a notepad or a Kleenex, has become the single most controlling force in our lives.

Money has only the power that we assign to it, and we have assigned it immense power. We have given it almost final authority. If we look only at behavior, it tells us that we have made money more important than we are, given it more meaning than human life. Humans have done and will do terrible things in the name of money. They have killed for it, enslaved other people for it, and enslaved themselves to joyless lives in pursuit of it.

In the name of money, humankind has done immense damage to Mother Earth. We've destroyed rain forests, dammed and decimated rivers, clear-cut redwoods, overfished rivers and lakes, and poisoned our soil with chemical wastes from industry and agriculture. We've marginalized whole segments of our society, forced the poor into housing projects, allowed urban ghettos to form, exploited whole nations to get cheaper labor, and witnessed the fall of thousands—in fact, millions—of people, many of them young, caught up in selling drugs for money, hurting others and wasting their own promise in a life of crime, enslavement, or incarceration. We've perpetuated age-old traditions that assign men and women different and unequal access to money and the power we place in it, subjugating women and distorting men's expectations and obligations with their privileged access to it.

Rarely in our life is money a place of genuine freedom, joy, or clarity, yet we routinely allow it to dictate the terms of our lives and often to be the single most important factor in the decisions we make about work, love, family, and friendship. There is little that we accept so completely as the power and authority of money, and assumptions about how we should feel about it. We challenge assumptions about every other facet of life: race, religion, politics, education, sex, family, and society. But when it comes to money, we accept it not only as a measure of economic value but also as a way of assigning importance and worth to everyone and everything else in the world. When we talk about success in life, money is almost always the first, and sometimes the only, measure we use for it.

In our private lives, we all, at one time or another, have

demeaned and devalued ourselves, taken advantage of people, or engaged in other actions we're not proud of in order to get or keep money or the power we believe it can buy. We've silenced ourselves to avoid conflicts or uncomfortable interactions over money. Our behavior around money has damaged relationships when money has been used as an instrument of control or punishment, emotional escape or manipulation, or as a replacement for love. Among families of great wealth, many have been poisoned by greed, mistrust, and a desire to control others. Their lives of privilege have cut them off from the essential experience of ordinary human interactions and authentic relationships. In lives where money is scarce, the struggle can easily become the defining theme that discounts the self-worth and basic human potential of an individual, a family, or even whole communities or cultures. For some, the chronic absence of money becomes an excuse they use for being less resourceful, productive, or responsible than they could be.

We are born into a culture defined by money, and our initial relationship with money is the product of that culture, whether it is one based primarily in poverty, in a country like Mozambique or Bangladesh, or a culture of affluence and wealth in a country like the United States or Japan. From our earliest experiences, we learn money's place and power in our families, our communities, and in our own lives. We see who earns it and who doesn't. We see what our parents are willing to do, and what they aren't willing to do, to acquire money or the things money buys. We see how money shapes personal perspective and public opinion.

In our distinctly aggressive American consumer culture, even our youngest children are drawn into that fierce relationship with money. Much as we did, only more so today, they grow up in a media milieu and popular culture that encourages an insatiable appetite for spending and acquiring, without regard to personal or environmental consequences. Distortions in our relationship with money emerge from a lifetime of these seemingly innocuous everyday experiences in the money culture. Personal money issues, as well as issues of sustainability and social equity central to the human economy and the environment, are clearly rooted in the soil of our relationship with money and the money culture into which we are born and which we come to accept as natural.

MONEY AND SOUL: THE GREAT DIVIDE

For most of us, this relationship with money is a deeply conflicted one, and our behavior with and around money is often at odds with our most deeply held values, commitments, and ideals—what I call our soul. When I talk about soul, I'm not referring to any religious interpretation. When I speak of "our" core values, or higher commitments, I'm not suggesting that we all think or feel the same about politics, religion, economics, and all the other issues, demands, and desires that dominate our day. I believe that under it all, when you get right down to it and uncover all the things we're told to believe in, or things we are maneuvered and manipulated to believe in, or even things we choose to believe in, what deeply matters to human beings, *our most universal soulful commitments and core values*, is the well-being of the people we love, ourselves, and the world in which we live.

We really do want a world that works for everyone. We don't

want children to go hungry. We don't want violence and war to plague the planet anywhere, even if it's a distant place. We don't want torture and revenge and retribution to be instruments of government and leadership. Everyone wants a safe, secure, loving, nourishing life for themselves and the ones they love and really for everyone. We all want a healthy planet, and an opportunity for everyone to have a chance of a healthy, productive life.

I also believe that under their fears and upsets, even the deepest ones, everyone wants to love and be loved, and make a difference with their lives. Speaking in spiritual terms, and not a specific religious sense, I believe people also want an experience of their own divinity, their own connectedness with all life and the mystery of something greater than we comprehend. The money culture has shaped us in many ways that we would not choose in a more conscious soulful process, driving us such that we unwittingly undermine and erode those most deeply human values and highest commitments, and at times turn away from the very ones we profess to hold dear.

THE SIREN SONG OF SUCCESS

In the early 1970s, as Bill launched his career in business, and the siren song of money started to sing in his ears, he and other young MBAs from the top business schools were recruited by a celebrated up-and-coming company that arranged deals for large-scale leasing of transportation and computer equipment. They made their money on a percentage of the deals, and they were entering a time of phenomenal growth in that market. The business began to grow more and more successful, faster and faster, and at one point the company executives set their goal at becoming a billion-dollar business faster than any other company in history. This was an ambitious, heady goal at the time, and entirely possible. It was tremendously exciting, and everyone—spouses included—became seduced by this target. I remember being excited that it was going so well for Bill and his colleagues, and thinking how fabulous this was, encouraging him and not interrupting his pattern of staying at the office later and going in earlier and having to go on business trips, even on weekends.

Our three young children—Zachary, a year old, Summer, who was three, and Billy, who was five—were the center of our lives, or so we thought. Our marriage and our relationship with our children were the most important things in the world to us, or so we said. Yet, if someone had filmed us during this time and looked at it objectively, they would have said—No, they don't care about the children. The kids are with the nanny, the wife is always off on these boondoggles with her husband, or shopping or entertaining, and they're missing out on the most important stages of their children's development, seeing those first steps, being there for good-night stories, kisses, or the spontaneity that builds relationships. They're able to purchase child care and purchase toys and a great house, but even when they're with their children their heads are spinning with what they need to do next to achieve financial goals or demonstrate to their friends that they know how to be facile with the emerging experience of wealth.

We felt we were sincerely devoted to our children, but if you looked honestly at how we actually spent our time and energy, you'd see that our actions were not consistent with our intentions.

We caught ourselves in that scramble in the mid-1970s. The

money was flowing in and everything we acquired or used the money for led to the desire for the next thing, the next purchase, or the next reason to buy more. To be socially literate, we felt we needed to learn about fine wine, and when we did, we needed a wine cellar. We bought a fast, hot sports car, and then needed another car, a station wagon, for our family life with the children. We had a wonderful house, but somehow it didn't seem finished without some impressive art. As soon as we began to learn about art, we wanted to buy at a higher level. Our friends began to have summer homes, so that seemed like the next must for us. Once we began to buy more expensive clothes, we needed newer, nicer shoes to match. Then our coats had to live up to the clothes they covered. And our watches had to keep pace. The list of upgrades was endless. In our social circle, vacations became like merit badges of the affluent lifestyle; if you wanted to fit in with the popular crowd, you were expected to take exotic vacations. Suddenly, driving to Yosemite or simply camping wasn't enough. It had to be skiing in Sun Valley or sailing in Hawaii. One thing led to another, and it all seemed so important. Something drove us, and we didn't stop to question any of it. All the while our kids were with the nanny and baby-sitters, growing up well stocked and well tended, but not with our presence. We were loving parents, but absent much more than we were comfortable with, and yet we would leave because it always seemed important that we go, and we knew that we'd be back home soon.

The launch of a global initiative to end world hunger—The Hunger Project—woke me up. When I first heard about a commitment to end hunger on earth, I felt that its mission matched deep feelings I held about responding to human suffering. I remembered when I was a child, a happy and contented child, that there was a point at which I had realized that somewhere there were people who were hungry, and it made no sense to me. It was upsetting to me that a child just like me somewhere on earth didn't have enough to eat. I remember thinking I couldn't let that happen. As a child, you have a thought like that and then go out and play. But that thought stayed with me, and decades later, when I heard The Hunger Project's message—that it was possible using existing resources to end chronic, persistent hunger on earth—it resonated right into the heart of my heart and took me back to that moment in my childhood when I had realized everyone wasn't taken care of and I wanted to do something about it. I felt a call from my soul that was so deep and profound that I couldn't deny it. In that moment, I began to separate myself from the chase.

Now, two and a half decades later, I can say that one of the unexpected gifts of my Hunger Project involvement was that in taking a stand to end world hunger I came to recognize, and had to address, my own inner hunger and the inauthentic and inappropriate way we were living. It was then that we purposely began to turn our resources—our time, our energy, our money, the accumulation of material wealth—toward our longing to make a difference with our lives.

While Bill continued to work with his company, we began to relate to it all differently. Rather than endlessly accumulate the money or use it to acquire more things, we began to see the resources he and his partners were earning as resources we could direct toward others, allocating money to people, programs, and projects that built a better life for all people. A former teacher myself, I decided to start a school for single and working parents. We involved our friends and other families in community-building activities and fund-raising. We dived into the work of personal and social transformation, taking courses and workshop programs ourselves, and encouraging others to do the same. We began to open our relationships from a narrow band of homogeneous people, all on a track for financial success and status, to a diverse collection of friends and colleagues from all kinds of backgrounds and cultures and all ways of life. Our circle became larger, multicultural, and from many different segments of society and economic circumstances.

Bill and his partners created a company foundation and we all experienced the joy and power of contributing, investing money in the things we cared most deeply about, programs that spoke to our highest commitments. We saw that we could make a significant difference by investing our money in ending hunger and we did, contributing to The Hunger Project and experiencing a kind of fulfillment that warmed and nourished our relationship with each other and with everyone. We realized that our previous scramble to accumulate and upgrade everything about ourselves and our life was another kind of hunger, and we addressed it head-on by realizing that what we really hungered for was to have lives of meaning. We hungered to make a difference and began to devote ourselves to doing that. Some of us turned our energies to hunger initiatives, some to education, some to poverty, some to stopping abuse or providing shelter and healing for victims of abuse.

This change of heart brought about a change in our relationship with money. Once we began to align our money decisions with these deeper core values and our highest commitments, we experienced a dramatic shift, not only in what we did with our money but also in how we felt about money, about our life, and about ourselves. Eventually, we came to know ourselves not for what we had or owned, but for what we gave; not for what we accumulated, but for what we allocated.

We saw a similar transformation occur among many of our friends. Regardless of their financial resources, when they connected with their generosity and commitment, they were moved to express themselves in a similar way. We realized that while we couldn't change the culture of money, we could see it more clearly. We could make more conscious choices about how we related to circumstances and how we responded to them. We didn't feel as caught or trapped by our fears and expectations around money, and the chase for more began to lose its grip. For each of us, money became more and more a way to express the longing and the fulfillment of soul.

MAKING A LIVING THAT AFFIRMS LIFE

Each of us experiences a lifelong tug-of-war between our money interests and the calling of our soul. When we're in the domain of soul, we act with integrity. We are thoughtful and generous, allowing, courageous, and committed. We recognize the value of love and friendship. We admire a small thing well done. We experience moments of awe in the presence of nature and its unrefined beauty. We are open, vulnerable, and heartful. We have the capacity to be moved, and generosity is natural. We are trustworthy and trusting of others, and our self-expression flourishes. We feel at peace within ourselves and confidant that we are an integral part of a larger, more universal experience, something greater than ourselves.

When we enter the domain of money, there often seems to

be a disconnect from the soulful person we have known our-selves to be. It is as if we are suddenly transported to a different playing field where all the rules have changed. In the grip of money, those wonderful qualities of soul seem to be less avail-able. We become smaller. We scramble or race to "get what's ours." We often grow selfish, greedy, petty, fearful, or controlling, or sometimes confused, conflicted, or guilty. We see ourselves as winners or losers, powerful or helpless, and we let those labels deeply define us in ways that are inaccurate, as if financial wealth and control indicate innate superiority, and lack of them sug-gests a lack of worth or basic human potential. Visions of possi-bility dissolve. We become wary and mistrusting, protective of our little piece, or helpless and hopeless. We sometimes feel dri-ven to behave in ways inconsistent with our core values, and unable to act differently.

The result is a deep division in our way of being, in our behavior, and in our sense of our own character and integrity. This dichotomy, this break in our truth, not only confuses us around the issue of money; it also keeps us from integrating our inner and outer worlds to experience wholeness in our lives, the exquisite moment when we feel at peace in the moment, a part of and one with life. This quieter experience of wholeness has been largely lost in our culture, overtaken by the noise and scramble around money. That gap exists for all of us—myself included—and is at the very heart of the toughest struggles in life for all of us.

Vicki Robin, in *Your Money or Your Life*, writes about people who, instead of making a living at their work, more accurately "make a dying," or, in some cases, make a killing. The work they're doing is unfulfilling, perhaps even detrimental to their own or others' well-being. Or perhaps they're embarrassed about their work. They hate it. They wish they didn't have to do it. They pretend that it doesn't matter, but in truth, their spirit—or someone else's—is being killed off. Caught up in the chase, they say they are making a living when they are really making a dying or a killing, but they don't see it, or can't admit it.

Money itself isn't the problem. Money itself isn't bad or good. Money itself doesn't have power or not have power. It is our interpretation of money, our interaction with it, where the real mischief is and where we find the real opportunity for self-discovery and personal transformation. The stories I'm about to share come from a journey through extremes, from circumstances of stunning wealth and shocking economic poverty, from people and places continents away from this country. But I have seen the same lessons play out closer to home, in the everyday struggles and choices we make with money, and our expectations, dreams, fears, and disappointments around it.

You may have to look closely to find the money thread in your own story, but it is there and it has meaning. You can begin the process of examination, and transform the mystery of money, and the field of play that money represents, into a different kind of place. Your relationship with money can be a place where you bring your strengths and skills, your highest aspirations, and your deepest and most profound qualities. Whether we are millionaires or "dollar heirs," we can actually be great with our money and be great in our relationship with it.

In a world that seems to revolve around money, it is vital that we deepen our relationship with our soul and bring it to bear on our relationship with money. In that merger and that commitment, we can create a new and profound spiritual practice. We can have our money culture both balanced and nourished by soul. Our relationship with money can become a place where, day in and day out, we can engage in this meaningful spiritual practice.

The chapters ahead are an invitation to confront our challenges with money, our fears around money, our addiction and attachment to money, our remorse and regret and hurts around money, and to embrace all of it as an arena for personal growth, a wonderful place in which to work on our own transformation. In that engagement we give money its soul.

2

Into India: Heart of Hunger, Soul of Money

Listen to your life. See it for the fathomless mystery it is. In the boredom and pain of it, no less than in the excitement and gladness: touch, taste, smell your way to the holy and hidden heart of it, because in the last analysis all moments are key moments, and life itself is grace.

—FREDERICK BUECHNER

On my first trip to India, standing on the banks of the Ganges River in Varanasi one night, I was intrigued by the sight of some small rafts adorned with flowers and torches, floating gently along with the current of the dark, velvety water. They bobbed along lightly, like pieces of some delicate carnival set adrift. I was taken by their beauty and wondered what festival was being celebrated—I wanted to join in. I asked a friend, who informed me that the lovely floral rafts were funeral pyres, cradling burning human remains downstream to a ceremonial end in ashes on the riverbank. It was a bit of a shock, but it was an appropriate introduction to the landscape and culture of India.

India is a land of surprises, a country of extraordinary beauty alongside unimaginable suffering. If there is a capitol of world hunger, it is India. There are more chronically malnourished, hungry, and starving people in India than anywhere else on earth, some three hundred million of them struggling to survive everywhere from the city streets and sewers of Calcutta to the parched, barren desert of Rajasthan where any living thing is an aberration.

I visited India for the first time in 1983, about five years into my career as a global activist and fund-raiser to end world hunger. That work thus far had taken me through the United States, Canada, and Europe, but this was my initiation trip to India. I came expecting to learn about the reality of hunger and poverty in their most staggering dimensions. As it turned out, it was in India where I also discovered startling truths about money and wealth, about human nature and human potential.

A WALK WITH RAMKRISHNA BAJAJ

They called him "Gandhi's fifth son," but Ramkrishna Bajaj was no blood relation to the great Mahatma, leader of India's non-violent movement for independence from Britain in the late 1930s. Rather, it was appreciation and Indian tradition that had moved a grateful Gandhi to offer to raise the little boy. Ramkrishna was the youngest son of Jamlalal Bajaj, the great Indian industrialist and silent financial backer of the independence movement.

We rarely think of the independence movement led by Gandhi as something that someone had to fund, but somebody paid for everything: the travel, the living expenses, the support that made it possible for Gandhi and others to be where they were needed and have what they needed to advance the cause of independence. Jamlalal Bajaj was that man, the deep pockets behind Gandhi and the independence movement. His was a huge and catalytic investment of money, and in gratitude for that investment, Gandhi, in keeping with Indian tradition, offered to raise Jamlalal's youngest child as his own. Gandhi already had four children, so when he adopted Ramkrishna, the Indian people called the boy "Gandhi's fifth son."

What began as an expression of gratitude proved to be a continuing blessing for India, as Ramkrishna himself grew into a great and good man. By age thirteen he was the leader of Gandhi's organized nonviolent youth movement, which numbered in the many thousands of young people. After years at Gandhi's side, sometimes in prison for months at a time for their passive resistance and civil disobedience, Ramkrishna grew into a respected leader and eventual patriarch of the industrial and financial empire his father had built. The Bajaj Corporation, or the House of Bajaj, as it is called in India, was one of that country's biggest companies. As the new patriarch, Ramkrishna proved to be enormously effective and generous, establishing several foundations that supported thousands of projects for the common good.

I felt privileged to have Ramkrishna Bajaj as my guide and mentor during those early trips to India. He was a fatherly figure and took me under his wing to educate me about this complex country of extremes and opposites; extreme beauty and exquisite spirituality, and abject poverty and horrendous suppression.

I remember stepping off the plane in Bombay and into a wave of heat and humidity. The smell of thousands of human beings so close together in that heat was overwhelming, as it is for most Westerners on their first encounter with India. At that time thousands of people—beggars and others—lived in the airport and on the edges of the roads to the airport, as well as in the streets of Bombay, on the sidewalks, in the doorways and stairwells—everywhere. People used any space anywhere to set up their little cooking pots to make chapatis, squatting around the little metal cooking can that was their fire. Some slept with no cover. Others had shelters made of paper and boxes, street trash and string. Many times a family of six or more would be huddled inside one of these makeshift huts.

We walked through the airport, and as soon as we got outside the baggage area we were confronted by beggars. They pulled at us, pushed in close for a response. It was overwhelming for me. By the third day in India, I was in a kind of shock. It was one thing to have been publicly speaking about ending world hunger, but it was another to be physically present to hunger in India. I hadn't seen the magnitude of the job, the immensity of it. Now I was face-to-face with it.

On that third day, I walked along the streets of Bombay with Ramkrishna, this man revered as embodying Gandhi's legacy, this man so celebrated as a great industrialist, a great philanthropist, a great spiritual leader, a great father, a great soul, and as we walked through the streets of Bombay I witnessed people who knew who he was, dropping to their knees and kissing his feet. At the same time, I also witnessed him ignoring the beggars; it was as if he did not see them, as if they were not there. He stepped over them, seemingly oblivious to their plight.

When you walk in Bombay, especially in certain parts of the city where we were going, you literally have to walk over people who are living in the streets. These people approach you for alms with their deformed hands outstretched or they hold their little blind babies in your face, or they pull on your clothes or whimper at your side. For a Westerner, someone like me, it is shocking to see, wrenching to witness, so I was very aware of these people. I couldn't notice or think of anything else. But Ramkrishna didn't react to them.

They didn't accost him the way they did me, either. It was as if there were some unspoken agreement or shield around him. He walked right through them without contact or comment, and I was astonished that such a great man, a man of such compassion, could be so blind to them. It was my first recognition of the light and the dark of India, and the light and the dark of even such a great man, that in order to function he needed to not see those people; not engage them and not even acknowledge that they were there.

The crushing poverty and hunger held other truths, too, that began to put Ramkrishna's behavior with the beggars in a different perspective. One sad fact is that begging is an industry in India—in other countries, as well, but especially in India. It's hard for us to think of it that way, but it is an organized industry there and in many places there are mafia-style bosses who encourage people to mutilate their children so the children will be more effective beggars. This practice effectively ensures that begging not only becomes a lifelong profession, but also creates a lineage of beggars.

The caste system has loosened its grip on India to some extent now, but in 1983 it was still very strong. It dictated the view of life as a closed system in which once you were a beggar you would never get out of that life. In that life view, you might pray to be born again as a more privileged Brahman, or born again in some other incarnation, but this time around, you and your children and your children's children would always be beggars. Knowing that, you wanted to become as effective as you could possibly be at begging.

Since success as a beggar depends on getting people to feel shocked or sorry or guilty so they'll give money, the syndicates and bosses would teach their street beggars ways to make their children look more pitiful. Pressured this way, the parents sometimes did something to scar their child's face, or they cut off their child's hand or leg so there would be a stump instead. Families actually mutilated their children to increase their shock value and revenue potential as beggars.

In my own country, I had seen plenty of ways that people hurt each other over money: in divorces and custody battles, or in exploitation of each other or the environment. It was easy to be critical about those wrongful choices made in the name of money. Now I also realized that I had always assumed that the poor, with no money to fight over, were somehow exempt from that particular corruption. However, in India I saw the cruel and self-destructive choices that poor people also make for money.

In this carefully orchestrated business of begging, those who designed the dishonesty and those who participated in it and perpetuated it were in a sick, unspoken collusion. The people who gave money from shock or guilt were appeasing their guilt, and in the process they were also becoming enablers, unwittingly supporting this brutal industry. The tragic victims were the children. The beggars' needs were deep and real, but the money gained did nothing to break the cycle of poverty. In fact, the money only perpetuated the perverse industry that demanded the mutilation and sacrifice of more children.

The days that followed delivered one lesson after another, one surprise after another, in which so many of the money-related mental pictures I had always carried around, and things I had assumed or thought I knew, were turned upside down. A whole new body of distinctions started to come into view for me around people we call poor and people we call rich, and I could see that the opinions and beliefs we have about rich and poor, and poverty and wealth, obscure more than they illuminate.

Here was the drama and theater of the beggars, a racket in which starving beggars played shock, shame, and guilt for all it was worth, and I felt caught in it. Not that they didn't need money to feed themselves or to treat their wounds, but in the begging and in the giving, there was undeniably a dishonest, dark side.

Here was a great man, Ramkrishna, who used his industry and wealth in so many ways to break the grip of poverty in his country, stepping blindly and without comment over those on the ground before him. Ramkrishna's company employed tens of thousands of people. He was at the top of Indian social status and he held both his business and social roles with tremendous responsibility and compassion; he was, in fact, a great philanthropist whose partnership and generosity were legendary. I also saw that in order to maintain his vision, purpose, and position in that society, he had to develop a certain kind of blindness in his everyday encounter with the overwhelming poverty on the streets. And he did.

So then do we all. We are all blind in some way about money, and we keep ourselves blind. Perhaps it is the fear and anxiety that if we see too much about the consequences of the ways we are earning it, or the real consequences of the choices we make with our spending, we will have to redesign our whole lives. If we really look into, for example, the brutality of child labor that is often associated with everyday products we buy at low cost from foreign countries, we would be shocked and immobilized. If we acknowledged the true environmental costs that we pay for the gift of seemingly limitless energy required to maintain our comfort, how would we need to change? If we really looked at the consequences and downstream impact of almost any industry that employs us or serves our wants and needs, the truth is we might be stopped in our everyday life. And if we really examined our beliefs and assumptions about other people in the context of money, we might need to open ourselves, our hearts, and our minds to people we have closed off from ourselves.

MOTHER TERESA AND THE PRISON OF WEALTH

I was raised as a Catholic, and all through my life I was deeply inspired by Mother Teresa. When I was a sophomore in high school I thought seriously about becoming a nun. Although I eventually broadened my spiritual life and career plans in different directions, Mother Teresa remained the most compelling role model in my life. In the 1970s when, as a young mother and wife, I began to fully embrace my personal commitment to end world hunger, I thought a lot about her and her work among the poorest of the poor in the slums of Calcutta and in places of hunger and poverty all over the world. On my first trip to India, as I felt overwhelmed by the horrific poverty that I saw, I thought about her and how she had placed herself in the middle of human suffering for her entire life, remaining a member of the community of the poorest of the poor even as she was celebrated by the most rich and powerful leaders of the world.

After many working trips to India, and a growing sense of connection there, I decided to seek out Mother Teresa. I wanted to meet her. Soon after, I discovered that someone in my circle of acquaintances in Delhi was a close associate of Mother Teresa's and was pleased to help me make contact.

It was May in 1991, and I was in Delhi to meet with World Bank officials regarding our hunger initiative when my friend contacted me early one morning to say that Mother Teresa could see me that same evening at seven o'clock. I was overwhelmed. I couldn't believe that this lifelong dream of being in her presence was coming true within a few hours. I canceled one of my meetings in the morning and went to Mass at a church in New Delhi. I went to a bookstore and bought three books about her, thinking that I needed to be more informed than I was in order to be with her. I fretted about what to say and what to wear. I went into a kind of whirlwind of worry, awe, and excitement over the privilege before me. I did the other meetings that I couldn't cancel, but I was far from present. My mind and my heart were totally engaged in the anticipation of an opportunity for which I had hoped all my life.

My friend arranged for a private car and a driver who knew the way to her facility, to pick me up at my hotel at six o'clock. He would take me into old Delhi, where, in a very obscure and poor part of town, the Missionaries of Charity housed Mother Teresa's orphanage for abandoned and orphaned children under two years old. My driver picked me up, and we drove through the streets of New Delhi into the old city. After about forty-five minutes of searching, we went down a very narrow street, to a spot where a modest sign hung at an entrance in a stone wall told us we had reached the Missionaries of Charity—Old Delhi Orphanage. My driver parked in the front courtyard to wait for me. As I walked up the three steps to the old door, I saw a large piece of crumpled newspaper on the doorstep and I stooped to pick it up. There inside the crumpled mass I discovered a tiny baby, still breathing, still alive. She was a girl, a just-born and very fragile little girl. I was shocked, and gently lifted her from her newspaper swaddling clothes and wrapped her carefully inside my shawl.

Opening the old wooden door, I stepped into a room lit by two lightbulbs dangling on wires from the ceiling. The clean concrete floor was painted blue, and there were thirty-nine cribs (yes, I counted them), each with one or two small babies inside. There were additional padded mats on the floor with more little babies on their backs cooing, or sitting up playing. Here were fifty babies under the age of two—now fifty-one with my newly delivered bundle from the doorstep—and the only sounds were those of babies cooing or playing, or the nuns and their helpers talking and singing gently to the babies and each other.

I handed the tiny infant girl to the nun who greeted me. She wore the familiar blue-and-white sari of Mother Teresa's order, and she seemed delighted to have another little one to care for. When I introduced myself and asked to see Mother Teresa, the nun who supervised the nursery told me that Mother Teresa was not there at the moment. She had gone to town to bail out of jail two young girls who had turned to prostitution; Mother

Teresa would bring them back and enlist their help with the babies in the orphanage. In the meantime, I was invited to wash my hands, put on an apron, and join the nursery staff in caring for these little ones. I went right to work.

First, I bathed a blind baby girl. She must have been about fourteen months old. Then I was given a tiny, deformed three-month-old baby with one leg that was a little stump. I sang as I bathed her small, malformed body. I have always been drawn to those in need and especially children who are handicapped or deprived in some way. This place was a kind of paradise for me, and I felt in a state of grace.

In stories about her, Mother Teresa had often been quoted as saying, "The way to know me is to know my work; I am my work," and now I could feel her presence as I fed and bathed and fell in love with these babies. I lost myself in this blissful enterprise and I don't know how much time had passed before I was startled by a nun's tap on my shoulder and her message, "Mother Teresa will see you now."

I was directed through a corridor past a chapel where there were about twenty nuns singing evensong. I was asked to wait in a chair by a doorway. In front of me was a stark hallway with no adornments. There was a very simple wooden table with two chairs against the wall. As I sat and looked down the long, dark hallway, a small bent figure emerged. I knew instantly that it was Mother Teresa.

She came toward me from the shadows, her familiar figure stooped over. She was smiling and glowing. She had next to her a black Labrador retriever who was clearly devoted to her and walked quietly by her side. There she was, Mother Teresa, right there in front of me. Speechless, I kneeled and kissed the ring on one of her small, gnarly hands. Then I instinctively kissed her sandaled feet. She placed her hands on the top of my head for a moment, then took my two hands in hers and asked me to stand up and go with her over to the chairs and table where we might sit and talk. We sat down together, and I was moved to tears as I began. I told her that her example and her commitment had been a flame of inspiration for me for as far back as I could remember. I told her that I had become completely committed and engaged in the work of ending world hunger and that at some level this life commitment had stemmed from her example and the courageous way she had chosen to live her life. I asked her to pray for my twenty-year-old son, who was ill, and my mother, who was struggling with cancer, and then we began to talk about my work.

She knew about The Hunger Project and knew about me. She knew that I was a leader in my organization, and she knew that one of my responsibilities was fund-raising. She told me that fund-raising was great work and that she admired me for the courage it took to be responsible for funding the work to end hunger.

She modestly described herself as "God's pencil," and told me that she could see in my eyes and by my work that I, too, was "God's pencil." This acknowledgment moved me deeply. In her presence, I felt an unconditional love and connectedness to the whole world so profound that I could not hold back my tears and so I spoke to her through them.

We were deeply engaged in this intimate conversation when we were interrupted by a scuffling noise and loud voices coming from down the hall.

First I smelled them, then I heard them: a middle-aged

Indian couple, a man and a woman, both very tall, very large, very heavily perfumed and clearly very rich. The woman came first, pushing ahead of her husband, moving aggressively toward our small meeting table. She had diamond studs in her ears and one in her nose. Her arms were covered in lavish bangles, many laced with precious stones. She was heavily made up and was wearing a blue and white sari covered with opulent gold and silver brocade and embroidery. She was very overweight and her flesh bulged through the open midsection of her taut sari.

Her husband was bigger, wider, and flashier than she was. He wore a turban with a topaz set in the center just above his forehead, and a white brocade kurta. He had a ring on every finger of both hands. In the quiet of this hallway, they seemed to me like monsters as they barged into our tranquil and intimate scene.

With no greeting at all either to me or to Mother Teresa, the large, loud woman shoved a camera into my hand as she and her husband pulled Mother Teresa from her chair and situated her against the wall between them. Then they pushed in like giant, grotesque bookends on either side of Mother Teresa and demanded a photograph.

"We didn't get a picture. We need to have a picture!" the woman complained loudly, and she motioned for me to snap a photo with her camera. I was livid. The beauty of my moment with Mother Teresa shattered in the rage I felt now at these rude and opulent intruders. As I snapped the photo, the tall woman fussed at Mother Teresa to look up toward her for a second shot. Mother Teresa was bent over at the neck from old age and osteoporosis, but without hesitating the woman put her hand under Mother Teresa's chin and forced it up. Shocked that anyone would treat Mother Teresa that way, but wanting them gone, I snapped the second photo. The woman then snatched her camera and she and her husband, without so much as a "thank you" to Mother Teresa or to me, disappeared in a noisy rush back down the hall and away.

Mother Teresa returned to her chair by the table and continued as if nothing had happened, finishing her thoughts on the topic of our earlier conversation. But I could hardly hear her, I was so full of anger and outrage toward this couple. I could feel the blood coursing through my veins; my palms were sweaty. It was time for our meeting to end. Tearfully, I said good-bye. She kissed both my hands, and I kissed hers, we embraced, and we parted.

I walked out through the nursery to my waiting car, and settled in for the forty-five-minute drive home. I was perspiring and breathing hard, running over and over again in my mind the dreadful scene of insult and entitlement that had just played out. I recalled the moment the large woman forced up Mother Teresa's chin, and I felt enraged all over again. I thought terrible thoughts about the intruders and felt a seething anger at the bossy, obnoxious, arrogant rich. My body was tense, and hatred ran through me.

Along the way, fifteen or twenty minutes into the ride back to my hotel, I became somewhat calmer. I realized with some shame how I had reduced myself to hatred and prejudice in the presence of one of the most inspiring spiritual beings on the planet. I thought back and realized that Mother Teresa had had no problem with the wealthy couple. To her, they were children of God, no less and no more than the orphans in her care, and she had treated them with love and respect and then calmly returned to her meeting with me.

I had always thought of myself as open and compassionate with everyone everywhere, but now I saw my own bigotry and where my compassion stopped. I saw my own ugly prejudice, a prejudice against the rich and powerful. These were not my people. These were people I could not embrace and include in my circle of love. They were rude. They were ugly. They were disgraceful. I also could see now that this chance encounter with this wealthy couple, behaving as they did, enabled me for the first time to confront and know my own prejudice. I could not have imagined the power this lesson would come to have in my life.

It was dark and late when I returned home to my hotel, exhausted from the day's roller coaster of emotions, from the moment I learned of the meeting early that morning to the actual moments of being with her, then the upsetting interruption, and my rage, then my realization and my shame. I lit a candle and sat down to write Mother Teresa a letter. I told her everything, including the unbridled rage, hatred, and resentment I had felt toward her visitors. I shared how shocked I was to meet my own prejudice and the limit of my own compassion, even in her presence. I asked for both her forgiveness and her counsel.

Weeks later I received a letter from her in her own hand. In her reply she admonished me, saying that while I had expressed compassion for the poor, the sick, the faint, and the weak all my life, that would always be a place where my self-expression and service would easily flourish. The vicious cycle of poverty, she said, has been clearly articulated and is widely known. What is less obvious and goes almost completely unacknowledged is the vicious cycle of wealth. There is no recognition of the trap that

wealth so often is, and of the suffering of the wealthy: the lone-
liness, the isolation, the hardening of the heart, the hunger and
poverty of the soul that can come with the burden of wealth.
She said that I had extended little or no compassion to the
strong, the powerful, and the wealthy, while they need as much
compassion as anyone else on earth.

"You must open your heart to them and become their stu-
dent and their teacher," she said in her letter. "Open your compassion and include them. This is an important part of your
life's work. Do not shut them out. They also are your work."

This was a shocking idea to me. Of course the rich were
human and had their woes, but I had never thought of them as
needy. I could begin to see it now. Their money bought them
material comforts and some level of protection from the incon-
veniences and impositions of more ordinary everyday life. But
their money and the lifestyle of privilege also cut them off from
the richness of ordinary everyday life, the more normal and
healthy give-and-take of relationships and useful work, the best
of the human experience. Often their wealth distorted their
relationship with money and only widened the gap between
their soulful life and their interactions around money. Sexual
abuse, psychological abuse, addictions, alcoholism, abandon-
ment, and brutality are part of the dysfunctional world that
hides behind walled communities, mansions, and darkened car
windows. Hurtful rejections, custody suits, legal battles for the
purpose of attaining more and more money harden family
members and shut them down from each other. The access to
money and power at high levels can amplify these situations and
make them ever more lethal and unbearably cruel.

Mother Teresa's admonition and my subsequent fund-raising work with the very wealthy taught me that, surprisingly, wealth is no protection from human suffering. I would come to learn that people with excess wealth—not all of them, but many—struggle in lives disconnected from the qualities of the soul. They live trapped in a prison of privilege in which material comforts are plentiful, but spiritual and emotional deprivation are real and painful. In that prison they lose touch with the values of the heart. They can become the manifestation of money's darkest side. For some, wealth only serves as a weapon that expands their capacity to do harm.

From the day I received her letter I made a commitment to open my heart and capacity for compassion and love to the rich and powerful with the same depth of commitment I devoted to the poor and hungry. As a global fund-raiser I had many opportunities to do that and have now seen intimately the vicious cycle of wealth and the damage it can inflict on those caught up in it. Money alone does not guarantee a fulfilling life, and excessive amounts of money more often become an obstacle to it.

HUNGER HAS BEEN MY TEACHER

In those early days of my work with The Hunger Project I was a shining and visible example of the power of commitment because in my soul I knew (and still know) that chronic, persistent hunger on this planet can be eradicated. That's where I stand, and when you take that stand and work from there, you take different actions than you do when you believe that hunger is inevitable and your effort is to try to make it "not so bad." When you know with certainty that things can be not just different but entirely resolved, you engage in the work in a more fundamental way. You don't wonder "if." You determine "how to." You look at root causes. You make different choices.

After five successful years of speaking and garnering resources in the United States and Europe to end hunger, when I finally did arrive in India and confronted for the first time the scale and complexity of chronic hunger there, I was devastated. I was sick. But there was no turning back. It wasn't as if I could say, "Oh, I see. I don't want to do this anymore because it looks too hard." That didn't even come up. Instead of falling back from a daunting task, or retreating from a situation that seems impossible, or compromising on the original commitment and saying you didn't really mean it, The Hunger Project drew its power for social action from the principles of personal transformation and empowering self-inquiry.

> Who do I need to be to fulfill on the commitment I've made?
> What kind of human being do I need to forge myself into to
>   make this happen?
> What resources do I need to be willing to bring to bear in myself
>   and my colleagues and in my world?

The Hunger Project's unique approach had been a perfect match for me, reflecting my own approach to life; I knew from experience that you can't fail if you live from there. You become a more powerful instrument of what's wanted and needed for the affirmation of human life. You deepen your humility and your courage. When you discard your own pettiness, center yourself in integrity, and reach into your soul for your greatness, it is always there.

For me, that translated into fund-raising. I knew that I could and I would raise any amount of money to get that job done.

Fund-raising to end hunger wasn't just a job or a fad or a political statement for me. It was an expression of my own soulful commitment, and as such, I could only do it in a way that would call on people to reconnect with their own higher calling, or soulful longing, to be the kind of people they wanted to be, the kind of difference they wanted to make, and see how they could express that with their money. So rather than feeling that fund-raising was a matter of twisting arms for a donation or playing on emotions to manipulate money from contributors, it became for me an arena in which I was able to create an opportunity for people to engage in their greatness.

It was in this soul-searching dimension of fund-raising, in these intimate conversations, that I discovered deep wounds and conflicts in the way people related to their money. Many people felt they had sold out and become someone they didn't like anymore. Some were forcing themselves to do work that wasn't meaningful. Many felt enslaved by their experience of being overtaxed by their government, or felt beaten down by their boss or by the burden of running a family business or employing others. Their relationship with money was dead— or, more accurately, *dread*—and there was hurt there. There was resentment. There were painful compromises, a kind of rawness. People were bruised and battered there. Not everyone, but many people were very unsettled and uncomfortable and just not their best selves in their relationship with money. They felt little or no freedom with money, no matter how much they had.

This lackluster relationship with money wasn't for lack of expert advice or practical tips. Money-management strategies were plentiful, but the concept of personal transformation was a stranger there.

What became clear was that when people were able to align

their money with their deepest, most soulful interests and commitments, their relationship with money became a place where profound and lasting transformation could occur. Their money—no matter what the amount—became the conduit for this change.

In the thick of everyday conversations about money, about how we earn, get, save, spend, or invest it, our conversations became a clearing in which people were able to focus on their money and their lives in a completely different and inspired way. In the space of that clearing, they were able to feel the rush of energy unleashed when they considered their money as a way to express their deepest, most soulful commitments.

This wasn't an occasional epiphany. It happened reliably, no matter what the circumstances of their lives. It didn't matter how much money they had to express their commitment. It was in the act of reseeing themselves in relation to their money, and expressing their soul's integrity through the medium of money, that they experienced the joyful reward.

So it was that in the striking beauty and severity of life in India, and in the conversations around fund-raising to end hunger, that one by one the flawed assumptions we hold about money, about soul, and about the gap between the two became clear to me, and a different truth emerged about money and the human spirit. I began to see how people could free themselves from money's grip and have money flow to and through their lives in ways that would nourish them and their world. But it required confronting some critical facts and fictions, the first and foremost: the lie of scarcity.

Part Two

SCARCITY AND SUFFICIENCY: THE SEARCH FOR PROSPERITY

3

Scarcity: The Great Lie

There is a natural law of abundance which pervades the entire universe, but it will not flow through a doorway of belief in lack and limitation.

—PAUL ZAITER

I have been engaged for all these years in the lives and circumstances of people, many of whom live in crushing conditions where the lack of food, water, shelter, freedom, or opportunity drives every move and every conversation. Others, by every measure, have bounty way beyond their needs—more money, more food, more cars, more clothes, more education, more services, more freedom, more opportunity, more of everything. Yet, surprisingly, in that world of over abundance, too, the conversation is dominated by what they don't have and what they want to get. No matter who we are or what our circumstances, we swim in conversations about what there isn't enough of.

I see it in myself. For me, and for many of us, our first waking thought of the day is "I didn't get enough sleep." The next one is "I don't have enough time." Whether true or not, that thought of *not enough* occurs to us automatically before we even think to question or examine it. We spend most of the hours and the days of our lives hearing, explaining, complaining, or worrying about what we don't have enough of. We don't have enough time. We don't have enough rest. We don't have enough exercise. We don't have enough work. We don't have enough profits. We don't have enough power. We don't have enough wilderness. We don't have enough weekends. Of course we don't have enough money—ever. We're not thin enough, we're not smart enough, we're not pretty enough or fit enough or educated or successful enough, or rich enough—ever. Before we even sit up in bed, before our feet touch the floor, we're already inadequate, already behind, already losing, already lacking something. And by the time we go to bed at night, our minds race with a litany of what we didn't get, or didn't get done, that day. We go to sleep burdened by those thoughts and wake up to that reverie of lack.

This mantra of *not enough* carries the day and becomes a kind of default setting for our thinking about everything, from the cash in our pocket to the people we love or the value of our own lives. What begins as a simple expression of the hurried life, or even the challenged life, grows into the great justification for an unfulfilled life. It becomes the reason we can't have what we want or be who we want to be. It becomes the reason we can't accomplish the goals we set for ourselves, the reason our dreams can't come true, or the reason other people disappoint us, the reason we compromise our integrity, give up on our ourselves or write off others.

It's the same in the inner city or the suburbs, in New York

or Topeka or Beverly Hills or Calcutta. Whether we live in resource-poor circumstances or resource-rich ones, even if we're loaded with more money or goods or everything you could possibly dream of wanting or needing, we live with scarcity as an underlying assumption. It is an unquestioned, sometimes even unspoken, defining condition of life. It is not even that we necessarily experience a lack of something, but that scarcity as a chronic sense of inadequacy about life becomes the very place from which we think and act and live in the world. It shapes our deepest sense of ourselves, and becomes the lens through which we experience life. Through that lens our expectations, our behavior, and their consequences become a self-fulfilling prophecy of inadequacy, lack, and dissatisfaction.

This internal condition of scarcity, this mind-set of scarcity, lives at the very heart of our jealousies, our greed, our prejudice, and our arguments with life, and it is deeply embedded in our relationship with money. In the mind-set of scarcity, our relationship with money is an expression of fear; a fear that drives us in an endless and unfulfilling chase for more, or into compromises that promise a way out of the chase or discomfort around money. In the chase or in the compromises we break from our wholeness and natural integrity. We abandon our soul and grow more and more distanced from our core values and highest commitments. We find ourselves trapped in a cycle of disconnection and dissatisfaction. We start to believe the profit-driven commercial and cultural messages that suggest money *can* buy happiness, and we begin to look outside of ourselves to be fulfilled. Intuitively, we know it isn't so, but the money culture shouts down the wiser inner voice, and we feel compelled to seek even the most transient relief and comforts that money can buy.

Some would suggest that scarcity is the true, natural, and inevitable basis for our relationship with money and resources. There is, after all, only so much of everything. More than two hundred years ago, around the time of the American Revolution, the Scottish philosopher and economist Adam Smith suggested that "the natural effort of every individual to better his own condition" was more powerful than any obstacle in its way, and he went on to articulate the founding principles of a modern (for the time) "free market" economy in which "the invisible hand" of self-interest was accepted as the dominant and most natural guiding force.

But how natural and accurate was that premise? The world of that day—that is, the world of the white, European, traditionally educated theorist Adam Smith—was one in which most white people dismissed indigenous people and people of color as "primitive" and "savage," rather than valued them as resourceful and wise in ways "civilized" societies would only begin to appreciate generations later. The dominant white classes of that day accepted, and practiced, racial, religious, and sex discrimination as a moral and economic assumption. In those days, self-interest and nationalism were not yet informed by an awareness of the global interconnectedness that today we recognize affects us, our wealth, and our security profoundly, and necessarily expands the boundaries of self-interest to include the well-being of all people, everywhere. The fundamental economic principles and structures of that bygone era were based on flawed assumptions and wrong thinking—about nature, about human potential, and about money itself.

Contemporary European author, Bernard Lietaer, former senior officer of the Belgian Central Bank and one of the chief architects of the Euro currency, in his book, *Of Human Wealth*, says that greed and fear of scarcity are programmed; they do not exist in nature, not even in human nature. They are built into the money system in which we swim, and we've been swimming in it so long that these shadows have become almost completely transparent to us. We have learned to consider them normal and legitimate behavior. He concludes that Adam Smith's system of economics could more accurately be described as the allocation of scarce resources through the process of individual greed. The whole process of Smith's "modern" economics actually has its roots in primitive fears of scarcity, greed, and the implementation tool—the process by which this became real—was money.

When we step out of the shadow of this distorted and outdated system and the mind-set it generates, what we discover is this: Scarcity is a lie. Independent of any actual amount of resources, it is an unexamined and false system of assumptions, opinions, and beliefs from which we view the world as a place where we are in constant danger of having our needs unmet.

It would be logical to assume that people with excess wealth do not live with the fear of scarcity at the center of their lives, but I have seen that scarcity is as oppressive in those lives as it is for people who are living at the margins and barely making ends meet. It is so illogical that people who have tremendous excess would be thinking they don't have enough, that as I encountered this time and again, I began to question the source of their concerns. Nothing in their actual circumstances justified it. I began to wonder if this anxiety over having enough was based on a set of assumptions, rather than circumstances. The more I examined these ideas and the more I interacted with individuals in a broad range of circumstances and a broad range of cultures and ethics, the more I saw that the fundamental assumption of scarcity was all-pervasive. The myths and the language of scarcity were the dominant voice in nearly every culture, often overriding logic and evidence, and the mind-set of scarcity created distorted, even irrational, attitudes and behaviors, especially around money. What I have found is that no matter where we are in the political, economic, or financial resource spectrum, the myths and mind-set of scarcity create an underlying fear that we, and the people we love or care about, won't have enough of what's needed to have a satisfying, happy, productive, or even survivable life.

This mind-set of scarcity is not something we intentionally created or have any conscious intention to bring into our life. It was here before us and it will likely persist beyond us, perpetuated in the myths and language of our money culture. We do, however, have a choice about whether or not to buy into it and whether or not to let it rule our lives.

THE TOXIC MYTHS OF SCARCITY

Myths and superstitions have power over us only to the extent that we believe them, but when we believe, we live completely under their spell and in that fiction. Scarcity is a lie, but it has been passed down as truth and with a powerful mythology that insists on itself, demands compliance, and discourages doubt or questioning.

In my work with people across the spectrum of money and resources, I found that it is possible to unpack this set of beliefs and assumptions, this kind of overarching way of seeing life, and get some distance from it, free ourselves from its grip, and see for ourselves—each of us in our own life—whether or not it's a valid way to live life. When we unpack the mind-set of scarcity, we find three central myths that have come to define our relationship with money and that block our access to more honest and fulfilling interactions with it.

Toxic Myth #1: There's Not Enough

The first prevailing myth of scarcity is that *there's not enough*. There's not enough to go around. Everyone can't make it. Somebody's going to be left out. There are way too many people. There's not enough food. There's not enough water. There's not enough air. There's not enough time. There's not enough money.

There's not enough becomes the reason we do work that brings us down or the reason we do things to each other that we're not proud of. *There's not enough* generates a fear that drives us to make sure that we're not the person, or our loved ones aren't the people, who get crushed, marginalized, or left out.

Once we define our world as deficient, the total of our life energy, everything we think, everything we say, and everything we do—particularly with money—becomes an expression of an effort to overcome this sense of lack and the fear of losing to others or being left out. It becomes noble and responsible to make sure we take care of our own, whoever we deem that to be. If there's not enough for everyone, then taking care of yourself and your own, even at others' expense, seems unfortunate, but unavoidable and somehow valid. It's like the child's game of musical chairs. With one seat short of the number of people playing, your focus is on not losing and not being the one who ends up at the end of the scramble without a seat. We don't want to be the poor suckers without, so we compete to get more than the other guy, determined to stay ahead of some impending doom.

The deficiency and fear reflect in the way we conduct our lives, and the systems and institutions we create to control access to any resource we perceive as valuable or limited. As members of the global community, our fear-based responses lead us at times—in the demand for foreign oil, for instance—to put our own material desires above the health, safety, and well-being of other people and other nations. In our own communities, we respond to the fear that *there's not enough* by creating systems that favor us or exclude others from access to basic resources such as clean water, good schools, adequate health care, or safe housing. And in our own families, *there's not enough* drives us to buy more than we need or even want of some things, to value, favor, or curry favor with people on the basis of their value to us in relation to money, rather than qualities of character.

Toxic Myth #2: More Is Better

The second toxic myth is that *more is better*. More of anything is better than what we have. It's the logical response if you fear there's not enough, but *more is better* drives a competitive culture of accumulation, acquisition, and greed that only heightens fears and quickens the pace of the race. And none of it makes life more valuable. In truth, the rush for more distances us from experiencing the deeper value of what we acquire or already have. When we eat too fast or too much, we cannot savor any single bite of food. When we are focused constantly on the next thing—the next dress, the next car, the next job, the next vacation, the next home improvement—we hardly experience the gifts of that which we have now. In our relationship with money, *more is better* distracts us from living more mindfully and richly with what we have.

More is better is a chase with no end and a race without winners. It's like a hamster wheel that we hop onto, get going, and then forget how to stop. Eventually, the chase for more becomes an addictive exercise, and as with any addiction, it's almost impossible to stop the process when you're in its grip. But no matter how far you go, or how fast, or how many other people you pass up, you can't win. In the mind-set of scarcity, even too much is not enough.

It doesn't make sense to someone who makes forty thousand dollars a year that someone who makes five million dollars a year would be arguing over their golden parachute package and need at least fifteen million dollars more. Some of the people with fortunes enough to last three lifetimes spend their days and nights worrying about losing money on the stock market, about being ripped off or conned or not having enough for their retirement. Any genuine fulfillment in their life of financial privilege can be completely eclipsed by these money fears and stresses. How could people who have millions of dollars think they need more? They think they need more because that's the prevailing myth. We all think that, so they think that, too. Even those who have plenty cannot quit the chase. The chase of *more is better*— no matter what our money circumstances—demands our attention, saps our energy, and erodes our opportunities for fulfillment. When we buy into the promise that more is better, we can never arrive. Wherever we are, it is not enough because more is always better. People who follow that credo, consciously or unconsciously—which is all of us to some degree—are doomed to a life that is never fulfilled; we lose the capacity to reach a destination. So even those who have plenty, in this scarcity culture, cannot quit the chase.

More is better misguides us in a deeper way. It leads us to define ourselves by financial success and external achievements. We judge others based on what they have and how much they have, and miss the immeasurable inner gifts they bring to life. All the great spiritual teachings tell us to look inside to find the wholeness we crave, but the scarcity chase allows no time or psychic space for that kind of introspection. In the pursuit of more we overlook the fullness and completeness that are already within us waiting to be discovered. Our drive to enlarge our *net* worth turns us away from discovering and deepening our *self-* worth.

The belief that we need to possess, and possess more than the other person or company or nation, is the driving force for much of the violence and war, corruption and exploitation on earth. In the condition of scarcity, we believe we must have more—more oil, more land, more military might, more market share, more profits, more stock, more possessions, more power, more money. In the campaign to gain, we often pursue our goals at all costs, even at the risk of destroying whole cultures and peoples.

Do other countries need American fast food or theme parks or cigarettes, or have American companies shrewdly expanded their markets internationally to increase their profits, disregarding the impact they have on local cultures, agriculture, economy, and public health, at times even in the face of widespread protests against their presence?

Do we need or even really want all the clothing, cars, groceries, and gadgets we bring home from our shopping trips, or are we acting on impulse, responding to the call of the consumer culture and the steady, calculated seduction by fashion, food, and consumer product advertising? Does a five-year-old *need* more than a few thoughtfully chosen birthday presents to feel celebrated? Whose interests are we really serving when we give children far more than they need or even appreciate at one time?

The unquestioned, unchecked drive for more fuels an unsustainable economy, culture, and way of being that has failed us by blocking our access to the deeper, more meaningful aspects of our lives and ourselves.

Toxic Myth #3: That's Just the Way It Is

The third toxic myth is that *that's just the way it is*, and there's no way out. There's not enough to go around, more is definitely better, and the people who have more are always people who are other than us. It's not fair, but we'd better play the game because *that's just the way it is* and it's a hopeless, helpless, unequal, unfair world where you can never get out of this trap.

That's just the way it is is just another myth, but it's probably the one with the most grip, because you can always make a case for it. When something has always been a certain way, and tradition, assumptions, or habits make it resistant to change, then it seems logical, just commonsensical, that the way it is is the way it will stay. This is when and where the blindness, the numbness, the trance, and, underneath it all, the resignation of scarcity sets in. Resignation makes us feel hopeless, helpless, and cynical. Resignation also keeps us in line, even at the end of the line, where a lack of money becomes an excuse for holding back from commitment and contributing what we do have—time, energy, and creativity—to making a difference. Resignation keeps us from questioning how much we'll compromise ourselves or exploit others for the money available to us in a job or career, a personal relationship or a business opportunity.

That's just the way it is justifies the greed, prejudice, and inaction that scarcity fosters in our relationship with money and the rest of the human race. For generations, it protected the early American slave trade from which the privileged majority built farms, towns, business empires, and family fortunes, many of which survive today. For more generations it protected and emboldened institutionalized racism, sex discrimination and social and economic discrimination against other ethnic and religious minorities. It has throughout history, and still today, enabled dishonest business and political leaders to exploit others for their own financial gain.

Globally, the myth of *that's just the way it is* makes it so that those with the most money wield the most power and feel encouraged and entitled to do so. For instance, the United States, with 4 percent of the world's population, generates 25 percent of the pollution that contributes to global warming. According to *Geo 2000*, a 1999 United Nations environmental report, the excessive consumption by the affluent minority of the earth's population and the continued poverty of the majority are the two major causes of environmental degradation. Meanwhile, developing nations adopting Western economic models are replicating patterns that, even in political democracies, place inordinate power in the hands of the wealthy few, design social institutions and systems that favor them, and fail to adequately address the inherent inequities and consequences that undermine health, education, and safety for all.

We say we feel bad about these and other inequities in the world, but the problems seem so deeply rooted as to be insurmountable and we resign ourselves to *that's just the way it is*, declaring ourselves helpless to change things. In that resignation, we abandon our own human potential, and the possibility of contributing to a thriving, equitable, healthy world.

That's just the way it is presents one of the toughest pieces of transforming our relationship with money, because if you can't let go of the chase and shake off the helplessness and cynicism it eventually generates, then you're stuck. If you're not willing to question that, then it is hard to dislodge the thinking that got you stuck. We have to be willing to let go of *that's just the way it is*, even if just for a moment, to consider the possibility that there isn't a *way it is* or *way it isn't*. There is the way we choose to act and what we choose to make of circumstances.

"LIFE SENTENCES" LIMIT OUR POSSIBILITIES

In any culture, myths communicate moral lessons, and scarcity myths have produced a legacy of beliefs—"life sentences"—that we embrace as folk wisdom or personal truths. When I was a child my grandmother used to say to her granddaughters, "Marry the money and love will come later." We used to laugh when she'd say that and she would giggle and have a twinkle in her eye, but to tell the truth, she believed it. It's what she had done. When she was married around 1900, she married the wealthiest man she could find and then found a way to love him.

She wanted to pass that advice on to us. Even though we laughed at her comments, they imprinted us. All her grand-daughters later had to break from that belief system in our lives if we were to be free to find loving partners with deeper creden-tials than cash.

In the mind-set and mythology of scarcity, we each struggle with our own life sentences about money. Some come to us in folksy phrases, like my grandmother's, that offer incomplete or flawed instruction: *Don't spend the principal. If you have to ask the price, you can't afford it. Money is no object. It's not polite to talk about money.* Sometimes it's important to be willing to spend the prin-cipal in meaningful ways; to consider price as a matter of princi-ple, even if you have more than enough to pay it; to be direct and open about money issues instead of uncertain or guarded.

Other life sentences are personal, of our own making, and are expressed in patterns of conscious or unconscious behavior around money. Early in my career as a fund-raiser, for instance, I worked almost completely on a volunteer basis, and was only comfortable asking for money for others. In my personal life, I was happy to let my husband handle the family finances, reliev-ing me of that nitty-gritty responsibility. However, over time, I realized that the unintended lessons I learned, the life sentences I was creating and which came to be limiting, were that I couldn't expect to earn a living with my work, and that I wasn't a full, responsible, and participating partner in my own family's financial life. I still give freely of my time and energy, and I still trust my husband with our family finances, but I also have expanded my experience to include the satisfaction of earning money and being more responsible for managing it. This has been a matter of personal growth for me, and a step toward cre-ating a more honest relationship with money.

Maybe those life sentences sound familiar to you. Or maybe you have worked for money most of your life, but have been reluctant to ask for well-deserved raises; or stayed at a dead-end job rather than investing the time and energy in searching for a new one, or getting training for a different kind of work. Maybe you enjoy an inheritance and feel entitled to family wealth, or maybe you feel guilty about it. Maybe you avoid balancing your checkbook or paying your bills because the black-and-white reality of those numbers says something you don't want to hear. Maybe you're afraid to assert yourself about money in a relationship, because you fear the repercussions; maybe your financial fears keep you from asserting yourself at all.

Most of our life sentences around money are the product of the limiting language of scarcity in our culture. In that parlance, the word *success* implies that a person is making an excess of money. A successful business owner is simply one who makes a lot of money. Not factored into that judgment are the quality of the product, the workplace, employee compensation, and management style, or the company's overall practice of civic partnership and contribution. In the language of scarcity, those who generate large profits from exploitive or unsustainable business practices show up as more "successful" than, say, teachers or public servants who earn less, but work to make our communities enlightened, caring, compassionate places to live and work.

The word *wealthy* has its roots in *well-being* and is meant to connote not only large amounts of money but also a rich and satisfying life. To the contrary, excess money often creates conditions of entitlement and isolation that diminish one's access to the genuine wealth of human connection and interaction.

Poor and *poverty* describe economic circumstances and environments, but too often these words are used in ways that discount the humanity and potential of individuals who have little money.

The "starving artist" life sentence has us accept that creativity is undervalued in our society. It suggests that those of us who rely on creative gifts to make a living can expect to be poorly paid, and the rest of us are entitled to exploit them or short-change them in money terms, and undervalue them in human terms.

These and other scarcity-based life sentences are mere constructions of language that have become embedded in our thinking, but once there they reinforce the myths of scarcity and give money enormous destructive power. A lifelong flood of messages from media, advertising, and marketing, from our parents and grandparents, from our friends reinforces and roots itself deeply in our thinking and leads us to believe that *there's not enough, you have to get yours, more is better*, and you have to play that game.

BUCKMINSTER FULLER
AND A YOU-*AND*-ME WORLD

It was in my work to end hunger and in the commitment it awakened in me that I began to see this whole construct of scarcity, and its pervasive mythology, language, and life sentences. I saw how it infused my own life, as well as the lives of my friends and family, and the lives of people with whom I worked in countries as poor as Bangladesh, and as rich as France, England, or the United States. In what proved to be a turning point for me, I had an opportunity to listen to the great futurist and humanist, R. Buckminster ("Bucky") Fuller. In the

1970s, Bucky was speaking broadly about mythologies in basic science that blocked us from an accurate vision of the world and its capacity to support a prosperous life for all.

Bucky later became a friend and mentor, but the first time I heard him speak I knew him simply as a controversial genius—a designer, engineer, and architect—who was giving a series of speeches around the world entitled "Integrity Days." I was a volunteer at his talk in San Francisco, and in an auditorium that held an audience of two thousand or so, I remember sitting in the second-to-last row of seats, watching this small, eloquent, and radiant older man on the stage express with great exuberance his insights and revelations about the way the world works. His ideas were not just eloquent, not just provocative, but for me completely revolutionary and transformational.

I was riveted by his talk and the distinctions he was making, but the one that changed my life was when he said that for centuries, perhaps thousands of years, we have lived in the belief that there's not enough to go around, and that we need to fight and compete to garner those resources for ourselves. Perhaps it had been a valid perception at one time, or perhaps it hadn't been, he said, but at this point in history—in the 1970s—we were able to do so much more with so much less that as a human family we clearly had reached a point where there actually was enough for everyone everywhere to meet or even surpass their needs to live a reasonably healthy, productive life. This moment represented a dramatic breakthrough in the evolution of civilization and humankind, he said.

Whether it was a recognition of something already true or a moment of transformation in the status of civilizations, he said, either way it could be the most significant turning point in our evolution because it meant we could move from a you-*or*-me world—a world where either you or I make it, and where we need to compete and fight to see who wins—to a you-*and*-me world, where all of us can make it. In that you-*and*-me world, all of us have enough food, enough water, enough land, enough housing, enough of the fundamental things for each one of us to live a fulfilling and productive life.

This new threshold completely changes the game, and it would take fifty years, he predicted, for us to make the necessary adjustments in our world so we could move from a you-*or*-me paradigm to you-*and*-me paradigm, a paradigm that says the world can work for everyone with no one and nothing left out. He said that our money system, our financial resources system, would need to adjust itself to reflect that reality and it would take decades for us to make that adjustment, but if and when we did, we would enter an age, a time, and a world in which the very fundamental ways we perceive and think about ourselves and the world we live in would be so transformed that it would be unrecognizable.

This statement, this uncommon vision and the revelation of the shift in the very basis of the way we relate to one another, completely captured me. It turned my world upside down. I remember being in tears in my seat, thinking about the implications of what he was saying. I remember thinking, this isn't just an interesting point in an erudite lecture. This is a moment of exquisite and profound recognition of something I have known in my heart all along, and he is voicing it, a revered scientist, a futurist, someone who has the knowledge and the credentials and who has done the research to back up this kind of thinking. That moment of profound recognition has never left me.

Bucky also was working from a changing worldview that had begun to emerge following the first manned lunar landing by the crew of *Apollo 11* in the summer of 1969. Historic and breathtaking photographs of the Earth from the moon gave humankind its first clear view of our planet as one complete, whole "spaceship Earth" as Bucky called it. In that moment we moved from being a part of the system to moving far enough outside the system so we could see Earth as a whole, and we could see its fragility, its beauty, its completeness, its exquisite integrity. I would venture to say this was the beginning of a global society, a global consciousness, global humanity, and from there this recognition of the finite but sufficient resources of this planet for all who live here—humans, plants, and animals alike—became the potential reality of the future.

It was with this view of our global community, and Bucky's insights and inspiration, that I engaged in the work to end hunger.

THE MYSTERY OF HUNGER AND OUR STRUGGLE WITH SCARCITY

Hunger and scarcity would seem to be obviously and inexorably linked. How could I work so intimately in settings where food and water are so scarce, and insist that scarcity is a lie? All I can say is that it is the harsh and surprising realities of that experience that have forced me to look beyond the obvious. I have struggled to understand the tragedy of hunger. Hunger isn't some mysterious disease. It's not a mutant gene or a wild force of nature. We know what to do when a child is hungry. We know what a starving person needs. They need food. There is nothing in the picture of global resources that explains why one-fifth of humanity is hungry and malnourished. The world is awash in food. We currently have more food on earth than we need to feed everyone several times over. Waste abounds. In several countries, including the United States, farmers are paid to not grow food. Cattle that are raised for slaughter consume enough resources to feed every hungry child and adult.

In 1977, when I first committed to working to end world hunger, I assumed that people were starving because they didn't have enough food, and if we just got food to the people out there who are hungry, that would solve the problem of chronic hunger in the world. It all seemed so logical. But if matching the world's food supply with the world's hungry people held the solution, what explained the stubborn, tragic statistics and realities of hunger that would seem to make us incapable of resolving it? How could it be that in a world with more than enough food to go around, 41,000 people, most of them children under the age of five, were dying *each day* of hunger and hunger-related causes?

Could it be that no one cares? When hungry children cry for food, they cry out not as Bangladeshis or Italians, or children from the poor side of our own town. They cry out as human beings, and it is at that level of our humanity that we need to respond. Is it that we can't hear those cries and respond as caring members of the human family? What would have so many of us turn a blind eye and deaf ear to a child's cry, and make a choice just to take care of "our own"—even when we have plenty to feed "our own" and others, too?

Yet, if caring were the answer, how could it be that even the massive donations of food and money that some people make don't lead to a lasting solution?

Could the problem be distribution? How could that be,

when American soft drinks are practically within an arm's reach of everyone on earth?

Could it be logistics? How could that be, when the most powerful nations like ours have logistical capabilities to deliver armed missiles and bombs for precise military strikes virtually anywhere in the world?

Could it be politics? Could we be so cynical and self-serving that we would let a starving child die because we disagree as adults about political or economic ideologies?

What *is* it that allows us to hear the cry and yet fail to respond effectively?

The more time I spent with people who live in hunger and with people who work or give money to feed them, the more clearly I saw that the cause of chronic hunger wasn't just the absence of food. What causes hunger and starvation is something more fundamental than that, because no matter how much food you might move from point A to point B, while it might make a huge difference to a number of people for a period of time, it does not resolve the hunger issue.

History teaches us that lesson. The flood of aid that went into Ethiopia in 1985 fed many people for a period of time, but did not resolve that country's hunger issue. Ethiopia remains a hungry, impoverished country. The food aid that was sent into Somalia during the crisis there in 1993 and 1994 fed a hungry few, but actually exacerbated the violence and corruption that was taking place during the civil war there. The food aid that flooded into Biafra during the Biafran war, the food aid to Cambodia during the Cambodian crisis—the aid was not a bad thing, some people were fed, but it also did not solve the long-term problem of chronic, persistent hunger.

In those events of massive infusions of food aid, time and again, to the point of becoming routine, the food supplies were stolen and resold by the corrupt power brokers who thrive on the greed and graft that is rife in embattled countries. Further, the massive amounts of food aid deflated the local market, meaning that those farmers who did grow grain could no longer sell it because free food was everywhere—at least for a time, as the scramble to hoard and control it played out. The disastrous cycle of aid, corruption, disrupted markets, and disastrous farming investments became part of a problem instead of a solution. The cycle only perpetuated the root causes of the crisis.

Ultimately, the societal effect of massive aid of this kind was that people at the receiving end, even those who got some portion of the food, became even more disabled, more impoverished, than they were before. They felt debilitated and helpless by the fact that they couldn't take care of themselves and had become welfare recipients, beholden to outsiders to bail them out again and again. They felt lessened and weakened, and the future prospect of their own self-sufficiency was often suppressed and diminished by the behavior they needed to exhibit in these situations to get their hands on the "free" food. Time and again, when money or aid flowed into communities through systems based on these scarcity assumptions, the relief was short-lived, and those on both sides of the transaction were left feeling ineffective.

I struggled with this question for years, as have others engaged in work to end hunger, in search of answers that might suggest a solution to this ongoing tragedy. When I considered the underlying beliefs held in common by most everyone everywhere—every system, every institution, every point of view, including those suffering from hunger—I saw that there were fundamental assumptions that disabled almost every effort to solve the problem. All of them could be traced to the myths and mind-set of scarcity.

No matter what our economic circumstances:

When we believe *there is not enough*, that resources are scarce, then we accept that some will have what they need and some will not. We rationalize that someone is destined to end up with the short end of the stick.

When we believe that *more is better*, and equate having more with being more—more smart or more able—then people on the short end of that resource stick are assumed to be less smart, less able, even less valuable, as human beings. We feel we have permission to discount them.

When we believe *that's just the way things are*, then we assume a posture of helplessness. We believe that a problem is unsolvable. We accept that in our human family neither the resource-rich members nor the resource-poor members have enough money, enough food, or enough intelligence or resourcefulness to generate lasting solutions.

The Hunger Project, by systematically challenging false assumptions about chronic hunger and food aid, exposed the myth of scarcity and opened new avenues of inquiry and possibility, eventually succeeding in making a significant contribution to the eradication of hunger by empowering people to author their own recovery. In every situation, from individuals to large populations of people, uncovering the lie and the myths of scarcity has been the first and most powerful step in the transformation from helplessness and resignation to possibility and self-reliance.

We often philosophize about the great, unanswered questions in life. It's time we looked instead at the *unquestioned answers*, and the biggest, most *unquestioned answer* of our culture is our relationship with money. It is there that we keep alive—at a high cost—the flame and mythology of scarcity.

4

Sufficiency: The Surprising Truth

> When you let go of trying to get more of what you don't really
> need, it frees up oceans of energy to make a difference with what
> you have. When you make a difference with what you have, it
> expands.

I t has been nearly ten years since my first encounter with
the indigenous Achuar people of Ecuador, but I can still
remember the experience of meeting them and being
among them for the first time—a completely different kind of
experience from my first encounter with hunger and poverty in
India. In the rain forest with the Achuar, I saw a people who
were naturally prosperous. They hadn't won some competitive
economic game to be prosperous. They were not prosperous at
anyone's expense. They hadn't beaten anyone at anything. They
were prosperous in the way they were with themselves and one
another, living consistent with the true laws, the unchanging
laws of the natural world, which ultimately govern us all.

Theirs was a culture with no money in it. It was something they encountered primarily when they ventured out of the forest. It was, for them, an odd, adjunct thing that was not a part of their everyday life or even their consciousness. With no money, no ownership, no accumulation of goods, and none of the conveniences of our Western lifestyle, still there was no suggestion of scarcity; no lack and no fear that there wouldn't be enough of what they needed. There was no chase for more, and no resignation or belief that they were living lives of less-than. They lived (and still do) in the experience and expression of *enough*, or what I call *sufficiency*. Instead of seeking more, they treasure and steward thoughtfully what is already there. In fact, their efforts today are devoted to protecting what is there—the rain forest—as a resource for all of us. For the Achuar, wealth means being present to the fullness and richness of the moment and sharing that with one another.

It is possible for those of us who live in money cultures to find the same equanimity and freedom in our own environment, and with money. Some of the greatest, most surprising lessons I've learned about sufficiency and our relationship with money have come from people with little or no money at all, like the Achuar, or from people confronted with the most formidable struggles for survival in situations we can hardly imagine. One such lesson unfolded in a remote village in Senegal.

Senegal is a small coastal country on the farthest west tip of the African continent. During the early slave trade days it was a prosperous French colony, and the historic slave owners' castles, with their prisonlike dungeons, still stand today, now tourist attractions and brooding monuments to the human and economic savagery of the time.

A large portion of Senegal is covered by the massive and encroaching Sahel Desert, which expands each year, toward the sea. The Sahel is a harsh environment, not friendly to life, even to the plants and animals that typically live in desert environments. The sand is fine, like dust, and a shade of pale orange. It is so fine and so pervasive that everything near the edge of the desert is covered with the yellowy orange sand: the streets, the houses, the plants, and the roads—even the people.

We were there, eighteen Hunger Project contributors and leaders, to meet with the people of a village several hours into the desert about their need to find a new source of water or a new place to live. As our drivers took the vehicles down the road from town and deep into the desert itself, we became covered with this very fine silty sand. It burrowed into our lungs with every breath. As we drove on the rough road into the orange wind, we saw fewer and fewer people, plants, and animal life and pretty soon there was nothing but barren land. It was hot and dry, over 95 degrees Fahrenheit, and I wore a hat and had a bandanna across my face to keep from breathing in the sand. It was so bleak that it seemed unimaginable that any human being could live in this climate.

For a while we were on a rough, unpaved road. Then it disappeared into the sand, and our drivers began driving on the open desert by compass only. Our Senegalese drivers knew the desert well, and there was a point at which the lead driver in the front vehicle stopped and turned off the engine. Then the other two did the same. After listening awhile, we could hear the faint sound of drums. Our lead driver smiled, turned on his engine, and began driving toward the sound of the drums. As we drove, the drums grew louder and louder, and soon on the horizon we could see tiny moving specks. As we drove closer and closer, we thought the specks were animals of some kind. Then as we grew near, we saw that they were children, dozens of children running toward our vehicles, bursting with excitement.

Here we were, in a place that showed no signs of life, being greeted by exuberant, cheering children brimming with vitality and aliveness. Tears welled in my eyes, and I could see my traveling companions were moved in the same way by this jubilant greeting. More little ones kept streaming toward us, and beyond them in the distance were two large baobab trees standing alone in the desolate vastness. The baobab is a lifesaving tree that can grow with almost no water, and provides shade and a windbreak for people who dwell in the desert.

Ahead of us, under the two baobab trees, about one hundred twenty people were gathered in the precious shade. Drummers were in the center of an opening in the crowd, and we could see that inside the circle some women were dancing. As the distance between us closed, the drumming filled the air with a vibrant energy and the celebration appeared to grow more intense. We picked up some of the children and gave them a ride in our cars. Others ran alongside. It seemed that this incredible scene had risen out of nothing. Here they were, men, women, and children dancing, drumming, cheering, clapping, and shouting greetings of welcome to our small visiting delegation.

We climbed out of our vehicles and dozens of women ran to us dressed in beautiful traditional Senegalese clothing with headdresses and long cotton boubous—long, loose, colorful dresses. The drums were beating, the children were shouting, the women were squealing with delight, the men were singing. It was a welcome like no other.

They seemed to know that I was the leader and they pulled me into the center of the circle, where the women danced around me and with me. I was swept up in the moment, moving my body in concert with theirs in a freeing, natural rhythm. They cheered and clapped. My fellow travelers joined me, and we danced and clapped and laughed together. Time and space seemed suspended. It wasn't hot or dry anymore. It wasn't sandy or windy. All that disappeared, and we were enveloped in celebration. We were one.

Then the drums suddenly stopped. It was time for the meeting to begin. People sat down on the sand. The chief identified himself and he addressed his comments to me. With the help of our translator, the chief explained that their village was several kilometers away, and that they had come to welcome us and were grateful for our offer of partnership. He said that they were strong and able people and that the desert was their spiritual home. But they and sixteen other villages to the east were at a point where the scarce water resources were pushing them to the edge of their options. Their people knew nothing but life in this desert, were proud people of this land, but knew they could not continue without some change in the water situation.

Government services were not extended to these people, even in times of crisis. They were illiterate people who weren't counted in the census. They couldn't even vote. They had little or no cachet with their government. They had tremendous resilience, but their shallow wells were nearly dry and they knew they would need something outside of their current thinking to see themselves through this next dry season.

The people were Muslim, and as we sat together in a circle to discuss the situation, the men did all the talking. The women were not in the primary circle, but sat in a second circle where they could hear and see, but they did not speak. I could feel the power of the women behind me, and sensed that they would be key in the solution. In this barren orange land, it didn't seem possible that there could be a solution, but the attitude, sense of resilience, and dignity of these people argued differently. There was a way through, and together we would find it.

Then I asked to meet only with the women. It was a strange request in this Muslim culture where the mullahs and the chief were empowered to speak for all, but they allowed it. The women from my group and the tribal women gathered together on the hot ground and drew in close. Our translator was a man, and the mullahs allowed him to join us.

In this circle of tribal women, several women assumed leadership and spoke right away, saying that it was clear to them that there was an underground lake beneath the area. They could feel it; they knew it was there. They had seen it in visions and needed our help to get permission from the men to dig a well deep enough to reach the water. The men had not permitted it, as they did not believe the water was there and also did not want the women to do that kind of work. In their traditions, only certain kinds of labor were allowed for women. Weaving and farming were allowed. Planning and digging a well were not.

The women spoke with convincing vitality and strength. It was clear to me that they knew what they knew, and they could be trusted to find the water. All they needed was permission from the men to pursue their clear instinct. That was the help they needed from an outside source. That was what they needed from us.

There was a rush of collective energy and commitment. I

looked around me. It was baking hot. There were thousands of flies. I had silt in my mouth and lungs. It was about as uncomfortable a place as you can imagine being in, and yet I remember that I did not feel any thirst or discomfort—only the presence of possibility amidst these bold and beautiful women.

When we set out into the Sahel desert, I had feared we were going to encounter people who were hopeless, starving, sick, and poor. These people definitely needed more food and water, but they were not "poor." They were not resigned. They were eager to create a way through this challenge, and they burned with the fire of possibility. They were a well of strength, a wealth of perseverance and ingenuity. They wanted our partnership—not handouts, or money, or food—and respect and equal partnership is what we brought.

After many conversations with both the women and the men, we made an agreement with the mullahs and the chief that we would start our work with the women because the women had the vision. With our partnership, the men agreed to allow the women to begin the work of digging the well. Over the next year, as the community rationed its existing supplies of water carefully, the women dug both with hand tools and the simple equipment we brought them. They dug deeper and deeper into the ground, singing, drumming, and caring for each other's children as they worked, never doubting that the water was there.

The men watched skeptically, but allowed the work to continue. The women, however, were anything but doubtful. They were certain that if they dug deep enough, the water would be there. And it was! They reached the underground lake of their visions.

In the years since, the men and women have built a pumping

system and a water tower for storage. Not just one, but seventeen villages now have water. The whole region is transformed. Women's leadership groups in all seventeen villages are the centers of action. There is irrigation and chicken farming. There are literacy classes and batiking businesses. People are flourishing and they are contributing members of their country. They face new challenges now and meet them with the same dignity and commitment. The women are now a respected part of the community in a new way, with greater access to leadership, and the tribe is proud that it was their own people, their own work, and the land they lived on that proved to be the key to their own prosperity.

SUFFICIENCY: RECLAIMING THE POWER OF WHAT IS THERE

We each have the choice in any setting to step back and let go of the mind-set of scarcity. Once we let go of scarcity, we discover the surprising truth of sufficiency. By sufficiency, I don't mean a quantity of anything. Sufficiency isn't two steps up from poverty or one step short of abundance. It isn't a measure of barely enough or more than enough. Sufficiency isn't an amount at all. It is an experience, a context we generate, a declaration, a knowing that there is enough, and that we are enough.

Sufficiency resides inside of each of us, and we can call it forward. It is a consciousness, an attention, an intentional choosing of the way we think about our circumstances. In our relationship with money, it is using money in a way that expresses our integrity; using it in a way that *expresses* value rather than *determines* value. Sufficiency is not a message about simplicity or about cutting back and lowering expectations. Sufficiency doesn't mean we shouldn't strive or aspire. Sufficiency is an act of generating, distinguishing, making known to ourselves the power and presence of our existing resources, and our inner resources. Sufficiency is a context we bring forth from within that reminds us that if we look around us and within ourselves, we will find what we need. There is always enough.

When we live in the context of sufficiency, we find a natural freedom and integrity. We engage in life from a sense of our own wholeness rather than a desperate longing to be complete. We feel naturally called to share the resources that flow through our lives—our time, our money, our wisdom, our energy, at whatever level those resources flow—to serve our highest commitments. In the context of sufficiency, and the flow of resources to and through and from us, our soul and money interests merge to create a rich, satisfying, and meaningful life.

Sufficiency is the truth. Sufficiency can be a place to stand, a context that generates a completely new relationship with life, with money, and with everything that money can buy. I suggest there is enough in nature, in human nature, and in the relationships we share with one another to have a prosperous, fulfilling life, no matter who you are or where you are in the spectrum of resources. I suggest that if you are willing to let go, let go of the chase to acquire or accumulate always more and let go of that way of perceiving the world, then you can take all that energy and attention and invest it in what you have. When you do that you will find unimagined treasures, and wealth of surprising and even stunning depth and diversity.

Living from sufficiency, thinking from there and generating that frame of reference for life is enormously powerful and important for our time. In our relationship with money, we can continue to earn, save, invest, and provide for ourselves and for our families, but we reframe the relationship with a new recognition of and appreciation for what we already have. In that new way of seeing, the flow of resources in our lives, rather than being something that is constantly escaping our grasp or diminishing, instead becomes a flood of nourishment and something we have the privilege of being trustees of for the moment. Our relationship with money ceases to be an expression of fear and becomes an expression of exciting possibility. The context of sufficiency can transform our relationship with money, with our resources, and with life itself.

I am not suggesting there is ample water in the desert or food for the beggars in Bombay. I am saying that even in the presence of genuine scarcity of external resources, the desire and capacity for self-sufficiency are innate and enough to meet the challenges we face. It is precisely when we turn our attention to these inner resources—in fact, *only* when we do that—that we can begin to see more clearly the sufficiency in us and available to us, and we can begin to generate effective, sustainable responses to whatever limitations of resources confront us. When we let go of the chase for more, and consciously examine and experience the resources we already have, we discover our resources are deeper than we knew or imagined. In the nourishment of our attention, our assets expand and grow.

This is especially true in our relationship with money, and the power of soulful commitment to expand and enhance our wealth. And it is especially true when we look at the struggles around money that weigh us down, and the profound release we experience when we align money and soul.

The struggle for sufficiency has nothing to do with the amount of money you have. It is all about the relationship you have with the money. Some of the greatest lessons I've learned about the struggle for sufficiency have come from people who have more money in the moment than most of us will see in a lifetime, yet they are living lives they find less than wholly satisfying. Overwhelmed by excess or crushed in the rush for more, the nourishing experience of sufficiency and enough is lost.

THE WOMEN OF MICROSOFT: RUSHING PAST SUFFICIENCY

In 1998 I was invited to speak to a group of senior-level executives at Microsoft, then the fastest-growing and one of the most profitable, if not *the* most profitable, companies in the world. I was excited to be going, slated as I was to speak to the Microsoft senior executive women's group about the status of women in the developing world. Having just returned from the fourth World Women's Conference in Beijing, I was eager to share what I had learned from the many reports and inspiring stories from women attending the conference. Some of those women came from countries that are impoverished and where women are subjugated beyond our imagination.

On the flight from San Francisco to Seattle, Microsoft had booked me in First Class—a more pampered environment than my usual coach seat—and as I looked at the comfortable seats and the well-dressed passengers filling them, I realized I was entering a rarified world and would be speaking to women who lived and worked in that world every day. The women attending the senior lecture group series were those at the top of the company's executive levels. In an earlier briefing I had been told that the average net worth of these women was $10 million, their average age was thirty-six, and most of them, more than half, had families. I realized I was traveling to the heart of a company that was on the cutting edge of global technology, and that I'd be speaking to a group who were pushing the edge of every envelope in that field, but also in their own lives as remarkably wealthy, successful women at remarkably young ages in their careers.

As I thought about them during the limousine ride to the Microsoft campus, I became more and more aware of the possibility of making a meaningful difference in their lives by connecting them with the most resource-poor women in the world, a population that numbers in the hundreds of millions. I thought about what this connection might mean to both groups and how privileged I was to be a person who walked in both of those worlds.

At Microsoft's sprawling corporate campus, I was escorted into an elegant office building, to a conference room for afternoon tea with a small contingent of the women who would be at the evening talk. I had asked for this smaller afternoon meeting because I wanted to know more about these women as a group and have some conversations with a few of them to learn how I could connect more easily later with women of this unusual life and career experience.

Over tea, these ten young, dynamic, and enormously confident women shared something about their home and work lives. Seven of them had husbands and children at home, and when asked to describe a sample day from their lives, they told of similar high-pressure routines: They got up early, often at 5:30 or 6 A.M., and for most of them, the only meal they had with their children was breakfast, if that. They had nannies and caretakers who lived with them. Six of the ten were married to men who also worked at Microsoft. Most of the women said they fed, tended, and dressed their children in the morning, and then either sent them off to school with the nanny or drove the children themselves, and then went to work and were on-line by 8 A.M. Most of them took no lunch break and worked through normal dinner hours until 9 P.M., and sometimes 10 P.M. They came home, had a late dinner with their husbands, kissed their sleeping children good night, and after dinner went back on-line until sometimes as late as 1 A.M. The next morning—for many, just a few hours later—they would begin again. Most nursed a quiet regret: Each day they promised to get home earlier, to get more sleep, to get more exercise, to do the things that were missing in their lives, and each day they failed to make any headway toward those commitments.

Then I asked them about their weekends. Most of them worked in the office on Saturdays. They would sometimes take a break to attend a child's dance recital or soccer game, but otherwise they were usually at the office until 5 or 6 P.M. on Saturdays. I asked about Sundays. Most said they stayed home on Sundays, but admitted they were drawn to the computer more than any other activity, and often were on-line at least half the day.

Each day, each week, each month they made promises to themselves, their husbands and children, to get through the next project, meet the next deadline, and then be home more, be more available, have more nurturing relationships with their children, but it rarely happened, and they felt a chronic frustration over these unfulfilled promises.

This pattern of work and family life was more the norm than

the exception among their colleagues, they said. All had plenty of money and could pay for any kind of services to support children and families, and that is what they did, more often than they liked to admit. Regrettably, they said, the competitive game they were part of at this powerhouse of a company demanded such full and complete dedication that, when it came right down to it, that was their priority. Their families came second. In every case they were disturbed and disappointed in themselves for some of the compromises they were making in their family lives.

Then I asked them about their knowledge of the world, who their friends were, and what kinds of conversations they were engaged in outside of work. Woman after woman shared with me that their life was their computer screen. Most of their conversations took place on-line and those conversations were about the development of new software, or meeting goals of performance and productivity. They knew little about the outside world, whether it was Seattle or the United States, and certainly not about people in developing nations or women in other parts of the world. They were enthusiastic to hear that I would be talking that evening about women in the developing world, but that had not been part of their conversations or in any way part of their reality. They didn't have time and they didn't have the psychic space to include anyone or anything other than what presented itself to get done in the moment.

We talked about their wealth. Aside from their material possessions, which they took little time to enjoy, they experienced very little satisfaction from the money. Very few of them were giving money away, and almost none of them took time for vacations. Their wealth—and using it as they did to buy child-care and home-care services—enabled them only to work harder and longer. It didn't give them freedom or vitality in the way they had once hoped, and even at one time expected, and their promise to themselves was that someday it would. Someday they would retire and live happily ever after.

That night there were about one hundred women at the senior executive dinner. Author and historian Riane Eisler spoke first and talked about the last one thousand years of the history of women, working mostly from the distinctions she had developed in her book, *The Chalice and the Blade: Our History, Our Future*. She described what she calls the dominator model of action in which men and traditional masculine principles prevail, and the differences between that and what she calls the partnership model characterized by more feminine principles of collaboration and partnership. Then it was my turn.

Advancing the conversation from Eisler's scholarly research and historical perspective, my talk was grounded in the detail of everyday life and the experience of women living in resource-poor situations such as Senegal or Bangladesh. These are women who work, as the Microsoft women did, sixteen to eighteen hours a day; whose lives are about providing for their own children and their families, and whose relationship to one another makes the harsh realities of their lives bearable. The Microsoft women were interested to learn that they, themselves, were among the top, tiny percent of the top 1 percent of women in the world who have the choices and opportunities to use financial resources the way they chose, and in the way they were shaping the life of their family. I invited them to connect with the one billion women who survive on somewhere between two dollars and five dollars a day.

I shared with them what I knew and had seen, about the developing-world women's commitment to their families, the singing and dancing that sustained them, their capacity to include their children not only in the hardship, but also in the celebration of life and love. I told them about the enormous hardship in which these women live their lives, about the suppression, marginalization, and subjugation that they experienced, and about the courage with which they lived through each day. And I told them about these women's experience being centered in appreciation, gratitude, and presence for the little that they had, but also the bounty of the relationships they shared, born of necessity. In these harsh circumstances everything ultimately was about the community. Everything ultimately was about caring for one another. Everything ultimately was about collaborating, partnering, and ensuring that everyone had a chance. In this connection and caring, these women not only survived, but experienced their true wealth.

The women executives responded with heartfelt reflections on their own lives and the possibility that the unchecked drive for advances at work might be coming at a higher price than any of them had ever intended or even consciously accepted—the lost time and irreplaceable experience of their young family years, or of meaningful relationships with people and life around them and beyond. The revelation that life might be completely passing them by became palpable in the room.

I wasn't encouraging them to leave their company or do anything other than make this connection and learn about their sisters around the world, but our discussion about these women living in harsh and unforgiving conditions, our focus on them, created an opportunity for these women executives to step back and look at the chase they lived each day, and think about whether they wanted to participate in it as blindly and fully as they had been doing.

The pause to reflect was significant for many of the women there. In that moment, the women were able to suspend their unexamined allegiance to the chase for more—more money, more status in the company, more accomplishments—and take note of the resignation they felt in the grip that the chase had in their lives. The moment also gave them the opportunity, within this circle of women, to reflect on the genuine satisfaction they derived from their work and their families, their appreciation for their own talents and accomplishments, and the company that affirmed and celebrated them as leaders. This conscious experience of satisfaction available to them through their families and careers was new to them.

I remember standing before them, seeing their faces reflect an experience of their fullness rather than lack. I remember their gladdening expressions when I invited them to find a partner and take a moment to list for each other all the things they appreciate and are grateful for in their families and immediate relationships at work and home. There was an overwhelming sense of fullness in the room as one by one they stood up and shared the recognition of the completeness and sufficiency in their own lives and how absent that experience had been previously in the rush for more.

These women were completely at the top of their game in their careers and the affluent family lifestyle, but the game they were playing had robbed them of any sense of victory or fulfillment, and the rules of that game were based on the condition of scarcity: They had to get more, more was never enough, and the chase was never ending. I saw in their stories that even when we promise ourselves that at some point we'll stop, that very promise is part of the fallacy and the slavish justification for keeping the game going, one more round, one more deal, one more you-name-it. I also saw the beauty and power of creating an environment where you could step out of that mind-set of scarcity even for just moment, and see that it is nothing more than a mind-set. It's not inevitable, not unavoidable, not hopeless. It's not *just the way it is*. I learned that even the most driven people can stop and take a look, and to do so for even a moment can have a profound and lasting impact on the way people proceed with their own lives.

In the years that followed several of the women wrote to tell me they were retiring, and they shared with me some of the insights and experiences that were flowing from that decision. Some of them wrote to let me know they had reframed their experience of working at the company and were living basically the same life, but seeing it from the lens of fulfillment and gratitude rather than fear, competition, and survival. Some of them became deeply engaged in social activism and traveled to developing countries with their families on their vacation time. Some became aware of the joy of contributing and investing money in philanthropic partnerships to overcome situations of hunger and poverty or gross inequities. Some had moved from working for the company to positions in the then newly forming Bill and Melinda Gates Foundation, now one of the biggest and most ground-breaking foundations in the world.

That evening was an encounter I will never forget. These women had so much; not only money wealth, but also a deep capacity for caring and connection that had been largely inaccessible to them in the context of their hurried, affluent lifestyles.

Their desire to be in relationships, with their families, with other women in conditions that called out for their partnership, and even simply with their own longings to make a difference, was a powerful expression of the soulful energy and possibility that is there in all of us. That night, it was the treasure of their awakening that filled my own heart.

SUFFICIENCY IS ALWAYS AVAILABLE

What is enough? Each of us determines that for ourselves, but very rarely do we let ourselves have that experience. What is that point at which we're fulfilled, where we have everything we want and need, and nothing in excess? Very few of us can recall moments in life when we have felt that. Like the Microsoft women, we mostly breeze right past the point of enough as if it's not even there. There comes a point where having more than we need becomes a burden. We are overcompensated, overstuffed, swimming in the excess, looking for satisfaction in more or different ways. The experience we crave of being fulfilled in life cannot be found in the chase for fulfillment or the chase for more of anything.

Each of us through our relationship with money, each other, and life can reclaim this territory of sufficiency, this territory of enough. We can rediscover fulfillment and satisfaction. The greatest teacher of sufficiency is nature and the natural laws of the earth—laws that have no amendments, laws that are not argued on the Senate floor. These are the laws we live by whether we acknowledge them or not.

The great environmentalist Dana Meadows said that one of the most fundamental laws of the earth is the law of enough. Nature, she once wrote, says we have "just so much and no more.

Just so much soil. Just so much water. Just so much sunshine. Everything born of the earth grows to its appropriate size and then stops. The planet does not get bigger, it gets better. Its creatures learn, mature, diversify, evolve, create amazing beauty and novelty and complexity, but live within absolute limits."

Nature's examples are everywhere around us, available at any moment to teach us what we need to learn to have a breakthrough in our relationship with life so that it is sustainable. This distinction of sufficiency allows us to transform our unsustainable culture to a sustainable one.

Can we individually and collectively in our relationship with money and all resources shift from the assumption that more, no matter what, is better? Can we recognize that better comes from not more, but in deepening our experience of what's already there? Rather than growth being external in acquiring and accumulating money or things, can we redefine growth to see it as a recognition of and appreciation for what we already have?

I suggest that sufficiency is precise. *Enough* is a place you can arrive at and dwell in. So often we think of "abundance" as the point at which we'll know we've really arrived, but abundance continues to be elusive if we think we'll find it in some excessive amount of something. True abundance does exist; it flows from sufficiency, in an experience of the beauty and wholeness of what is. Abundance is a fact of nature. It is a fundamental law of nature, that there is enough *and* it is finite. Its finiteness is no threat; it creates a more accurate relationship that commands respect, reverence, and managing those resources with the knowledge that they are precious and in ways that do the most good for the most people. I can see in the environmental movement that the quest for sustainability may be more accurately located in recognizing and affirming that we do have what we need—not that it's disappearing and that we have to save it because it's diminishing, but that we have what we need, exactly what we need, and therefore we must make a difference with it. We must know that it is a finite and precious resource, but it is enough.

This way of seeing, which is consistent with the laws of the natural world, offers a new set of principles or set of assumptions for a whole new culture around money. It teaches us how to be stewards of money rather than gatherers of money. It teaches us how to bring quality and intelligence to our use of financial resources in ways that reflect our inner wealth rather than the flamboyant display of the accumulation of outer riches. In so doing, whether one is an American billionaire or a Guatemalan peasant, an inner-city single mother or a middle-class midlevel manager, the experience of enough, sufficiency, and respectful stewardship of financial and other resources redefines life in such a way that sufficiency and fulfillment are available to all. There is no sacrifice in this—there is satisfaction.

Sufficiency as a way of being offers us enormous personal freedom and possibility. Rather than scarcity's myths that tell us that the only way to perceive the world is *there's not enough, more is better*, and *that's just the way it is*, the truth of sufficiency asserts that there is enough for everyone. Knowing that there is enough inspires sharing, collaboration, and contribution.

We may not be managing our lives and the world in a way that that experience is available to us all the time, but in truth there is enough and any real abundance or plenty flows not from excess, but from our recognition of sufficiency, the affirmation that there is enough. As Buckminster Fuller said in the 1970s, this is a world that can work for everyone with no one and nothing left out, and we have the power and the resources now to create a you-*and*-me world rather than a you-*or*-me world. *There is enough for everyone.* To access that experience of *enough*, however, we have to be willing to let go—let go of a lifetime of scarcity's lessons and lies.

In the contemporary folktale *Hershel and the Hannukah Goblins*, by Erik Kimmel, a host of grisly goblins is bent on destroying a small town's holiday celebration, but Hershel outwits them all, one by one. To one greedy goblin, Hershel offers a pickle from a jar, but when the goblin reaches in and grabs a handful, he is outraged to find his full fist is stuck in the jar. Angry at being trapped, he flies into a rage at Hershel, who says, at last, "Shall I tell you how to break the spell?"

"Yes!" the goblin shrieks. "I can't stand it anymore!"

"Let go of the pickles," Hershel replies. "Your greed is the only spell holding you prisoner."

We aren't mindless, greedy monsters, but the fear of scarcity has us wrapping our hands around as much as we can get and grasping for more. As long as we hold on to that fear we're trapped by it, hands full, but hearts fearful and unfulfilled. When we let go of the fear and the unconditional drive for more, we liberate ourselves from its grip. We can pause to consider how we're living with what we have, and whether our money practices are serving our soulful commitments.

When we let go of trying to get more of what we don't really need, we free up an enormous amount of energy that has been tied up in the chase. We can refocus and reallocate that energy and attention toward appreciating what we already have, what's already there, and making a difference with that. Not just noticing it, but making a difference with what we already have. When you make a difference with what you have, it expands.

Anne Morrow Lindbergh understood the exquisite distinction of enough when she wrote, in her book *Gift from the Sea*:

One cannot collect all the beautiful shells on the beach. One can collect only a few, and they are more beautiful if they are few. One moon shell is more impressive than three . . . Gradually one . . . keeps just the perfect specimen, not necessarily a rare shell, but a perfect one of its kind. One sees it apart by itself, ringed around by space—like the island. For it is only framed in space that beauty blooms. Only in space are events and objects and people unique and significant and therefore beautiful.

In the many years I've worked and interacted with people in the world of fund-raising, whether they are people we would call wealthy or people we would call middle class or of lesser economic means, the experience of fulfillment and sufficiency becomes accessible to them when they take the resources they have, at whatever level those may be, and choose to make a difference with them. When they use what they have to support their highest ideals and commitments, and express their deepest values, their experience of their own true wealth expands.

THE BUSINESS OF SUFFICIENCY

I used to assume the world of business was far removed from me and my work, although I felt that the principles of sufficiency must be as valid and valuable in the context of business as they were in philanthropy, global socioeconomic initiatives, or personal transformation. The world of day-to-day business just seemed more over-there than right-here. In my fund-raising work, I dealt almost exclusively with individuals and rarely approached businesses or corporate-backed foundations for money. Our paths just didn't cross.

At the same time, I have seen that business and entrepreneurial energy grounded in the principles of sufficiency leads to success and sustainable growth, while the notorious business failures of recent years—Enron, for instance—offer ample evidence that business rooted in the get-mine-and-get-it-fast mentality of scarcity only creates financial instability and eventually proves unsustainable, even if the short-term gains seem highly profitable.

I realized during the writing of this book that many of the people who encouraged and urged me to write the book are among the most successful entrepreneurs, business minds, and corporate leaders in the world. Some are billionaires, multimillionaires, and others whose wisdom in matters of business, economics, and money is highly respected. Our lives intersected mostly outside the business arena, through mutual interests as activists and philanthropists. I know them as friends and colleagues in that context.

Over the years, consulting at times, or simply observing, I have witnessed the phenomenal success of businesses where sufficiency is embraced as the guiding principle, making creative, efficient use of resources, and combining social responsibility with a deep commitment to service and quality. These are businesses in Japan, England, Sweden, Germany, the United States, and other highly competitive environments. They haven't abandoned the pursuit of profit or the commitment to increase their market share. They have simply pursued their goals with conscious attention to integrity in product development, manufacturing and pricing, labor and management, and the consumer experience.

Paul Dolan, president of Fetzer Vineyards and Winery, is a fourth-generation wine maker who loves the industry, loves the land, and loves the world of food and wine. He is a remarkable executive and cutting-edge leader in developing sustainable practices for his company and his industry, and he is an active philanthropist, and an involved partner in our work to preserve the rain forests.

Paul invited a group of us, all partners, like himself, in The Pachamama Alliance rain-forest preservation work, to visit him one day at the Fetzer Vineyards in Hopland, California. He wanted to show us the extraordinary transformation under way in his company—changes now rippling through the wine business in America.

Paul and his colleagues have positioned themselves with great clarity in their relationship to money, as a socially responsible *and* profitable business. The company's mission statement includes these commitments:

> We are an environmentally and socially conscious grower, pro-
>   ducer and marketer of wines of the highest quality and value.
> Working in harmony and with respect for the human spirit, we
>   are committed to sharing information about the enjoyment of
>   food and wine in a lifestyle of moderation and responsibility.
> We are dedicated to the continuous growth and development of
>   our people and our business.

This mission is in full operation in every inch of the property owned by Fetzer and in each one of the people who work there. Fetzer is an ever more environmentally sustainable operation, growing its grapes organically, demonstrating to the industry that pesticides, chemicals, and manipulation of soils through non-natural means is no longer necessary or even viable.

In the fields where gophers used to be a problem, there are houses for owls. The owls limit the population of gophers naturally and create beauty by their own presence in the whole region. Wherever there has been a problem with a certain kind of insect, Fetzer has made an inviting home for its natural predator.

The company has brought this same attention to environmental safety and sustainability to every aspect of its business. From wine making and maintenance to the fleet of electric trucks and carts used to get around the grounds, the company strives to operate in environmental integrity. In every step of the process of bringing wine to market, Paul and his colleagues are creating environmentally sustainable and earth-honoring practices that are also producing more excellent, more taste-full, and more outstanding wines. His love for the land, his love for his people, his love for his industry, and his commitment to responsibility and moderation for the citizens who enjoy wine with their food inspired all of us. The spirit with which he was running this business was dazzling, and what was even more powerful was his absolute commitment to demonstrating the sufficiency of soils, plants, animals, insects, and the entire natural cycle if it is honored and well cared for and understood.

Finally, what really speaks to his wine colleagues and competitors, and to the world, is the expanding financial success of Fetzer Vineyards. The vineyards are a wonderland of sustainable environmental practices, the wines are of the highest quality, *and* the revenues meet and exceed expectations each year. Paul is now committed to using the example of his award-winning wines and his profitable business practices to transform the entire industry in the United States and the world.

In being with this gentle, fine man, I saw how deeply he embraces the principles of sufficiency, and is creating a place and a conversation in the industry where those principles and profitability merge.

Socially responsible businesses are everywhere now, breaking new ground and demonstrating new practices that earn money honorably and don't deplete the world's resources irrevocably. Odwalla Juice, Patagonia outdoor gear, Ben & Jerry's ice cream, Working Assets phone company, the Body Shop, Esprit, Interface Carpet—the list goes on and on. Socially responsible investing is the largest growing asset class in America. There are appropriate opportunities everywhere to live in the domain of sufficiency and choose consciously those products and services that respect resources and honor the distinction of enough.

Could it be that the surprising truth, the revelatory truth of our time, is that our relationship with money is based in an unexamined, unquestioned set of assumptions that are myths and lies and that spur us to act in ways that rob us of the satisfaction and fulfillment we're looking for in life? Could it be that the key to turning around a runaway, unsustainable economy, culture, and almost frightening time in the evolution of civilization is in confronting and embracing the surprising truth that there is enough, we have enough, *we are enough*, and that at the heart of every circumstance is that possibility and that opportunity?

In the chapters ahead we will establish the principles of sufficiency and the steps toward living a life grounded in sufficiency. In that context, we will look at money in a new way, look at money as a flow, like water, rather than a static amount of something we have to accumulate. We'll look at the power of what really makes things grow in value—depth, quality, and fulfillment—through the action and potency of appreciation. We'll look at how existing resources, when brought together in collaboration, create a new source of prosperity. And we'll see how the principles or truths of sufficiency, which are consistent with the laws of the natural world and the deeper instincts of our own human nature, can be the new governing principles of our time.

Part Three

SUFFICIENCY:
THE THREE TRUTHS

5

Money Is Like Water

Money is a current, a carrier, a conduit for our intentions. Money
carries the imprimatur of our soul.

I met Gertrude in a church basement in Harlem, and it
was from Gertrude, a woman most people would call relatively poor, that I learned some of the most powerful
lessons I ever learned about money. It was from Gertrude that I
learned that money is like water.

It was 1978, very early in my life as a fund-raiser with The
Hunger Project, and I had been asked by some community leaders to do a fund-raising event in Harlem. I wasn't so sure it was
a good idea to go try to raise money in Harlem, but I had been
asked to come and I said I would on this particular Wednesday
night. Then I got a call to come meet early in the morning that
same day with the CEO of a huge food company in Chicago. It

was a very well known food company, one of the giants in the industry, and although the timing would be tight flying from Chicago to New York, I committed to making both meetings.

With the scheduling problem resolved in my mind, I turned to other important matters. I started thinking about the actual meeting with this food company fellow, possibly the biggest potential contributor I had ever approached. What worried me most immediately was what to wear. What image did I want to project? Would my clothes reflect in some unintended negative way on my mission? I was asking myself questions that usually didn't even cross my mind. The way I was approaching this meeting felt very uncomfortable, very foreign to me. And it only got worse.

I can still recall how it felt when I stepped into the elevator in this building in Chicago. It was a towering skyscraper, and you couldn't get up to the company's offices with just one elevator. You had to take a series of them, going from one bank to the next. As I went higher and higher, I got more and more nervous, and began to perspire. The higher I got, the more separate I felt from the rest of the world. Even the air and the sound quality changed until it became this richly quiet, awe-filled atmosphere. I felt as if I were making a pilgrimage to a mountaintop. The air seemed thin and I felt a bit faint.

I hadn't been given many details about this contribution, but I had been told this: The food company had recently suffered some public-relations setbacks—they had been guilty of some nasty things and had an image problem—and the company leaders felt that making a donation to The Hunger Project and being seen as supporting the end of world hunger might help clean up its image.

I was ushered into the CEO's office. There he sat at his desk, and I sat facing him on the other side. Behind him were floor-to-ceiling windows that displayed a spectacular view of the city skyline, but the backlighting made it so that I could barely see his face. I only had fifteen minutes of his time, so I spoke quickly about the mission and work of our organization and the challenges of ending world hunger. I talked about the courage of the hungry people and the partnership that we all needed to provide them in their courageous commitment to feed themselves and their children and build the conditions for a healthy and productive life. When I was done and had made my request, he opened his desk drawer and pulled out a preprinted check for $50,000 and passed it across the desk to me.

It was clear that he wanted me gone as quickly as possible. The perfunctory presentation and the tone of his voice told me that he had no genuine interest in our work, in connecting with resource-poor people or in making any kind of a difference in the work to end world hunger. This was purely a strategic move. He wanted to off-load the guilt and shame from public mistakes the company had made. And he wanted to have the company look good in the media. In purely financial terms, it was to be a simple transaction: Handing me this check for $50,000 bought his company an opportunity to mend its reputation. But as he slid the check over to me, I felt the guilt of the company coming right across that desk with the money. He gave me the money *and* the company's guilt.

Our meeting felt awkward, but I was a fund-raiser, and a pretty new one at that, and I had a flight to catch. I put the check in my briefcase. I thanked him and in somewhat of a daze I headed back through the maze of inner rooms and outer rooms, and down the several banks of elevators.

As I went down floor after floor, I had an odd feeling in the pit of my stomach—and I knew it wasn't from the elevator ride. I didn't feel happy even though I felt I should. This check was the largest amount of money I'd ever been handed by a single contributor, and I knew everyone back at The Hunger Project would be thrilled. But I also felt I had received the company's guilt and shame with the money. I felt dirty, and sick to my stomach. I went down the final bank of elevators and hailed a cab for the airport, feeling unsettled about it all, but unsure of what else to do.

I arrived in New York in the middle of a rainstorm, and made my way to Harlem, to an old church building. I walked down the steps to the basement room where about seventy-five people had gathered for the fund-raising event. The surroundings couldn't have been more different from the penthouse office that I had left only a few hours before. It was raining, and there were leaks all over the room where we were meeting. Buckets were strategically placed all around the outer walls catching the dripping water. There was a constant background noise of the rain outside and the *plink, plink, plink* inside from the leaking walls and ceiling. I felt both relieved and self-conscious, more comfortable in this community gathering than in the corporate suite, but also aware that I was the only white face there, and the silk dress I'd picked to impress the CEO now felt officious and silly. I looked out at the audience, and I knew that the people sitting there did not have much money to give. I spoke to them about The Hunger Project's commitment to Africa, as I thought it would be the most relevant to their own lives and their heritage. When it came time to ask for donations, my palms were sweating and I began to wonder if it was the right thing to do. I went ahead and made the request, and the room fell absolutely silent.

After what seemed like a long silent pause, a woman stood

up. She was sitting on the aisle in a row near the back. She was in her late sixties or early seventies, and she had gray hair parted down the middle and swept up into a tidy bun. When she stood up she was tall, slender, erect, and proud.

"Girl," she said, "my name is Gertrude and I like what you've said and I like you," she said. "Now, I ain't got no checkbook and I ain't got no credit cards. To me, money is a lot like water. For some folks it rushes through their life like a raging river. Money comes through my life like a little trickle. But I want to pass it on in a way that does the most good for the most folks. I see that as my right and as my responsibility. It's also my joy. I have fifty dollars in my purse that I earned from doing a white woman's wash and I want to give it to you."

She walked up the aisle and handed me her fifty dollars. It was in five-dollar, ten-dollar, and one-dollar bills. Then she gave me a big hug. As she headed back to her seat, other people started coming up and making their own contributions in singles and five-dollar, ten-dollar, and twenty-dollar bills. I was so moved that I was crying. I couldn't hold all the bills in my hands, so at one point, I opened my briefcase and put it on the table to act as a kind of basket for the money. These moments, with people streaming up to give their money, had the feeling of a ceremony. There was a sense of integrity and heart. The amount of money that we received—maybe $500 at the most—was more precious to me then any I'd ever seen before. I realized that at the bottom of that same briefcase, underneath all these bills, was the $50,000 check. As I saw it, I also realized that Gertrude's fifty dollars felt more valuable to me and ultimately would do more to end hunger than the check for an amount one thousand times more.

The money I received from Gertrude carried the energy of her commitment to make a difference—the stamp of her soul—and as I accepted the money, I felt inspired by her and renewed by her expression of integrity and purpose. I felt my organization's principles and programs affirmed, not only by her fifty dollars, but also by her contribution of spirit. Gertrude's money had come from the soul and not from a bank account intended to ease guilt or buy admiration. She set that standard for everyone in the room that night, and I felt the money they gave was "blessed money." The precise amount of the money and how much it would buy was secondary to the power of the money as it moved with purpose, intention, and soulful energy in the act of contribution. Gertrude taught me that the power of money is really derived from the intention we give it and the integrity with which we direct it into the world. Gertrude's gift was great, and her clarity helped me regain my own.

The next day I mailed the $50,000 check back to the food company executive, and was relieved to feel I was returning the guilt and shame that it carried, too. I felt unburdened. With the check I sent a letter suggesting that the CEO choose an organization they felt committed to and thanking him for considering us. I didn't hear back from the CEO at the time, but years later he would contact me again in a way that brought our first awkward transaction to a surprising and beautiful completion, which I'll share later in this chapter.

SCARCITY VS. SUFFICIENCY: HOW DO WE FEEL THE FLOW?

Gertrude taught me that money is like water. Money flows through all our lives, sometimes like a rushing river, and sometimes like a trickle. When it is flowing, it can purify, cleanse, create growth, and nourish. But when it is blocked or held too long, it can grow stagnant and toxic to those withholding or hoarding it.

Like water, money is a carrier. It can carry blessed energy, possibility, and intention, or it can carry control, domination, and guilt. It can be a current or currency of love—a conduit for commitment—or a carrier of hurt or harm. We can be flooded with money and drown in its excess, and when we dam it up unnecessarily, we keep it out of circulation to the detriment of others.

In this condition of scarcity, money shows up not as a flow, but as an amount, something to collect and hold on to, to stockpile. We measure our self-worth by our net worth, and only and always *more is better*. Any drop on the balance sheet is experienced as a loss that diminishes us.

Grounded in sufficiency, money's movement in and out of our life feels natural. We can see that flow as healthy and true, and allow that movement instead of being anxious about it or hoarding. In sufficiency we recognize and celebrate money's power for good—*our* power to do good with it—and we can experience fulfillment in directing the flow toward our highest ideals and commitments. When we perceive the world as one in which there is enough and we are enough to make the world work for everyone everywhere, with no one left out, our money carries that energy and generates relationships and partnerships in which everyone feels able and valued, regardless of their economic circumstances.

Mother Teresa never kept any cash reserves. When I visited her at her orphanage in India, I asked her if she had any advice about fund-raising. She replied that her method of fund-raising was to pray, and that God had always provided what she needed, never more, never less. She operated with no reserves, trusting that God would always provide, and in her experience God always did. She operated more than 400 centers in 102 countries, and they always seemed to have exactly what they needed. Not excess, not more. But not less, either.

Most of us can't imagine living in that way and I'm not even suggesting it, but the knowledge that Mother Teresa operated a successful multimillion-dollar operation just that way, makes you think anew about money and flow.

ALLOCATION VS. ACCUMULATION

Years ago my colleague and mentor Joan Holmes, president of The Hunger Project, challenged contributors "to be known for what you allocate, not what you accumulate." I never forgot those words, and started to become conscious of the patterns and habits I saw people following in that regard and the resulting impact on their lives—including my own.

In indigenous economic systems, the centering principles are those of sustainability and sufficiency. The values of sharing, distribution, and allocation—not accumulation—are the way of life. The concept of "the commons" and its protection for the use of all prevails rather than individual ownership and personal "holdings." In these cultures everything is transferred and shared from person to person, regiven, rereceived, and passed on, always increasing in value.

The myths of scarcity that drive popular culture and popular wisdom promote owning, holding, collecting, and accumulating. In the context of sufficiency, accumulation well beyond the point of enough stops the flow of resources from finding their way to their highest use. Ironically, the condition of scarcity breeds accumulation to excess, which only diminishes the value of what we have too much of. We become burdened by our excess; it clutters our thinking and our lives. We become attached to our possessions and, in a way, start to think that what we have is who we are, and it becomes harder and harder to share anything because as it diminishes in value from the flood of excess, we feel less valuable ourselves and *must* acquire more.

True wealth, or well-being, can't be found in a static balance sheet, no matter how large the accumulation of financial assets. Wealth shows up in the action of sharing and giving, allocating and distributing, nourishing and watering the projects, people, and purpose that we believe in and care about, with the resources that flow to us and through us. Accumulation in moderation—saving money—is part of a responsible approach to personal finances. But when "holdings" hold us back from using money in meaningful, life-affirming ways, then money becomes an end in itself and an obstacle to well-being.

Just as blood in the body must flow to all parts of the body for health to be maintained, money is useful when it is moving and flowing, contributed and shared, directed and invested in that which is life affirming. When blood slows down and begins to stop or clot, the body becomes sick. When water slows down and becomes stagnant, it becomes toxic. Accumulating and holding large quantities of money can have the same toxic effect on our life.

As Gertrude so clearly demonstrated, money flowed through her life, not in a way that ever showed up for her as finite, not in a way that it was ever accumulated to any great degree, but in a way that she was able to receive it and direct it consistent with her highest commitments and values. When we see money as something that flows through our lives and through the world, we realize that it doesn't really belong to anyone; or we could say it belongs to everyone and the opportunity we have is to allow this resource, just like water, to move through the world in a way that nurtures the most people, and the highest purpose.

It could be said that a great fund-raiser is a broker for the sacred energy of money, helping people use the money that flows through their lives in the most useful way that is consistent with their aspirations and hopes for humanity. It could be said that the best financial advisor is really someone who can inspire a client to do the same—to invest money in ways that contribute the most to a meaningful, fulfilling life. It could be said that each of us has the opportunity in our own lives to steward the flow of money; whatever level comes our way.

In Haiti there is a saying—"If you get a piece of cake and eat the whole thing, you will feel empty. If you get a piece of cake and share half of it, you will feel both full and fulfilled." The happiest and most joyful people I know are those who express themselves through channeling their resources—money, when they have it—on to their highest commitments. Theirs is a world where the experience of wealth is in sharing what they have, giving, allocating, and expressing themselves authentically with the money they put in flow.

MONEY CARRIES THE SOUL'S ENERGY

Just as Gertrude described the trickle of money as something she took pride in passing along, and wanted to pass it on to "do the most good for the most folks." For each of us money in any amount acts as a carrier of energy and intent.

People and families of very few financial resources, and those of enormous financial wealth, have turned their financial flow toward causes and commitments that make their hearts sing, and their money carries the same joyful, life-affirming energy into the world to make a difference. These people are not living in fear of losing what they have or fear that there isn't and never will be enough. They are experiencing the blessing of resources, the appreciation and recognition of having just what they need or more than they need, and focusing on making money a con-duit, or expression of their gratitude and purpose. Some of the most important social institutions and catalytic transformations in the world have been financed by these enlightened people, many of them people of modest means.

I have also worked intimately with families and individuals possessing great fortunes, some of whom have been deeply wounded by their wealth. Contrary to our beliefs, many of these lives are an exercise in excess and emptiness. Where wealth and privilege are the prevailing conditions, and where money defines life and character, the fear of losing it is often profound. People behave defensively and even desperately to hold on to the money, to get more and more of it, and use what they have as a carrier for their own need to control others. Life becomes a game they must win at all costs, and the money they control amplifies their ability to conquer, demean, and diminish others so they can stay on top. Their relationship to other people can harden in strategy and mistrust, with heartbreaking internal conflict and power struggles. Alcoholism and drug abuse are rampant in families that are considered part of the "polite society" of the wealthy. Violations of personal trust and intimacy show up in sexual abuse and violence. These families of wealth are no strangers to the most insidious abuses that the money culture fosters.

HEALING A FAMILY: BARBARA'S BRAVE CHOICE

Time and again, I have seen people give money in a way that freed them from the trap of accumulation and acquisition, and opened them to a new experience of life in contribution. Barbara, a woman in her late sixties, was the recipient of a five-generation New England family fortune. That fortune had defined her family so far back, that no one in the family or outside the family had any other sense of the family, but its money. For as long as anyone recalled, they had lived in the understated refinement of "old money," not a terribly flashy life by contemporary standards of wealth. Family members existed to serve the fortune, to protect it, to represent it, and to use it to advance the superior and untarnished standing of the family in the public eye. In their choices of clothes, schools, friends, and even marriages, they were expected to live in deference to the fortune and those family members who controlled it. The value of any individual in the family was a reflection of her or his place in the hierarchy of power, prestige, and access to that family fortune.

For Barbara and her two sisters, this inheritance had become a kind of curse, manifested in alcoholism that crippled one generation's ability to responsibly parent the next generation, and produced yet another generation of dysfunctional rich children.

When I met Barbara in the early 1990s, she was a recovering

alcoholic struggling to help her three adult children face their own addictions and other problems. Under pressure from the family to hold on to the fortune, and fearful of squandering it, Barbara and her relatives had given almost no money away. Instead, it had been used to respond to the constant crises that roiled behind the Ivy League façade. Personal and financial disasters were a constant state of affairs for many of her relatives and her adult children. She saw the family money being expended and depleted in ways that distressed her and drained not just her fortune but also her spirit.

Our first conversation began with Barbara's interest in becoming a contributor to The Hunger Project. In that conversation, she spoke of her desire to bring meaning to her life and for her fortune to have more meaning in the world. She made her first contribution anonymously, knowing that her family would be angered by a big pledge of what they considered to be ultimately and eventually "their money." As her commitment and generosity grew, however, she took the bold step of making her activities and contributions known to family members. As she had predicted, they were angry—at first. Then she actively recruited their involvement in the hands-on work, inviting them to join in the partnerships with people who, not so unlike themselves, were struggling to become self-sufficient under difficult circumstances.

One by one, her children and other family members stepped outside their self-focused lives and into the larger world of experience that such genuine partnership offered. They came to know themselves differently, in selfless collaboration with other people, and as useful, productive, capable partners in making a difference. The transformation in their individual lives, and in the condition of the family, was remarkable. Barbara succeeded in changing the energy and the flow of the family money. She invested it with her intent to heal and build strong families— her own and others—and the money carried that energy and that healing full circle.

KNOW THE FLOW: TRUTH TELLING ABOUT WHERE THE MONEY GOES

Do you know the flow of money in your life? Are you mindful of how it comes to you? Are you consciously allocating where you want your money to go? When you can see the way money flows through your life, it gives you power to see where you are in your relationship with it and where you want to go with it.

If you want a clear picture of your priorities in life, who you are and what you care about, look at your checkbook, your credit-card bills, and bank statement. That's where you can see the flow in black and white. Maybe the money is going to cars and clothing, maybe to education or to travel.

The way money flows to you and through you to other purposes isn't unrelated to your life. Does your money come to you through work, relationships, or perhaps existing wealth that carries the energy of nourishing, generative commitments and values? Or does it come to you through work or relationships that deplete or exploit you, other people, or the environment? An unhealthy relationship with the way you acquire money is something that can suppress your life. The way we earn it and the way we spend it have an effect. It matters. It does make a difference. To bring that consciousness into your relationship with money, to true the course of that flow, is a courageous, empowering, and important practice.

Knowing the flow is an examination without blame. We can witness how money comes to us, how we spend it, save it, invest it, give it to others, and in this personal financial fact-finding mission begin to see the flow as a representation of our values. Sometimes what you discover is a fit with who you think you are, and other times it's just not. When it's not, then there is an opportunity to reexamine the flow and how you actively manage and direct it. Without a judgment of good or bad, when you know the flow, it gives you the necessary self-knowledge to make conscious choices that align your spending with your vision of yourself and your highest commitments.

DIRECTING THE FLOW:
OUR POWER AS CONSUMERS

It doesn't take a family fortune to direct dollars into the world with the power of your commitments and integrity. In my years of partnership with Barbara, and ultimately thousands of other contributors, I have seen this transformative power of money in any amount. Each of us, as individuals, gives money this generative power when we make even the most routine choices with intention. We can consciously put money in the hands of projects, programs, companies, and vendors we respect and trust, and even approach paying taxes as a way of expressing our commitment and investment as citizens.

We have much more power than perhaps we realize to direct our financial resources in ways that support, empower, and express what we believe in. It takes courage to direct the flow, but with each choice, we invest in the world as we envision it. We can consciously choose, for instance, whether to spend our money on products or entertainment that are violent and destructive to the psyche of our children, or invest in activities that enrich their experience of life and deepen their appreciation of it. We can choose whether to buy into the imagery of success or style, or to invest our money in ways that nourish the inner life. We can use this grand resource of money to affirm those companies whose products and people support the well-being of our children and our communities, or we can get caught up in spending to get more simply because we can, and find ourselves accumulating things that eventually only burden us with excess, clutter our homes, and end up in a landfill. I know because I've done it myself!

SHOPPING FOR AYAH: MY WAKE-UP CALL

When my first grandchild, Ayah, was born in 1999, I was ecstatic to have a grandchild. I couldn't wait to shop for her. Every baby store, every advertisement, captured my imagination and took me into the world of beautiful pink treasures for a baby girl. When she was three months old, my daughter-in-law Halima and I decided to go shopping for baby clothes. All the gift baby clothes she had received when Ayah was born were starting to get too small, and it was time to buy some new things. Because of our busy weekday schedules, we planned our shopping trip for a weekend when we could devote a day to it. We planned to meet at a big shopping center in Marin County, about half an hour from my home. Halima was coming from Oakland with the baby, and my daughter Summer was coming in from her place in Sausalito. Three women and a baby—this was going to be one power-shopping trip!

Shortly before I left the house, the phone rang and it was my son Zachary, Ayah's father. I could tell by the tone of his voice that he wanted to tell me something serious. "Mom," he said, "I know you're going shopping today with Halima and I want to tell you how important it is for us that we purchase things for our daughter that are produced and made in ways we feel good about."

He then went on to list the stores they didn't want us to buy from. One trendy national chain store had been known to use child labor in Indonesia. Another respected department store had no policy against using toxic dyes, and Zachary and Halima didn't want their money going to support the company.

Zachary continued, kindly but firmly, asking me not to buy Ayah more than she needed—they didn't want to begin a pattern of excess. And he asked me to buy things only from those stores or brands that represent natural, sustainable manufacturing and fair labor practices. He and Halima wanted the things they purchased—and the things I purchased for their daughter—to be consistent with their values, he said. And he named a few stores where we would most likely find those brands.

I remember being totally shocked by the conversation. His words didn't match the picture of the shopping spree that had filled my mind. It hadn't occurred to me to think in those ways about buying clothes for my new granddaughter. My upbringing, my training, my way of seeing and being with this new baby were filled with the voices of my culture and my family history, and I hadn't noticed that I was completely sucked in. I had bought into the craze of the marketing that targets grandmothers. They had me figured right. I'd fallen for it totally. Here I am, a social activist, someone working to stop child labor in developing countries and clean up the environment, yet completely blind to the fact that I was ready to buy anything and everything for my adorable granddaughter, with no consciousness about where it came from, who made it, how it was made, and any consequences that came from that.

I also saw that I would have purchased much more than she needed. What was parading across my mind was an endless supply of pink dresses, booties, and bonnets, and that pointless parade was brought to a halt by the conversation with my son. I knew he was right. Halima, too, had communicated the same standards to me in conversations past. And yet, how easy it was to get caught up in the impulse to buy, and leave my conscientious consumer habits for another day. All my training in the field, all my witnessing of conditions of cruelty and sweatshops in Asia, all my commitment, had been obliterated in the great glee of this marathon shopping event for my granddaughter. It had taken my son's wake-up call to see that I had never taken all those lessons and applied them to real life. Not my own life, anyway; not just now.

Red faced, but grateful, I promised to honor his request. I met my daughter and daughter-in-law at the shopping center and we shopped with a kind of consciousness I had never known before. We looked at labels. We asked questions. We learned about fabrics and origins of materials. We chose stores where the people were knowledgeable about the craftspeople behind their products, and we bought exactly the right amount of clothing for the next few months of little Ayah's life.

By the time we were done, I no longer felt daunted by what had seemed to be limitations imposed on my shopping spirit. I was excited! The joy of buying my granddaughter lovely things was made even greater by the satisfaction of having invested my money in the services of companies and craftspeople who had knitted the sweaters or quilted the blanket. I felt good about paying the store clerks for their thoughtful and attentive service. We concluded our shopping trip with a sense of satisfaction and fulfillment, not overladen with more than Ayah could use, but with an appropriate amount of clothing and baby equipment for the next few months of her young life. It was satisfying to direct the flow of my money and invest it with my own values, allocating it to people and places I felt good about.

FUND-RAISING: A WINDOW INTO FLOW AND SOUL

I love to ask people for money. Fund-raising is a calling for me, not the dreaded assignment or burdensome obligation it is sometimes made out to be. Fund-raising is hard work, but I also believe fund-raising is sacred work. It offers a powerful and privileged opportunity to be in intimate conversation with another person about the nature of his or her highest commitments and values. These conversations enable them to move the money that flows through their life toward those highest commitments in some way. Fund-raising is all about flow: freeing it, inviting it, channeling it, and enabling people to experience themselves in the nourishment of that flow, wherever they are along its way.

In fund-raising from people all over the world, I have found that everyone everywhere wants to contribute their money to make a difference in the world—whether they have only a few Indian rupees or Zambian kwacha or they have millions of yen or hundreds of thousands of dollars. When all is said and done, they want to put their money in flow. Philanthropy at any level enables people to get back in touch with that relationship with money. In philanthropic interactions, we can return to the soul of money: money as a carrier of our intentions, money as energy, and money as a currency for love, commitment, and service; money as an opportunity to nourish those things we care most about.

When we are in the domain of soul, we imbue the money that flows through our lives with that energy. This kind of soulful relatedness creates a flow of what I call blessed money, money that has surprising power to it. Although I have done very little fund-raising from corporations and foundations, I know that ultimately the decisions in those entities are also made by people, and when people are engaged soulfully and authentically, the commitments they make with money can and do nourish the world.

In addition to the privilege of being in that kind of an intimate and inspiring interaction with others as a fund-raiser, I have also seen people come into their wealth. By that, I mean deeply experience it, and in many cases for the very first time. This has happened even with people who are below any poverty line we could draw in any country on earth, and it has happened with people who are among the world's billionaires. The experience of true wealth comes from sharing, expressing that you have and are enough. This beautiful quote by the Indian poet Rabindranath Tagore expresses that experience of sufficiency:

> I lived on the shady side of the
> road and watched my neighbours'
> gardens across the way reveling
> in the sunshine.

*I felt I was poor, and from door
to door went with my hunger.*

*The more they gave me from
their careless abundance the
more I became aware of my
beggar's bowl.*

*Till one morning I awoke from my
sleep at the sudden opening of
my door, and you came and
asked for alms.*

*In despair I broke the lid of my
chest open and was startled into
finding my own wealth.*

Fund-raising has afforded me an opportunity to stand in the flow—in rivers and trickles of money—and help direct it to endeavors that address the most profound needs and aspirations of life on earth. Ending hunger. Improving health and literacy. Caring for children. Tending to the sick and dying. Protecting the Earth and wisely stewarding natural resources. Creating healthy, thriving communities that support and affirm life around the world.

Many people like me do this as our life's work, for organizations that provide the structure that enables the flow of money and commitment to reach from here to there and back again. But ultimately, everyone—you, me, your friends and your neighbors and the man ahead of you in line at the grocery store and the woman in the car behind yours—we all stand in the flow of money and have the opportunity to direct it. Each of us can discover in that flow our own sufficiency, our own prosperity, our own sense of enough, and our own wealth.

A CEO'S UNFINISHED BUSINESS

I never forgot Gertrude. My memory of her has stayed with me in every fund-raising interaction that I have had since the night in 1978 when she shared with me in the Harlem church. The lessons I learned from her live on in ways I could not have imagined. The impact of that day would have changed my life no matter what the final outcome, but several years later, the other piece of that day's business came to a surprising conclusion.

The Hunger Project had grown into a much bigger and more visible organization, and our track record of results had become more substantial month by month and year by year. Five or six years after my awkward meeting in Chicago with the executive of the large food company, and my decision to return his check after my epiphany in Harlem, I received a letter from him. He had since retired, and had received a very lucrative exit package for his work as the head of the company. In this letter, he shared that he was living in a kind of bounty that was well beyond his needs. He said that the interaction between us years ago would have been easily forgotten but for the letter I sent and the strange occurrence of the money being sent back. In his retirement he had looked back on his long and fruitful career, and one thing that had stood out for him was our interaction and the return of that $50,000 check with the letter explaining that we were looking for committed partners. It stood out for him as a seminal moment when all the rules of corporate America that he had so deeply learned—that you do anything and everything to increase profits—all those rules had been broken by someone outside his world returning the company's money.

Reflecting from retirement on meaningful moments, he realized that he did, in fact, want to make a difference in ending world hunger. He did want the money under his control to make a difference, and he could see now that it was possible to make a meaningful contribution to ending world hunger. So from his own pocket, and in affirmation of his own commitment, he made a personal contribution to The Hunger Project many times in excess of the $50,000 that had been returned. He did it from his soul and it was for him, he said, a fulfillment of something that had been left incomplete. It was his way of completing this piece of unfinished business.

As for me, I will never forget opening that letter, seeing that check, and realizing again the power of money when it is imbued with purpose, integrity, and aligned with our soul. It was a triumph! A triumph for Gertrude, a triumph for fundraising, and a triumph for this man who spoke with such deep generosity about an interaction that uplifted his life.

No matter how much or how little money you have flowing through your life, when you direct that flow with soulful purpose, you feel wealthy. You feel vibrant and alive when you use your money in a way that represents you, not just as a response to the market economy, but also as an expression of who you are. When you let your money move to things you care about, your life lights up. That's really what money is for.

6

What You Appreciate Appreciates

In the context of sufficiency, appreciation becomes a powerful practice of creating new value in our deliberate attention to the value of what we already have.

W hat you appreciate appreciates. It's true in our money culture, where a desirable house in a desirable neighborhood appreciates in dollar value from year to year. It's true in our personal relationships, where our appreciation of someone's special qualities can make them bloom before our very eyes. It's true in business, where a company's commitment to its employees fosters pride and excellence in their work. And this simple but powerful act we call appreciation expands the freedom, creativity, and ultimately the success we experience, particularly in our relationship with money. Appreciation is the beating heart of sufficiency.

In the context of sufficiency, appreciation becomes a powerful, intentional practice of creating new value through our deliberate attention to the value of what we already have. Our attention enlarges and enriches our experience of whatever is before us.

We have the opportunity to direct our attention in the way we relate to money, and when we do it empowers us. It becomes who we are and what we are about. When we allow jealousy, envy, resentment, and even vengeance to become the focus of our attention and intention, we become jealous, envious, resentful, vengeful people with our money. When we direct our attention to creativity, courage, and integrity, we become expressions of those qualities in whatever we do in our interactions with money.

When your attention is on what's lacking and scarce—in your life, in your work, in your family, in your town—then that becomes what you're about. That's the song you sing, the vision you generate. You engage in lack and longing and what's missing, and you call others to that same experience. If your attention is on the problems and breakdowns with money, or scarcity thinking that says *there isn't enough, more is better* or *that's just the way it is*, then that is where your consciousness resides. Those thoughts and fears grow from the attention you give them and can take over your life. No matter how much money you have, it won't be enough. No amount of money will buy you genuine peace of mind. You expand the presence and the power of scarcity and tighten its grip on your world.

If your attention is on the capacity you have to sustain yourself and your family, and contribute in a meaningful way to the well-being of others, then your experience of what you have is nourished and it grows. Even in adversity, if you can appreciate your capacity to meet it, learn, and grow from it, then you create value where no one would have imagined it possible. In the light of your appreciation, your experience of prosperity grows.

We can use our appreciation—our conscious attention and intention—to develop some mastery in the arena of money and transform our relationship with money into an open space for growth and freedom. That's the truth, and I learned it first from people we would call poor. I learned it in places around the world where there is almost no water and no food, and no explanation for the fact that people survive at all.

THE MAGNIFICENT SEVEN

Bangladesh is an Asian country of more than 130 million people on a landmass the size of Iowa. It once was a land abundant with tropical rain forests, a diversity of plants and animal species, and a bounty of natural resources. In the 1900s the land was denuded of its forests by foreign interests that came and went, and the land was ravaged by war and the results of poor land tenure polices. Absent the trees and vegetation that once had thrived, seasonal floods took an even greater toll on the land and the people. Listed by the United Nations as the second poorest country in the world in the late 1970s, Bangladesh became the recipient of another kind of flood, a flood of aid, and within a short time had become almost completely dependent on aid from outside sources. Bangladesh began to have a global reputation as needy and helpless, a giant begging bowl of a nation, and within Bangladesh itself, the people came to see themselves that way, too. Bangladeshis had become convinced they were a hopeless, helpless people dependent on others for even minimal survival.

In what had become a common cycle of disintegration of villages and communities, the people in villages near the district of Sylhet were giving up, making plans to leave the region and look for subsistence work elsewhere, or send the men off to larger towns and cities to find work and send money home to support their indigent families.

Sylhet is in the northern hill region of Bangladesh, just high enough to escape the floods that submerge the surrounding lowlands periodically each year. The dry hills had surrendered long ago to an invasive jungle of prickly scrubby brush, a plant whose only fruit is poison berries. The plants all tangled together look like a massive briar patch—inaccessible, dangerous, and thick. An overgrown area had been deemed government land and was off-limits for development by local farmers. But the scrubby, poisonous plant that grew there kept spreading and invading the small plots of land that the villagers would farm, taking over the crops and poisoning the land.

For generations the villagers had scraped a meager existence from the small plots of land the government had given them, but even that was becoming an impossible task. Young people had turned to begging on the roads and stealing. Crime was at an all-time high. So it came to be that the villagers had given up on their difficult, unproductive land and were ready to take drastic action. Many were prepared to abandon the village and move their families elsewhere, or abandon hope for an intact family, and instead send the men elsewhere to find jobs. The conversation among villagers was urgent and pragmatic. Where could they move or send the men that would allow them to grow enough or earn enough to provide for their families? There was also talk of asking for U.S. financial aid to enable them to buy food and other goods without work at all. They had given up. They were tired and they were resigned. They felt the answer must be somewhere else and with someone else. They felt they just couldn't make it on their own.

About this time, The Hunger Project was beginning to work actively in Bangladesh. There were plenty of independent relief agencies in Bangladesh already doing heroic and inspiring work, but what seemed to be making sustainable improvements were the initiatives that came from the Bangladeshis themselves. The now-famous Grameen Bank, created by Dr. Muhammed Yunus, is a micro–credit program providing small-business loans to hardworking, cash-poor women, and BRAC, a village development initiative created by Bangladeshi leader Faisal Abed, had created significant success where outsiders unfamiliar with the people had failed.

These successes and experiences in other regions had affirmed our conviction that the Bangladeshi people were the key to their own development and that outside aid was systematically and psychologically turning them into beggars instead of the authors of their own future.

As the first step in the process of forging an effective partnership, together we looked deeply into the Bangladeshi culture, their attitudes and beliefs about themselves, their resignation and hopelessness. It became clear that after so long subsisting on aid, the people had lost touch with any sense of their own competence or any vision of their country as capable of success. In our meetings together, the Bangladeshi leaders determined that the thing that was missing, which, if provided, would enable these people to become self-reliant and self-sufficient, was a vision of their own strengths and capabilities. The Hunger Project committed, as a partner, to develop a program designed to enable the Bangladeshis to reconnect with a vision for themselves and their country, with an awareness of their available assets, and strategies to put their ideas into action. Out of that commitment and partnership came the Vision, Commitment and Action Workshop. It called upon participants to engage in a series of group-discussion and visualization exercises enabling them to imagine and envision a self-reliant, self-sufficient Bangladesh: the healthy, thriving Bangladesh they had fought for years ago in their struggle for independence.

In Bangladesh, because there are so many people, when you call any kind of a meeting, hundreds, even a thousand people can show up. People often gather in the village parks and squares. In Dhaka, the capital, there is a public park that holds easily a thousand people or more, and that is where we launched some of the early Vision, Commitment and Action Workshops. We publicized the meeting, and at the appointed time the park was packed with people. If you can picture it, this is no beautiful pastoral retreat, but a park with barely a blade of grass, packed with hundreds of these small, brown, beautiful people seated on the ground very close together, lots of babies and small children, people of all ages sitting attentively, tentatively, listening for whatever we could offer them that might be helpful.

The program opened with music, a few introductions and inspired words by community leaders, and some initial interactive exercises to bring the crowd's energy and focus to the task at hand. Then we began the program, asking everybody to close their eyes and envision what a self-reliant, self-sufficient Bangladesh would look like:

What would it look like if Bangladesh were a country that

was exporting its finest-quality goods? What would it be like if Bangladesh were known for its art and music and poetry? What if Bangladesh were a contributing member of the global community, instead of the big recipient, the big begging bowl receiving aid? What it would be like if Bangladeshi leadership, including Bangladeshi women, Bangladeshi men, and Bangladeshi young people, were a contribution to society? What would that look like?

At first, people sat there very still, eyes closed, expressionless, shoulder to shoulder in the park. A hush settled over the crowd, and the sea of faces remained still, eyes closed, in thought. After a few minutes I noticed tears streaming down one man's face, and then another and another. People were still sitting with their eyes closed, but they were silently weeping. And then it was not just three or four, or ten or twenty faces with tears streaming down. In this crowd of more than a thousand, it was hundreds of weeping faces. It was as if they had never in their lifetime even thought they could be self-reliant or self-sufficient or a contributing nation, that they had never imagined they could be a nation that made a difference for other nations, that they could be a nation that stood out, that had qualities that people admired, a unique role to play in the world community. It was a brave new thought.

When we completed this visioning meditation, and people shared with one another the visions they had seen for their village, their family, their school, their home, their business, their children, and their grandchildren, the vision became rich and real, palpable and exhilarating. A new future was born.

In the next section of the workshop the participants were invited to commit to their vision. They were asked not merely to envision, but to commit to being the people who would make that vision real. You could see them drop their anxiety and fear, letting go of their sense of lack and inadequacy, and step up to their own creation and commit to it. In that exercise you could see people's posture and countenance change. People seemed to visibly strengthen. Their sense of resolve and determination was contagious, and the impossible seemed possible. They finally broke into small groups to collaborate and design the actions they would take to fulfill their commitment to make their vision real. The actions were practical, local, doable, but in alignment with their new commitments and in service of their vision. People seemed to resee themselves, their family, their village, and their country as able, resourceful, and potent—self-reliant and self-sufficient.

Soon these workshops were being repeated in gatherings all over, some in cities, others in villages, some just within families, and every Sunday for thousands in the square at Dhaka.

Now it happened that on a trip to Dhaka, one of the leaders of a village in Sylhet attended a Vision, Commitment and Action Workshop nearly by mistake. His name was Zilu. He was visiting his cousin in the city, and this cousin invited him to come along to the park to see what this workshop was all about. Zilu didn't want to go. He wanted to talk to his cousin about moving his family from Sylhet in with his cousin, to share their home, so the family could leave their desolate village, hoping that Zilu could get work in the city and give them a chance for a new life. His cousin prevailed, however, and they attended the workshop together.

Zilu was completely captivated by the workshop experience, and his awakening to his own commitment to his village and the surrounding community. He stayed in Dhaka another three days and participated in a training to be a workshop leader himself. He then took the training and the vision back to Sylhet.

Back home, he called his six closest male friends together and delivered the workshop to them. With a shared vision now, and unlimited commitment to develop the human and natural resources of their own region, the seven men came up with an idea and created a plan for a new agribusiness venture designed to bring the whole region out of poverty into self-reliance and ultimately into prosperity. They called it the Chowtee Project: A Bold Step for Self-Reliance.

I arrived in Sylhet just four months later, in April of 1994, with seventeen travelers who were major donors to The Hunger Project. Zilu had invited us there to show us the progress he and his friends had made in the area and to thank us for the contribution we were making to his country and his people. He and his friends, whom we came to call the Magnificent Seven, told us the story of their region's transformation and showed us the results.

Zilu shared how he had returned from the workshop at Dhaka that December day inspired to look with new eyes at the resources he and his people had before them, and determined to develop a vision, a commitment, and a plan of action. Once his six friends joined him in this commitment, their next step was to look at the resources they already had but had previously overlooked. There, at the edge of town, was the fallow, hard-scrabble government land covered with poison berry brambles. The seven men met with government officials and got permission to clear seventeen acres of the tangled vegetation that had taken over their land. Then they went to the community for the money needed to buy equipment and supplies. People drew from their meager savings to support the initiative, and the men were able to collect the needed thousands of taka—then about $750. Finally, they delivered their own version of the Vision, Commitment and Action Workshop to six hundred people in the village of eighteen thousand.

Those six hundred people got to work, building a road along the edge of the land and starting the clearing effort. Impressed with their vision, clarity, and commitment, the government gave them a hundred acres more to develop. They trained the young people who had turned to begging and crime to cultivate and farm instead. They trained destitute women, many of them widows, to farm. In clearing the land, they were surprised to discover a previously unknown lake and small stream abundant with fish.

The entire area was now under cultivation, providing food, fish, training, and employment for hundreds of people. All eighteen thousand people in the immediate area had benefited from this activity, and an area that had been wracked with poverty was now becoming self-sufficient and beginning to flourish. The crime rate had dropped by an astounding 70 percent.

We walked the fields with Zilu and the rest of the Magnificent Seven, and visited the fisheries and the training fields. We were overwhelmed by the people's vitality, joy, and success. I realized as I walked with them that they had accomplished this feat with almost no help from the outside. They had had what they needed all along—the land, the water, the intelligence, the muscle, and the capacity to put it all together—but had lost touch with those resources and capabilities in the climate of "Third World" aid and the hopelessness and presumed incompetence that had come with it. Once they were inspired to see themselves differently, to see themselves as strong, creative, and capable, their commitment knew no limits. Success was inevitable.

Looking at the fields, once impenetrable jungle and brush, I thought about our own lives, and that which covers over the soil of our dreams, that which temporarily blocks our inner vision or capacity to see. In their world, it was the jungle and the confusing message of aid telling them that they were incomplete and needy and not able to make it on their own. They had bought into that, and as long as they did, they couldn't see the resources in front of them. Once they had focused their attention on their own unlimited inner resources, the outer resources materialized, suddenly accessible. They could begin to see that what they needed had been there all along.

I never forgot the Magnificent Seven. When you are crushed by the victim mentality, as they were, your ability to dream and envision is crushed, too. It goes dead. When I find myself groping for what's beyond my grasp, I hear their words in my head and know that if I can relook from the inside out and access and appreciate what's already there, what's already available, then its power, utility, and grace will grow and prosper in the nourishment of my attention.

APPRECIATIVE INQUIRY:
A POSITIVE THEORY OF CHANGE

The power of appreciation has been recognized as a tool for building organizational success, whether it is in a community of farmers, a group of factory workers, a company with thousands of employees, or a handful of volunteers on a community service project.

David L. Cooperrider, Diana Whitney, and their team of researchers and consultants in the field of organizational theory and human development introduced the concept of "appreciative inquiry" as a formal model for change. In their book, *Appreciative Inquiry: Rethinking Human Organization Toward a Positive Theory of Change*, they suggest we shift our frame of reference from one of "problem solving" to one that seeks to identify the sources available in any collection of people for inspiring, mobilizing, and sustaining positive change.

How would our practices surrounding change be different, they ask, if we started with the positive presumption that "organizations, as centers of human relatedness, are 'alive' with infinite constructive capacity"?

In appreciative inquiry we "search for the best in people, their organizations, and the relevant world around them." Appreciative inquiry involves "systematic discovery of what gives 'life' to a living system when it is most alive, most effective, and most constructively capable in economic, ecological, and human terms." Look for what's working instead of what's not, they say, and "instead of negation, criticism, and spiraling diagnosis, there is discovery, dream, and design."

So much of our life around money is centered in scarcity's problem-based assumptions, and the spiraling diagnosis and chase for solutions beyond our grasp. If instead, you can put your full attention and appreciation on what's there, then you experience the bounty available in the moment. You experience sufficiency, and that's what you're about. You generate that vision and you call others to that experience. In the context of sufficiency, every aspect of your life becomes an asset by virtue of your ability to embrace it, learn from it, and make something of it. What you appreciate, and the way you direct your attention, determines the quality of your life.

This power of appreciation is available to all of us, anywhere and anytime. Your own country and your own culture may be different from Bangladesh and its culture, but the anxiety, fear, resignation, and hopelessness we feel at times around money issues can be precisely the same. In appreciation of all that we are and already have, we can resee the possibilities, identify a vision, make a commitment, and act on it.

AUDREY: FINDING HER WORTH

Audrey was forty-two years old, a full-time homemaker, wife, and the mother of two young daughters, when she filed for divorce from her emotionally abusive and adulterous husband. They had been married nearly twenty years, and under pressure from her husband, Audrey had passed up higher education and career opportunities as a promising artist to be a full-time homemaker. At different times over the years, Audrey had turned her attention to her dream—having her own business designing children's clothes—but she had been discouraged from doing so by her husband and his parents. They told her she wasn't smart enough, and she believed him.

Her husband came from a very rich family and had plenty of money, but he had used legal loopholes to make his assets off-limits to her.

In the divorce proceedings, with each punishing exchange of settlement proposals with her estranged husband, she felt newly wounded by his reminder—now expressed in low dollar amounts—that he viewed her and the time and life she had invested in their marriage as worthless. "I am without value" was the money mantra, the punishing life sentence that she had carried with her from her marriage experience, and now it was the official message, in legal language, of the divorce settlement.

Day by day, court date by court date, she grew increasingly depressed, angry and discouraged at her sense of being cheated, first out of her dream of a lifelong marriage, and then, from a practical standpoint, cheated out of a share of the money she felt was her due. She grew pessimistic about her ability to find work.

Her worst fears loomed large. What if she couldn't make money enough to get an apartment and keep custody of her children? What if she turned out to be inept and unemployable, as her husband had always told her she was? Overcome with fears and self-doubt, she couldn't get past images of disaster to imagine a prosperous future for herself and her children. Many days she was immobilized by both her anger and her fear of failure.

Audrey and I met when she was at this low point—in income and self-esteem—and we used the prism of her relationship with money as a way to find new insights to empower her recovery.

We turned our conversation to identifying Audrey's true assets: her talents and skills, hopes and dreams, and the resources she had in her circle of family and friends. After so many years of feeling worthless, it wasn't easy for Audrey to see herself as having any assets at all, any inner wealth to speak of.

We began with a head count of those people who Audrey knew offered unconditional love and appreciation for her, who believed in her. They were assets, too. She pictured her two daughters and the close and loving bond they shared, having nothing to do with money. She pictured her parents and her brothers, who could offer little in the way of material support, but who were steadfast in their expressions of love and encouragement. She thought of her closest, most trusted friends of long standing, and then of other, more recent friendships, and how each one contributed to the climate of love and well-being in her life. None of these relationships relied on money as the glue that held them together. Love and appreciation was all there was.

She named each person—there were about twenty, all told—and then I asked her to name the qualities that, at one time or another, they had let her know they appreciated about her. She laughed self-consciously, but went ahead and named the things she recalled her friends having said. Like me, they knew her as clever, creative, smart, generous, enthusiastic, determined, and with a great sense of humor.

We identified these qualities of character as assets more valuable and unlimited than any possessions she might own or any money she might have in a bank account. These were assets that some people work a lifetime to develop, qualities that money can't buy. Audrey already had them!

As we sat talking and Audrey turned her attention to the wealth of these friendships, her own assets of character and material resources, she could feel a change and I could see it. She straightened a bit in her chair; her expression lifted and her voice became more confident. She described a shift in the way she felt now, relative to the challenge. Her fears felt smaller. She already felt more self-reliant and less needy, although she did have needs, and undaunted by her circumstances, though her circumstances were challenging. She felt some fear still, but now she also felt more confident in the firm ground of her own resources and the affirmation of others.

"Now imagine it is twenty-five years from today," I said.

"That would make me seventy years old!" she said, laughing.

"So imagine you are going on seventy, and think of your girls grown and maybe married, and you have grandchildren and you are in an incredible time in your life, you've made peace with the past and with yourself, and you can look back and see. How did you get through that period right after your divorce? What were the possibilities and opportunities you found and created for your daughters? What was it that got you through those first few years?"

Audrey paused and then spoke, a little hesitantly at first.

"I stopped letting fear stop me," she said. "I was afraid, but I did it anyway. I trusted myself."

"And what will you tell those grandchildren of yours about how you made it through that difficult passage with money?" I asked. "What was your breakthrough that allowed you to find your sufficiency?"

She paused again, as if listening from a distance to her wiser, older self, reporting from the future. Then with a strong voice this time, she answered.

"I stopped waiting for someone to tell me what to do. I realized I'd have to try a number of different things and I just did it. I developed a belief in myself. Where I had spent years putting my belief in a man, now I put just a quarter of it toward believing in myself, and that freed up three-quarters of that energy for other things besides making a living. I think women should look at how much energy they put into their relationships and consciously take a quarter of it and put it into their own relationship with themselves, and they would go as far as I have gone."

"And how did you earn a living? What was the breakthrough there?"

Audrey paused again, then looked apologetic. "When I try to

think of that, I keep getting scared and stop looking," she said. But she refocused her attention to envision her future.

"I started my children's clothes business and it became our bread-and-butter—it kept us going," she said.

We talked about her desire to build on her passions and talents to make a real *living*, which is different from making enough to pay the rent, or making a killing, as her ex-husband and his parents had. In just the space of our conversation, she had been able to step back and see how much of her energy had been consumed by her money fears and the unquestioned assumption that she was incapable of making a good life for herself and her children. She had said it herself: If she took all the energy that was tied up in anxiety, worry, and fear, and focused it on her assets and on her commitment and strategies to achieve a vision, she now knew in her heart that she would be successful.

In the months that followed, Audrey kept me posted on her progress. With growing confidence and the encouragement of her friends and family, Audrey began to turn her attention to her marketable skills and take steps to learn how to build her own business.

One evening she attended a seminar on women in business and immediately discovered a world of contacts, small-business support groups, and workshops on the very issues she needed to learn about to start her own enterprise. Soon she was part of a mentoring program, in which successful businesswomen from the community partnered with women like herself, as teachers and advisors. She attended more classes, learned about the money flow in business and how to manage it wisely. Everywhere she went, when she took a new sample of children's outfits to show a friend, someone passing by wanted to buy it.

Strangers would share their enthusiasm for her product and her vision, and Audrey's excitement grew.

Step by step, Audrey researched the manufacturing and sales aspects of her dream company, refined her product designs, and created a business plan. People she met in the process were impressed by her creativity, enthusiasm, and keen business sense, and she was able to secure a number of part-time jobs as her planning continued. As she devoted more and more attention to creating her own business, her circle of friends and business contacts grew and continued to encourage and support her inspired effort.

Over time, her relationship with money changed. Instead of living in awe of it, or in constant fear of not having enough, she lived prudently with what she had, and focused her attention on creating a viable business doing what she loved. Her relationship with money shifted. No longer was she a victim or passive participant beholden to her ex-husband and angry or fearful of being cut off. Now she was growing to know her own earning power and her own value as a creative, generative entrepreneur in business and in life. She wrote into her business plan a commitment to become a resource for other women, through jobs sewing, manufacturing, and selling her product line.

There were down days and difficult ones, but when Audrey focused her attention—even for just a moment—on the simplest aspects of her own sufficiency, she recovered her courage and energy, and even joy, in that moment. Each time she was able to find the courage she needed to continue; not excessive courage, but *enough*, she said later, laughing. Even more surprising, she said, was that each time she was ready to move forward one more step with her plans, as luck would have it, she found precisely what she needed—the right contact, the right studio, the right suppliers, the right investors—and by the end of the next year, Audrey had launched her company and was off to a promising start. From the scraps of a torn life, she had crafted a masterpiece.

JAMES: LOST AND FOUND
AND TURNED AROUND

It would be easy to assume that all this talk about appreciation and sufficiency is really aimed at people like Audrey or the Magnificent Seven, those who have so little that they must learn to appreciate what little they have or sink in despair. It is just as true of people with great wealth and surplus. They can, and often do, become lost in a sea of excess, flooded with things, houses, cars, and stuff, such that they lose any sense of an inner life or meaning beyond the money. Mother Teresa once noted what she called "the deep poverty of the soul" that afflicts the wealthy, and had said that the poverty of the soul in America was deeper than any poverty she had seen anywhere on earth.

James knew that place and that poverty of spirit. He had grown up in a small town in Missouri, where his family owned the primary industry in the town. The family name was his curse—anyone who knew him knew that he was rich and would never need to work, and they automatically assumed he was a spoiled rich kid. They treated him with envy and contempt.

James had a huge heart and wanted to be seen as a normal contributing member of society, but he saw his name and his fortune as a terrible burden that kept him from being able to relate normally to people and to the world around him. He resented, in fact hated, his family name and this burden of his fortune. He felt he needed to escape from the environment he was in to find any genuine sense of self-worth, in essence to prove himself. The emptiness inside of him was getting deeper and he was tortured by a sense of worthlessness, guilt, and shame.

We had met in college and although I can now look back and see retrospectively the pain he was in, I didn't see it at the time. He was merely another classmate, studying, taking tests, drinking beer—being a college kid.

I reconnected with him years later at the home of a mutual friend, and he looked older than his years, but was still the elegant, handsome man I remembered from school. He asked me to join him for lunch a few days later, saying only that he needed some advice. Over lunch, he shared his story. James was an alcoholic. He also was now the father of two children and in the middle of a second divorce. He had money enough for a lifetime of luxury, but he felt lost and sad, and fearful that people would find out that his personal life was in shambles. He wanted to change, but didn't know how.

Like nearly every other relationship in his life, James's relationship with money was a place of hurt, conflict, distrust, disappointment, and very little clarity. The deep and long-ignored emotional issues that had plagued him since childhood had only compounded with a lifetime of neglect, and the family's ready cash had enabled him to finesse his way around difficult moments in marriage, family, friendship, and life itself. Having done nothing of significance himself to earn the money, James's bitter secret was that he suffered deep self-doubt. He felt worthless, save for the very money he hated. He had the money to do anything, but his life had become nothing more than an expensive and increasingly complex charade, masking alcoholism, failed relationships, superficial friendships, and a profound feeling of uselessness.

He was a caring man, a man who wanted to do good in the world, wanted to make a meaningful contribution with his life. He wished that he could start over, but he felt trapped by both his financial excess and his personal failures.

We began to talk regularly, and while James embarked on the slow and arduous repair of relationships with the people in his life, we focused on his relationship with money. He blamed his problems on the family name and fortune he had been expected to cultivate. He unloaded a lot of emotional baggage as an angry, unhappy rich kid, and some more about his failed marriages and people he felt had been opportunists in his life. Then, after a time, the need to blame and rail against his money and his past seemed to fade. He began to talk about the man he yearned to be.

How would his life look if he were living it true to a deeper vision? How would his relationship with his children and his ex-wives be different if he were to act with integrity toward them, including in the financial settlements of divorce? Beyond the loving responsibility of caring for his children, what higher commitments stirred his heart? What kind of difference did he want to make in the world?

Envisioning a life he could love opened James up to new possibilities and gave him a new experience of himself. As we put our attention on that vision, it was like fanning a tiny ember in a bed of dark coals. The possibilities glowed, and more specific ideas began to emerge with definition. He felt a special affinity for struggling young people, and wanted to work with them. He volunteered in a local school, and as he learned more about the struggle of children with learning disabilities, he discovered his own talents in working with them. The more he worked with the students, their teachers, and the special-education teachers who often assisted in the classroom or provided special assistance through tutoring, the more he began to understand the complexity of the children's needs and the efforts to address them.

The money that had been a burden all his life now appeared as a resource to support organizations working with special-needs children. He also stepped up in his community as an advocate for the schools and school funding, to benefit all children. His own painful childhood became an asset that enabled him to relate with greater sensitivity to those children with whom he worked. The chaos of his troubled life began to calm, and he began to appreciate even that chaos as a passage from a confused and troubled time to one with purpose, meaning, and fulfillment.

His children joined him in his work as a volunteer with other children, and as a single father, this new engagement with his own children enriched their relationship; their appreciation of each other grew. James's hard work and devotion to the school and the students, and his children, not only turned around the lives of many of those children, but his own life, too. The money that had seemed a curse for so long now became the instrument of his release into a new, rewarding life of connection and contribution.

The poet Rainer Maria Rilke wrote (translated by Robert Bly):

> *I love the dark hours of my being*
> *in which my senses drop into the deep.*

I have found in them, as in old letters,
My private life, that is already lived through,
And become wide and powerful now, like legends.
Then I know that there is room in me
For a second huge and timeless life.

The time had come for James's second huge and timeless life.

BUDDHA'S WISDOM

Buddha told his followers that whatever they chose to give their attention, their love, their appreciation, their listening, and their affirmation to would grow in their life and in their world. He likened one's life and the world to a garden—a garden that calls for sunlight and nourishment and water to grow. In that garden are the seeds of compassion, forgiveness, love, commitment, courage and all the qualities that affirm and inspire us. Alongside those seeds and in the same garden are the seeds of hatred, the seeds of prejudice, the seeds of vengeance, the seeds of violence, and all the other hurtful, destructive ways of being. These seeds and many more like them exist in the same garden.

The seeds that grow are the seeds we tend with our attention. Our attention is like water and sunshine, and the seeds we cultivate will grow and fill our garden. If we choose to invest our attention in the seeds of scarcity—acquisition, accumulation, greed, and all that springs from those seeds—then scarcity is what will fill the space of our life and the space of our world. If we tend the seeds of sufficiency with our attention, and use our money like water to nourish them with soulful purpose, then we will enjoy that bountiful harvest.

The Magnificent Seven and the Bangladeshis, Audrey and James couldn't be more different. But for each of them, the power of appreciation enabled them to expand and deepen their experience of their true wealth and self. In the context of sufficiency, they each found a new freedom in their relationship with money or issues around money, and in that, a path to their own prosperity. For any of us, in the fertile soil of our appreciation, new possibility takes root, and it grows without limits in the lasting light of our attention.

7

Collaboration Creates Prosperity

There are no haves and have-nots. We are all haves and our
assets are diverse. In the alchemy of collaboration, we become
equal partners; we create wholeness and sufficiency for everyone.

It was Friday night. I had been in a meeting all day and
was exhausted. I was on my way home from Sausalito to
San Francisco when the brakes on my car began to fail a
few blocks from the Golden Gate Bridge. I pulled into the nearest gas station. The fellow there couldn't fix brakes, but he
pointed me in the direction of an auto-repair garage down the
street. I drove at a crawl—without brakes—the short distance,
but as I rolled up in front of the garage, I could see I was out of
luck. It was after seven o'clock. The garage doors were closed
and the office light was off. But a soft light shone through the
garage-door windows, and desperate as I was, I went over and
peeked in, hoping to find a merciful mechanic. Instead, I saw a
party of thirty or forty people in progress. All the automotive

equipment had been pushed aside and in the center of the bare concrete floor, surrounded by party lights and decorations, was a sleek, shiny, grand piano. The party was going strong, but the piano sat silent. I ventured in, found the garage owner, a man named Rico, champagne glass in his hand, and I asked if anyone might be able to help me. I explained my problem. "I'll pay you anything to fix my brakes so I can get home," I said.

Rico laughed and said, "No way, lady. We're having a party and we're in full swing." But then he said jokingly, "Our piano player is a no-show, though, and if you can play the piano, we'll fix your car." Everyone laughed, but, as it happens, I *do* play piano, and that is what I did. I played for their party for nearly an hour, and, surrounded by these people laughing and singing and dancing, the mechanic cheerfully fixed my brakes. When the job was done, they sent me on my way, refusing any payment and toasting our new friendship. I drove home safely—no longer tired and exhausted but exhilarated and energized. I had showed up with exactly what they needed, and they had provided exactly what I needed. Our encounter was filled with the delight of serendipity, and the satisfaction of having been perfectly able to help one another.

Collaboration and reciprocity are natural, and yet in the world we inhabit, competition and the fear of scarcity often block us from seeing these ways of being with one another. In a you-*or*-me world, reciprocity and collaboration don't fit. A you-*and*-me world is full of collaborators, partners, sharing, and reciprocity. In that world, our resources are not only enough; they are infinite. When we bring the practice of collaboration and reciprocity into conscious view in everyday life, a kind of alchemy and prosperity await discovery all around us.

Connections forged in a mind-set of scarcity—acting on the

belief that *there's not enough, more is better,* or *that's just the way it is*—no matter how strong they may seem in the moment, are inherently self-limiting. Grounded in a lie, they only undermine our chances for long-term survival and sustainability. The kinds of connections that truly protect and preserve us are those that emerge from the context of sufficiency and the sharing, diversity, reciprocity, and partnership found there. We find sufficiency and sustainable prosperity when we think of our resources as a flow that is meant to be shared, when we put our full attention on making a difference with what we have, and when we partner with others in ways that expand and deepen that experience.

Potlucks, car pools, time-shares, play groups, quilting bees—these activities, these ways of sharing with and caring for each other, enrich our lives more than we realize, and perhaps more than money ever will or could. Collaboration leads us to and grounds us in sufficiency. You can see it in the way connections grounded in sufficiency value the diversity, knowledge, creativity, experience, and wisdom of all partners equally, and allow us to experience ourselves as active participants in a vital, generative process. Collaboration becomes the circuitry through which the energy, attention, and resources of sufficiency flow and are continually renewed. Implicit in collaboration is the trust that says there is enough and we will figure out how to use it together wisely.

Think of an effective collaboration you've been involved with, and the way in which working through the issues deepened your sense of self and your appreciation and respect for your collaborator. Think about the generosity you needed to exhibit and the openness it required of you and your partner or partners. Think of the satisfaction of the outcomes produced collectively and the experience of true wealth in the fruit of the action.

Reciprocity allows us to acknowledge each other in appreciation of our unique gifts. Reciprocity is like the breath we breathe in—no more than what we need. We breathe out exactly the amount that must be released. It is sufficient and it is precise and it is life affirming. To recognize, lift up, and shine a light on the beauty of reciprocal relationships and interactions in our lives is to uncover vast reservoirs of existing wealth that we have taken for granted. In reciprocity there is nourishment and joy: I am there for you and you are there for me.

As an activist and fund-raiser for work that is grounded in sufficiency, and as someone who tries to live that way myself, virtually every day of my life I see the power of collaboration to bridge the age, race, gender, religious, ethnic, and socioeconomic gaps that often divide us. The benefits of collaboration are apparent in turnaround stories like those of Sylhet in Bangladesh, or the village in Senegal where the women dug their well, or so many others in which chronic struggle has been transformed into celebrated success. The quieter, sometimes unseen, victories have been in the similar transformation of the inner landscape of people's lives, those struggling in poverty and those struggling in material wealth. There, collaboration has led to self-discovery, personal growth, healing, and an experience of sufficiency that was inaccessible before, the happiness that money could not buy.

In our relationship with money, collaboration frees us from the obligatory chase to acquire more in order to feel we have enough, and becomes an opportunity to make a difference with what we have. It puts money its rightful place, as just one of many resources we may have to offer that are valued and needed.

And it keeps our money in flow, so that whether it is a river or a stream or a trickle in our life, it circulates in ways that do the most good for the most people—including ourselves!

TRACY: SHARED RESOURCES AND SHARED RICHNESS

One of my closest and most beloved friends is a woman named Tracy. Her life path has been challenging, and yet she has always had exactly what she has needed for herself and her children. At every turn, she has found the wealth and alchemy in collaboration, and I continue to be moved by the principles of sufficiency from which she lives.

Tracy is a mother of two and lives in a small community in northern California. She and her husband separated in the late 1980s, and when her husband left Tracy thought her life was over. She had little money. She had no husband. She had two small children and a heart full of despair.

Somewhere deep in her soul, Tracy had always felt drawn to living in other cultures. When her marriage broke up, she decided she wanted to go somewhere far, far away to clear her head and her heart, and to think more openly about the future for herself and her children. She had done some work for The Hunger Project in Japan and had become close friends with a colleague there, Hiroshi Ohuchi, a Japanese professor at Tamagawa University. Hiroshi and his American wife, Janet, had three children, ages twelve, ten, and eight; Tracy's young daughter, Sage, was seven, and her son, Sebastian, was five.

Tracy wrote to Janet and Hiroshi telling them of her despair over the divorce and her desire to be someplace different where she could think more clearly about her situation. Janet immediately invited her and the children to visit for the winter holidays. The Ohuchis lived at the foot of Mt. Fuji, far from other people, had no television, and were homeschooling their children. The Ohuchi family welcomed Tracy and her two children with open arms, and eagerly incorporated them into their home and their lives. The five young children became fast friends.

For the duration of their planned visit, every day brought new and joyful dimensions to their friendship and new appreciation for each other's gifts. Tracy brought magnificent organizational strengths to the family and household, a flair for fun cooking, and a genius for creating special times to be shared by all. At the end of the holiday period, when the time came that Tracy and her children originally had planned to return to the United States, a new possibility presented itself. As the family story now goes, Tracy said, "I can't remember why we were going back" and Janet responded, "No one ever said you have to go . . . we'd love to have you stay!" From that joyous moment came what each now calls a fourteen-month gift, a mutual gift of shared responsibility, friendship, and extended family.

Tracy, a former teacher, worked with all five children doing homeschooling, helped with cooking and meal preparation, contributed creative ideas to keeping the three adults and five kids organized and happy, worked part-time for The Hunger Project, practiced Buddhism with Hiroshi, sang old folk songs with Janet and the kids, and slowly was able to heal herself in the nurturing environment of the Ohuchi family.

The Ohuchis offered warmth, comfort, and joy that Tracy and her children needed after the breakup of the family. The Ohuchis, meanwhile, were dealing with the fatal illness of their infant daughter. With Tracy and her children's participation in the family, including the baby's funeral, a heartbreaking experience was shared and made more bearable. All of them flourished. All had exactly what they needed, and by collaborating and opening their hearts to one another, they found a sense of plenty, that exquisite experience of enough. The Ohuchis felt blessed to be able to share their home and family life with their friends. Tracy found the time and place for the spiritual healing she needed, as well as to co-write a book with her daughter and do productive work with The Hunger Project. The combined family of five children grew up in an environment that was immensely richer than it would have been had they lived in separate households.

Each family provided what they had at that point and stage in their lives: The Ohuchis had stability, a steady paycheck coming in, and a home that was peaceful and spacious enough for all. Tracy and her children provided liveliness, laughter, and creativity all tied together with a spiritual base and discipline. Both families were facing the most wrenching emotional times of their lives, and in one another they found compassion and strength.

When Tracy and her children eventually returned to the United States, she described the pleasure and benefits of living in an extended family with some dear friends, and they, with their two children, decided to embark on a group-living situation. They found a house together—a lovely place that neither family could have afforded alone—in a location with good schools and ample outdoor play areas for the children. Since the other couple worked outside the home, Tracy wanted a business that would allow her to be home after school for the four elementary-school-age children. Tracy discovered she had a talent for interviewing and writing, and she began a freelance writing business chronicling the life stories of elderly people for their families. The business has thrived, and the two families have lived together for eleven years, to the satisfaction of all. Tracy now earns a living doing what she loves most, while her children have enjoyed excellent educational opportunities and a beautiful, warm, nurturing living environment and an extended family that has further enriched their lives. Although Tracy's income is low- to middle-income by American standards, (about $35,000) she and her children lack nothing.

The journey that began in Tracy's despair over divorce and her fears about money and supporting her children eventually proved to be a path to a collaborative, joyful life shared with close, loving friends and family. Her friends, in turn, felt fortunate in the opportunity to share their lives with Tracy and her children.

Tracy lives from a context of sufficiency. From there, she has had the space and heart to be both *generous*—contributing whatever she has without fear of loss—and quietly *trusting* that the universe will provide. She has told me she is guided by Mother Teresa's advice to "work as though everything depended on it, and leave the rest to God." Tracy herself is a constant inspiration in the way she has developed deeply in herself and in her children the distinction "enough" that is so lost in our culture. It is from there, from having enough and being enough, that she has reaped the harvest of collaboration, the alchemy of reciprocity. Her young-adult children thrive, centered in their own gifts and committed to use those gifts to make a difference in the world.

THE TRUE "LAW OF THE JUNGLE": COLLABORATION AND COMPETITION IN BALANCE

Nineteenth-century scientific and economic theorists painted a harsh picture of the natural world, describing competition for food and other resources as the inevitable and defining force by which Nature balanced population and resources, and selected in favor of some species and against others. Political economist Thomas Malthus saw famine, disease, poverty, and war as divinely wrought natural scourges intended to control overpopulation. Charles Darwin went on to describe "survival of the fittest" in large part as the competition for scarce resources, as the basis for the evolution of species. Contrary to those models of Nature as innately, intensely, and almost exclusively competitive, more recent scientific study has illuminated the powerful role of mutuality, synergy, coexistence, and cooperation in the natural world and the more accurate picture of life that presents.

Even a cursory look at the world food supply and world population tells us that there is enough food to feed everyone, but that other factors keep some populations oversupplied and even overfed while others are malnourished and dying from hunger. Chronic hunger isn't "Nature's way" of limiting population or improving the species. In fact, it is less about Nature and more about flawed government, politics, and economic systems of our own construction.

The idea that scarcity and competition are *just the way it is* is no longer even viable science. Respected evolutionary biologist Elisabet Sahtouris notes that Nature fosters collaboration and reciprocity. Competition in Nature exists, she says, but it has limits, and the true law of survival is ultimately cooperation.

Nature expresses itself in balance and purpose. Nature thrives in sufficiency. A lion kills what it needs to maintain itself and no more than that. A healthy lion doesn't go on killing rampages. It wants and takes only enough. Different species of plants and animals coexist, each providing something essential to a balanced environment that supports all life. Sahtouris and others note that contrary to the competitive theme that "survival of the fittest" connotes, a more accurate description would be "survival of the cooperative and collaborative." In my own experience, that truth has expressed itself particularly powerfully in the rain forest, where every step you take brings you face-to-face with the extraordinarily rich and delicate interconnectedness of all life.

The late environmental scientist Donella (Dana) Meadows, with whom I worked closely as a friend and colleague at The Hunger Project for twenty years, in her book, *The Limits to Growth*, and other writings made a convincing case for this more enlightened understanding of the natural world. In her works and in the way she lived, she brought into view the overlooked world of "enough" that exists and supports life on this planet.

Contrasting economic assumptions with those apparent in Nature, she once wrote that while the laws of economics drive the condition of scarcity with an assumption that we must consume, produce, compete, and dominate more and more, and faster and faster, Nature in balance models competition *and* collaboration within a context of coexistence; creation, production, and consumption on a timetable expressed in the natural cycles of life, growth, and death. She wrote:

Economics says: Compete. Only by pitting yourself against a worthy opponent will you perform efficiently. The reward for successful competition will be growth. You will eat up your opponents, one by one, and as you do, you will gain the resources to do it some more.

The Earth says: Compete, yes, but keep your competition in bounds. Don't annihilate. Take only what you need. Leave your competition enough to live. Whenever possible, don't compete, cooperate. Pollinate each other, build firm structures that lift smaller species up to the light. Pass around the nutrients, share the territory. Some kinds of excellence rise out of competition; other kinds rise out of cooperation. You're not in a war; you're in a community.

Nature offers so many other lessons that illuminate our behavior around money, if we choose to be more fully open to the insights and reconsider old assumptions. For instance, recent research suggests that the "fight or flight" response that has for so long been described as the normal human response to a threat or to fear actually is characteristic primarily of males. The characteristic female response to a threat is to connect and collaborate with others. From a range of sources in enlightened scientific discovery, we are beginning to see this larger truth about the natural world. Competition and conflict comprise an undeniable part of Nature, but not the predominant one, as suggested by those who excuse human greed and violence as a natural phenomenon. It is a mistake, or a manipulation, to use Nature as a metaphor or model for human behavior, yet focus on only one facet of it—the competition, aggression, and violence—to define an inevitable world of winners and losers, and to suggest *that's just the way it is*.

Of course Nature includes conflict—some wild animals will

fight to the death for dominance, for mating partners, for food, and territory. But even in the animal community, that is only one behavior in a complex array of behaviors, many of which are characterized by nurturing, exploring, or communicating important information about the location of food, water, and predators.

Nature isn't a model separate from us. We *are* part of the natural world, complete with all its complexities. As part of the natural world, we can accept fear and aggressive behavior as natural, but only as extreme behaviors in a larger context of a cooperative, collaborative, symbiotic relationship that is generative and life supporting. It is just as reasonable for us to draw from those life-affirming natural behaviors and images for our inspiration—in fact, it is more so—because it is those types of relationships, those qualities of behavior, that offer the best models and best practices for a generative relationship with money, for human survival, and a sustainable future for our Earth.

THE TROUBLE WITH CHARITY AND THE "HELPING HAND"

"If you are coming to help me, you are wasting your time," an indigenous saying goes, "but if you are coming because your liberation is bound up with mine, then let us work together."

As a fund-raiser, I facilitate collaboration and have been deeply engaged in the world of giving and receiving. As beautiful as that sounds, I have also seen the dark, dishonest side of what at first looks so apparently genuine and good. It is difficult to imagine how charity could have a dark side, or be dishonest, but it is true.

I encountered the dark side many years ago in Chicago, when I accepted that $50,000 check from the food company CEO, realizing belatedly that it amounted to guilt money, a pay-off intended to make up for some public relations faux pas. I saw it in Bombay, when it became apparent that the beggars would mutilate their children to shock and shame visitors into giving money, and the money they got that way only perpetuated the manipulation, and ultimately the cycle, of begging. I've seen it in the way some wealthy donors use giving as a way to polish their public image, or use the promise of money to extract special attention or privileges from those desperate for dollars; and in the way organizations, programs, and people sometimes compromise themselves to cater to the rich, in hopes of currying favor and the big check.

The dark side shows up in struggling countries where massive amounts of aid—money, food, or other supplies—from helper nations end up in the hands of corrupt officials, serving to strengthen their greedy grip on the lives of those who struggle, or where the recipients become invested in dependence. It is there in even the most routine charitable giving and receiving, when it is charity at arm's length: the guilt giving, the off-loading of money from those who have it to those who don't, which only perpetuates the lie that there are "haves" and "have-nots" rather than partners of varied resources meeting in a transaction that benefits *both*.

The painful legacy of excess and misguided charity was evident in Ethiopia when I was there in the early 1990s. Six years before, "Live Aid" had taken place, the biggest television fund-raising event in history at that time, and succeeded in drawing world attention to the devastating famine taking place in 1984 in the Rift Valley of Ethiopia. Millions of dollars of aid had been raised and food had been sent to stop more deaths. Ethiopia and the Ethiopian people were at the center of the world stage for several weeks. The televised images of their gaunt, starved faces and emaciated bodies pulled the heart-strings of the affluent world such that charitable contributions flooded into the agencies working to alleviate the famine and help the people.

Although much good was done with that money and many lives were saved, when I visited there six years later I encoun-tered people who were still on the brink of death, who had lost their sense of self-reliance and who were waiting for the world to save them again. Now, without the headlines and television images, they were helpless and hopeless in a situation of drought and despair, and the world community had moved on to other crises. There was talk of "donor fatigue" and the aid had dwin-dled to practically nothing.

By being charitable for those weeks, the affluent world had perhaps done more to relieve its own discomfort about the situ-ation than really addressing the Ethiopians' situation, and as soon as that crisis was out of fashion, attention and money went elsewhere. The Ethiopians, on the other hand, had learned that they needed to be able to continue to hold up a starving baby to get the attention they desperately needed to keep some form of aid flowing in their direction. Much as the organized beggars of Bombay had learned to present themselves advantageously for alms, this charity relationship based on pity and sympathy for "the needy" began to show up for me as a kind of pornography of poverty that demeaned all parties.

I have seen its cost again and again in my work in the devel-oping world. I see people with a dependency hangover. I see the consequences of a welfare state worldwide that goes beyond rich and poor, that is actually inside of institutions, families, nation-to-nation relationships where people "help" other people in a way that is patriarchal—from the top down—and creates dependents, and dependence, instead of supporting self-reliance and healthy interdependence. It diminishes everyone.

Whether it is between nations, or within the smaller space of our own communities or families, when people giving money think of themselves as benevolent saviors, people who are deemed "recipients" cannot establish or distinguish for themselves their worth or their own self-reliance. The benevolent savior misses the vital human experience of healthy interdependence, and the people receiving the money often see themselves as unworthy, instead of the worthy, valuable partners that they could be. There is no way that rich people can really change anything with money without the passion and commitment of partners who know how to do what needs to be done. It is only when that on-site wisdom is valued, honored, and embraced in partnership that lasting gains are made. Absent the commitment to confront the challenges we face together as a human community, charity doesn't solve problems. It separates us from the problem temporarily and gets us off the hook. Our societies have trained us to give and accept help, when, in fact, what is needed is full engagement, collaboration, and partnership.

There is a distinction to be made between charity and solidarity as we experience it in collaboration. Tad Hargrave, a young activist and facilitator for Youth for Environmental Sanity (YES), has eloquently put it this way:

Charity is made complete when it is grounded in solidarity ... While charity may help those on trial by the system, solidarity may put the system itself on trial. It not only gives resources, but it actively works to change the very systems that unfairly put resources into the hands of some at the expense of others. Solidarity says, "I don't want to benefit unfairly from a system that is unjust." . . . Solidarity is born of knowing that we are all connected and so the choice of "us" versus "them" is a false one.

COMMITTED PHILANTHROPY: MONEY AND SOUL IN CONCERT

If there was one surprise waiting for me in my career as a fund-raiser it was this: Some of the world's greatest, most inspired philanthropists don't have much money. Some do have money; great and even gross amounts of money. But philanthropy in the United States and around the world is as much a product of hardworking wage earners, everyday kind of people, as it is a practice of the rich and famous. According to the *Giving USA Annual Report on Philanthropy*, in the year 2000 more than $200 billion was given to the not-for-profit sector, and of that $200 billion only 5 percent came from corporations, 7 percent came from foundations. Eighty-eight percent came from individuals. So the bulk of the giving and generosity comes from individuals, and of those people who give 88 percent of the money, 75 percent of them made less than $150,000 a year.

The generosity of people in countries where poverty is the prevailing condition is astounding. In Africa for example, people who live in rural villages, as in most parts of the world, depend on one another and the generosity of their own community to make anything extraordinary happen. For example, for a child from an African or Mexican village, who has a chance to go to college, often the entire village will come together to contribute whatever they can to make that possible. Or they'll pool their resources if there's an opportunity to send someone to travel to a conference in the United States or Europe. I remember a young teenage boy who was sent to a Hunger Project conference in Germany by the three hundred people in his Nigerian village, whose names he read to us all when he arrived.

The people I'm talking about aren't people of what we would call means, but they have a little stash of money they save for that kind of an opportunity to support someone in their community or extended family. Religious or spiritual communities can be places where that kind of private cooperative funding also becomes a way that people express their love or support in small contributions that add up.

We think of philanthropy, and it's often a word reserved only for the rich; but I see all these acts of generosity, sharing, and kindness as philanthropy, and we're all capable of participating in it all the time.

Another misimpression is that people with resources are giving to people without resources, but that's rarely the way it works. What really works is when everyone is giving the assets or resources they bring to bear to make a vision come true. Some of those resources are financial. Some are sweat equity. Some of them are devotion and passion for what everyone wants to happen. Whatever they can contribute, everybody's participation is an equal asset. When we release the kind of overimportance of the money that gives it more weight than anything else, we see everyone as having and giving their assets, and everyone standing together and contributing to the vision.

That's when it's really healthy. That's when money isn't given more meaning than it deserves; it's just another way to participate, and it's what some people have to share.

On one trip to Ethiopia for The Hunger Project, I traveled with several other women to a rural community called Lallibela, where we had been asked by a small group of older women to meet with them about a project they had in mind. This was a very harsh and unforgiving part of the rural area, not what most of us would consider a fertile place for any enterprise. Most people would call these women elderly and most people would call them poor, but we sat in a circle on the hard ground, the sixteen of us, and we were sixteen women ready to think and work together to make something happen. Some of us had come from and would return to the affluent world of the United States. Some of us had been born here and would live and die in this barren, rugged region.

The Ethiopian women were much older than us, in their sixties and seventies, and some were widows with little or no means of earning a living. These women had a dream to build a teahouse, a modest teahouse along a path where many of the farmers traveled to bring their goods to the Lallibela market. The teahouse would be a boon to both the weary farmers and other travelers on this route, and to the women, as a means of earning enough to support themselves. They wanted to work, but they were fairly frail, couldn't farm anymore, and couldn't walk to market anywhere, and had needed to come up with something that would allow them to stay in one place.

The vision they had of the house was very simple and they had already begun building this round, one-room structure, with pieces of fallen branches or dead trees in the area. They had been able to build their teahouse with all the materials right there on the land, but what they didn't have were teacups and saucers and a kettle, the things that would really make it a teahouse and not just a resting spot. So my group of women arranged to buy those supplies and contributed that to the project. We also established a small fund to assist with the ongoing costs of supplies to be delivered periodically from the nearest city by a young woman who was a development worker and was happy to be their purchaser and keep the teahouse stocked. She provided her youth and physical strength. We provided the financial support, which we were eager to do, to be partners in this teahouse venture with these women. It was a perfect collaboration, and I remember thinking that we were all just women putting in our piece of a larger picture to make something extraordinary and important happen. It was such a joyful, beautiful experience. We weren't giving these "poor old women" money. We were all collaborating in service of them and of everyone who walks on this path to the market—and our desire to make a difference.

In the context of sufficiency, philanthropy and service become an expression of interconnectedness. Committed philanthropy enables people to invest their wealth, not only in dollar amounts, but also with the energy of their intention. They become "vested in" a new future for all of us, whether that is to improve the facilities of the local school or to abolish nuclear weapons on earth or to empower women in Indonesia. In directing the flow of money to their highest commitments, they invest money with soul, and embrace and express sufficiency. I call this "real" investment and it creates no recipient. It is an opportunity for us as a human family to partner with one another with whatever resources are part of our life. In that context, financial investors experience that they have enough and that they have the capacity, the longing, and the ability to share.

They partner with people who are on the ground at work making the new school facility happen or being engaged in doing the groundwork to preserve a rain forest or working in the Indonesian villages expanding their literacy or farming or educational skills. These collaborations are equal partnerships in service of a vision that all parties share. Everyone is sharing their wealth—that which they experience to be a sufficiency, an enoughness, a prosperity in their own life and work.

The human hand must open to receive, but also to give and to touch. A human heart must also open to receive as well as to give and to touch another heart. That openness and reciprocation, that image of the open hand and heart, connects us not just to others, but to the feeling of fullness and sufficiency in ourselves.

FAITH STRONG:
CONNECTION BUILDS KINSHIP

Faith Strong was in her sixties when she decided to use philanthropy to shift her own inherited wealth from a family legacy of self-interest to a serious investment in global partnerships to advance health and social equity, particularly for women in conditions of subjugation in male-dominated cultures. As she contributed and worked with The Hunger Project, she became increasingly interested in empowering women working to create self-reliant communities in these challenging environments. On a trip to Senegal to meet her West African partners, there, in a ceremony and festive celebration in a village, she found a kinship and a partnership with eight Senegalese women who wanted to start a micro-credit program for their own and five neighboring villages.

The resources each woman brought to the partnership were different. One was the natural leader of the group. Another was excellent at accounting and tabulating figures. A third was a natural communicator and promoter, and people always wanted to do what she was doing. Another was very good with food storage in this difficult environment. Another was excellent at poultry farming. Faith was good at providing financial resources. So nine women in total, including Faith, came together with a common vision of a micro-lending program for all the women in these five villages. The program would enable them to begin food-storage businesses and poultry farming to earn money to feed their families and improve the lives of their people.

As it had been for those of us in the teahouse venture, Faith gave the resource she had, they gave theirs, and together they invested in a common vision. Everyone was empowered. No one was a "recipient." Each woman was valued for her gifts. That is the role of money in transformed philanthropy.

Philanthropy is not just for rich people who feel magnanimous, guilty, or embarrassed about having more than they need, or for anyone looking to prove their righteousness through sacrifice and charity. Our world is more evolved than that, and we have an opportunity now to retire traditional charity as we've known it, and in its place create partnerships in which a shared vision is realized through solidarity and the collaboration of know-how, sweat equity, and cash resources. These partnerships already exist in the form of organizations like The Hunger Project, the Peace Corps, Save the Children, Planned Parenthood,

Habitat for Humanity, Katalysis: North-South Partnership, the Grameen Bank, The Pachamama Alliance in communities, projects, and programs all over the world. People from diverse circumstances are bringing their resources together to create solutions. This is the new philanthropy: contribution and service in collaboration. When you are in that space, that place, problems dissolve, miracles abound.

BANGLADESH: MONEY, SOUL, AND A NATION IN RECOVERY

The story of the Magnificent Seven shows the power of the partnership in which an organization provided vision and leadership workshops and training so local community leaders or activists could recover their sense of power. In its simplest terms, these ongoing workshops brought people together to envision a self-reliant and self-sufficient Bangladesh, a Bangladesh that could be a contribution to the world community—a country that needed no handouts; a country whose people contributed their intelligence, courage, skills, and stamina; a people of industry, and of creativity; a people with their own arts and literature; a nation that could sit proudly at the table as an equal player in the United Nations.

The situation in Bangladesh has improved dramatically, in the past twenty years, now with a passionate vision of what could be, the commitment to garner their inner resources to the task, and the continued contribution of resources and partnership through many other international organizations that contributed other resources.

Much has changed in a relatively short period. Today,

women have an average of three to four children instead of the eight or ten they used to have. Average incomes have doubled. Nongovernmental agencies and independent economic-development initiatives are some of the most effective grassroots movements in the world, alleviating poverty and resolving hunger.

The conversation of national life there today includes poetry—they are a nation of prolific poets, and their poetry is a source of national pride. In cafes and marketplaces, poetry readings are often at the center of gatherings, and now more and more Bangladeshi poetry is beginning to be published in other languages. Bangladeshi fabrics and fashions are now available worldwide.

The transformation of Bangladesh continues, with huge challenges ahead, but already there has been significant progress. Many people are rediscovering their self-sufficiency and are able to see themselves in partnership as peers, not as needy people being rescued. They see themselves as the authors of their own development working potently with equal partners who brought different resources to the collaboration. They have made a conscious choice to stop striving only to get more and more and more aid, and are turning their energies toward identifying their own capabilities and doing more with what they have. They are taking responsibility and a leadership role in the broad collaboration of international partners.

At a meeting I attended there in 1991, a recent comment by the prime minister was the inspiration for talk on the street as well as in the halls of power. He had spoken proudly of his people: "What we have are not 120 million mouths to feed, but 240 million hands that are ready to go to work. What we have are

240 million eyes that are ready to see the world anew. What we have are 240 million ears ready to listen to one another."

Looking at his own country and seeing its beauty, he said, "We are poets, we are weavers, we are musicians, we are intellectuals, *and* we are able to manage disaster, flood after flood. We are among the most creative and resilient people in the world. We don't want charity. What we want is partnership."

Through tens of thousands of organizational partnerships and millions of individual partnerships and collaborations, Bangladesh is expressing and deepening its strength and its well-being and is becoming a contributing player on the world stage.

THE PROPHECY OF THE EAGLE AND THE CONDOR

In continuing work with the Achuar indigenous peoples, they have told us that our alliance with them is the fulfillment of a long-told indigenous prophecy of collaboration for survival, called the Prophecy of the Eagle and the Condor. For thousands of years, South American shamans and elders across the continent have told that at the beginning of the fifth Pachakuti (a Pachakuti is a cycle of five hundred years)—the era we live in today—a reunion would come to pass between the long-separated "people of the Eagle" and "people of the Condor."

The prophecy story relates that in the beginning all the earth's people were one, but long ago they divided into two groups and each followed a different path of development. The people of the Eagle were highly scientific and intellectual. The people of the Condor were highly attuned to nature and the intuitive realm.

The story goes on to say that at this current juncture in earth's history, the Eagle people—the people of the intellect and the mind, people with a highly developed sense of the aesthetic and cognitive skills—will have reached a zenith in their amassing of scientific knowledge, technology, and technological tools, expression of high art, and the ability to build and construct. The Eagle people will even develop tools and technologies that will expand the mind, and they will be producing technical miracles of unimagined power and breadth. The enormous accomplishments and technologies of the people of the Eagle will bring tremendous material wealth to leaders of the eagle world. At the same time, they will be spiritually impoverished to their peril, and their very existence will be at risk.

In this same era, the people of the Condor—people of the heart, the spirit, the senses, and the deep connection with the natural world—will be highly developed in their intuitive skills. They (the indigenous people) will reach a powerful zenith in their profound ancient wisdom, their understanding and relatedness with the natural world and the great cycles of the earth, their connection with the great spirits, the animals and the plant kingdom, and their capacities to move through the many spiritual dimensions that they inhabit. At the same time, they will be hungry and impoverished for knowledge that will enable them to be successful in the material world, and they will be disadvantaged in their interactions with the material world of the eagle in a way that their very existence will be at risk.

It is clear that our Western culture represents the people of the Eagle. Indigenous people of the world are the people of the Condor.

The prophecy says that at this time in the earth's history, the

Eagle people and Condor people will rejoin. Remembering that they are one people, they will reconnect, remember their common origin, share their knowledge and wisdom, and save each other. The eagle and condor will fly together in the same sky, wing to wing, and the world will come into balance after a point of near extinction. Neither the eagles nor the condors will survive without this collaboration, and from this rejoining of the two peoples, a new alloy consciousness will emerge that honors the Eagle people for their remarkable accomplishments of the mind, and honors the Condor people for the deep wisdom of the heart. Together—and only together—the crisis will be resolved and a sustainable future will emerge for all.

In our work with the Achuar people, I have seen the clear, unmitigated alchemy of collaboration. My husband, Bill, has become clearer, deeper, and richer in his own gifts as a modern world businessman, now integrating the profound qualities of holism, reciprocity, and heart wisdom so central to our indigenous partners' way of being. I have seen my own strengths grow and my deficits diminish as I integrate their ancient ways of knowing and understanding of the natural world into my own heart and soul. We have watched them retain and deepen their intuitive power while becoming clear, knowledgeable players on the modern world stage, adding skills and qualities that are central for success in the new world they inhabit.

This increasing and deepening richness in this alliance as well as my years of work with hunger and poverty, affluence, and wealth, have shown me that collaboration and all its tributaries—reciprocity, partnership, solidarity, alliance—flow from the truth of sufficiency. It's all here, now. It is enough. We are each other, and our resources abound.

This ancient prophecy offers timeless wisdom for our contemporary lives, even as we live them in "eagle" country, where science, technology, and material goods have become such defining elements. The Eagle and Condor story is a parable for our own time and our own telling, a reminder that collaboration is an essential part of our human story, the truth of sufficiency, and the key to a prosperous, sustainable future for us all.

Part Four

CHANGE THE DREAM

8

Change the Dream

We have dreamed it: therefore it is. I have become convinced that everything we think and feel is merely perception: that our lives—individually as well as communally—are molded around such perception: and that if we want to change, we must alter our perception. When we give our energy to a different dream, the world is transformed. To create a new world, we must first create a new dream.

—JOHN PERKINS, *The World Is As You Dream It*

Since 1995, Bill and I have been immersed in work with the Achuar people in Ecuador, an intact, prosperous, healthy, and incredibly wise ancient indigenous culture we never would have dreamed we would be partnered with—but it was in fact a dream and a friend that brought us together.

In 1994 I traveled to Guatemala with John Perkins, an author, environmental activist, and friend, who has worked with shamans in South America for more than thirty years. John took us to Ecuador the first time we went into the Amazon rain forest and introduced us to all the key people with whom we began working when we founded The Pachamama Alliance—or more accurately, when the Achuar "found us" through their initial out-reach to us.

My trip to Guatemala with John was nearly ten years ago. He and I led a group of donors and activists on a journey to see the Mayan indigenous people in the hill region of Totonicapan. During the trip, a small group of us had the opportunity to par-ticipate in a ritual dream and vision ceremony with a venerated shaman there. This particular stop on the itinerary was a rare opportunity, since history had made the indigenous leaders wary of white people like us, and the shaman would not ordinarily have seen us. But John drew on the trust and friendship of three decades, and had been able to arrange this session between our group and the shaman.

We gathered that night at the place the shaman had prepared for our ceremony. He welcomed us and invited us into a circle to have a different kind of journey, the kind of inner journey you do in the powerful trance and dream space the shaman creates. In most indigenous cultures, dreams are a powerful communication medium; people discuss their dreams and draw meaning from them, consult their dreams before making important decisions, and consider their dreams a means of communicating their desires and intentions and in making them known and real to others.

It was my first experience with a shamanic ceremony, and as I let myself be drawn into that dream state, I had a remarkable experience. In my dream, I became a large bird and experienced myself flying over a vast, green forest. As I looked down I saw disembodied faces floating up from the forest floor toward me. They were faces of men that were painted with geometric designs, and they wore yellow and red feather crowns. As they floated toward me, and then back into the forest, they seemed to be speaking in a strange language that I didn't know. The dream was very vivid and clear, very haunting and quite beautiful. Then I heard a loud drumbeat and awoke.

The shaman beat the drum, and as everyone in the group was roused from their inner space, he invited us each to share what we had seen and heard in our dream. We spoke one by one, some having dreamed and others not. Those who had dreamed typically dreamed they were some kind of animal—a wolf, a butterfly. Some people had simply fallen asleep. Some had had very vivid visions. Some mild. My vision was clear, and I shared it. The shaman and John said that these visions, and particularly mine, could possibly be a communication, but they didn't speculate on the source. At the end of the ceremony we all returned to our lodging and I thought of it as a powerful and exotic experience, but didn't have a sense of any particular meaning.

We concluded our trip and I went home, back to the United States, and on to my work with The Hunger Project, but the visions from the dream returned, again and again, sometimes in my sleep and sometimes in waking moments. Two weeks after I returned from Guatemala I traveled to Ghana, West Africa, for a board meeting; the visions continued. Home again, still they persisted, to the point that they were becoming a real interruption and imposition in my life. As beautiful as these visions were, they wouldn't go away.

I talked with John about it and he said again that in the context of shamanic practice and the dream culture, the visions were significant. He also recognized in my description of the facial markings and feather crowns that these could be the markings and traditional feather crowns of the Shuar and Achuar people in the Ecuadorian Amazon. He had worked with the Shuar for many years and knew them well. The Achuar, however, were an isolated group that had had little contact with outsiders, but whom he had recently learned were planning to initiate that contact. He shared with me the remarkable conversations he had had with Achuar warriors deep in the Amazon rain forest which were the beginnings of the invitation or "call" for modern world people to come to them.

Consistent with the ancient Prophecy of the Eagle and Condor, the Achuar had seen in their own prophetic dreams that contact with the modern world was inevitable. It would come whether they wanted it or not, sometime around the year 2000, and in threatening and dangerous ways. Informed by that prophetic dream, they had decided to initiate the thing they most feared, contact with the modern world, but to do it on their terms, with people they felt they could trust. They wanted to begin to learn about the modern world so they could be prepared for the unfriendly contact when it came. To this end, they had partnered with an Ecuadorian man they trusted, Daniel, and begun work to create a lodge inside their territory where people from the modern world—the Eagle people—could come and have an encounter with them—the people of the Condor—and their pristine rain forest territory.

So it was that Daniel, who also was a longtime friend and partner of John's, recruited John, who then recruited me, to bring about this meeting with people from our part of the world and the Achuar leaders. At the time, I was in the thick of my work with the hunger initiative. I was traveling constantly to sub-Saharan Africa, India, and Bangladesh, as well as raising money and working with staff and volunteers in Asia, Australia, Europe, and across the United States. I had no time or space to consider the problems facing this region of Latin and South America. I had never been to South America and although I had some consciousness about rain forest destruction and the fragility of the world's rain forests, I was glad to know that other people were working on that. I had my hands full.

However, when the invitation, or really the "call," came from this remote, indigenous people deep in the Amazon, it was a call I could not deny. So John and I helped organize a group of twelve travelers from the modern world to meet with the Achuar leaders. The group was composed of people of enormous quality and integrity—people with open hearts, each of whom had a global voice of some kind in their own issue, and some understanding of the importance of the rain forest to the sustainability of all life. These were people with the humility to be open to indigenous wisdom, who would respect the ways of the shaman and the way of life in the Achuar community.

Led by John and Daniel, we traveled to Ecuador and began our journey from Quito, the capital, through the Valley of the Volcanoes, down the eastern side of the Andes, through the Pistaza River Canyon to the beginning of the vast Amazon basin, which stretches east across the entire continent. After taking a small military plane into a dirt landing strip in the rain forest, we moved deeper into the jungle and ultimately into Achuar territory by flying in an even smaller plane that left us on a dirt runway as far away from the civilized world as one can get.

It was there in Achuar territory that we had an encounter with the leaders of the Achuar people that has completely changed my life. Here in this rain forest, abundant and over flowing with beauty and life, were people who wore the face paint and yellow-and-red feather crowns I recognized from my dream. They looked like they had come from another age, but they were as sophisticated in their ways and as evolved as the most evolved of all of us.

Their request of us was that we partner with them in a way that would enable them to begin to understand the ways of the modern world so that when the threat came that they had seen in their visions, they would be ready, competent, and capable to deal with it. They wanted us to support them in organizing and strengthening their governing federation. They requested our support and partnership in setting up an office in a town called Puyo at the edge of the rain forest, where other Amazonian indigenous federations had established their headquarters to enable them to interface with the outside world. We agreed to become their partners in this endeavor. Bill and I took responsibility for the budding relationship and with the other participants we put together the funding to ensure that the expenses of setting up the office in Puyo would be covered for the next two years. Over the next seven years, this relationship took over our lives. Although I was deeply immersed in my work to end world hunger and had expected to stay in that work for the rest of my life, this was clearly an intervention and interruption in that plan that demanded to be respected. It was not part of my plan, but it was clearly part of my destiny.

Bill, at that time, was fully engaged in his business and he, too, was stunned by this unexpected interruption in our life, but he also yielded to it, realizing that it was part of his destiny as well. This encounter was the beginning of The Pachamama Alliance. *Pachamama* means Mother Earth or Mother Universe in Quichua, the language of the Andes, and is understood as such for many of the different peoples throughout the Amazon. This project has now grown to include many other indigenous groups that border and surround the Achuar territory, and has become the central focus of our lives.

The Achuar are an ancient dream culture. Dreams are central to the way they perceive the world and where they get their wisdom and information, so they take their dreams very seriously. They consider them a critical part of their way of being. I had never paid much attention to my dreams and didn't have much memory of them, but in this particular experience, that first, vivid dream had tremendous power, and it was clear to me, over and over as events unfolded, that it was an important part of my life path and I needed to pay attention to it.

Allowing this unusual dream culture to permeate our way of being has created an alloy of consciousness and a working partnership all through this part of the Amazon. As partners, we are finding breakthroughs in seeing the way through to sustainability. The future we dream, and which is emerging as reality, is one in which these pristine ecosystems are protected and the indigenous people who are the natural custodians of these forests are respected for their intelligence and vision. In partnership with these indigenous groups and other organizations, we are now engaged in projects and programs that are transforming the previous threat into opportunities for their ancient wisdom and clear vision to enable us all to see new pathways to sustainability worldwide.

Our culture teaches no special respect for dreams. Yet, I am reminded of Martin Luther King, Jr.'s "I Have a Dream" speech, and the fact that even in the United States, the power of a dream shared can change the most entrenched reality. A dream *is* a catalyst for change, first in the dreamer, and again and again in the dream shared.

John Perkins heads his own organization called the Dream Change Coalition and in his many years of interactions with indigenous Amazonian peoples they have told him over and over again that the job is to "change the dream" of the modern world. The indigenous shamans and elders, with whom John has studied for years, teach that "the world is as you dream it." The dream we have had in the modern world, they say, is a dream of more— more factories, more companies, more freeways, more houses, more money, more buildings, more cars, more everything. These wise elders and shamans point out that that dream is now becoming a nightmare rippling across our great earth, and wreaking havoc.

In our interactions with the Achuar people of Ecuador and the other indigenous peoples with whom we now have begun to work, the message is the same: "Change the dream." They say that we really can't change our everyday actions because at their root will always be the dream we have for our future and we will always act consistent with that dream. However, they say, the dream itself can be changed in the space of one generation and the time is now to do the work that will change the dream.

I have looked deeply into what our dream is and where it comes from. I have seen that we must redream, learn to question the cultural dream of *more* and begin to create a dream and a future that is consistent with our reverence toward, respect for, and affirmation of life. Changing the dream may really mean to see the world completely differently—as indigenous people do. They see a world that is totally sufficient, animated with spirit, intelligent, mystical, responsive, and creative—constantly generating and regenerating itself in harmony with the great diversity of resources that support and collaborate with one another through the mystery of life. They see human beings as part of that great mystery, each human being having an infinite capacity to create, collaborate, and contribute.

Historically, the world as we have envisioned it has seemed to be a world where fixed, finite resources are declining so fast that we must compete in any way and at any cost to be among the people who can survive and be on top. From that view or understanding, from that dream, we run the world in a way that fewer and fewer people have a real chance to win. We strive to eliminate the competition. We erode our true wealth, the creative power and ingenuity of all people, the wealth that is inherent in all of life.

It has become obvious that the mechanistic, materialistic view of the world is inaccurate and incomplete. Scientists and philosophers are seeing that the objective view of reality is incomplete—that subjective reality is a dynamic, unpredictable, creative, ever-changing, and mystical process.

Indigenous people live, breathe, and participate in that kind of world and have a dream that is derived from that dynamic experience of reality. In inviting us to change our dream, they may be asking us to wake up to the dream that currently drives our actions—a dream that is actually a dangerous trance, a dream that is on automatic pilot: the dream of acquiring and accumulating ever more in the face of limited fixed resources, a dream that all growth is good, regardless of the human and environmental costs. They may be asking us to look at what our trance or dream is doing to us and the world we live in, the plants, the animals, the sky, the water, each other.

They may be inviting us, imploring us, to resee that what we need is already and always there. As Gandhi said, "There is enough for our need but not for our greed."

It is not my intent to idealize the Achuar or the indigenous cultures. The Achuar people were historically, and at the time we were called to meet them, known for their reputation as highly skilled warriors. In the context of their culture, they fought over matters of honor, not property, but there is no denying they kept the neighboring indigenous people at a distance in large part by their fearsome reputation.

It may be a kind of providence that the ancient prophecy which ultimately prompted them to reach out for partners from a modern culture to save the rain forest, in effect delivered them into a new opportunity for sufficiency through a relationship with money and through the new experience of collaboration rather than isolation. This opportunity, grounded in the principles of sufficiency, invited them to create a new role for themselves as leaders rather than warriors, key players in what has become a global movement. While they have shared their prophecy with us and urged us to change our dream, it is also clear that the prophecy they honor with this new collaboration has effectively changed their dream as well. Their concern now is to align their developing relationship with money to serve their highest commitments as experienced, responsible custodians of the rain forest and leaders in creating a sustainable global community.

As Buckminster Fuller said, "everyone has the perfect gift to give the world—and if each of us is freed up to give the gift that is uniquely ours to give, the world will be in total harmony." As the indigenous people say in their prophecy of global collaboration for survival, we need to re-member each other, reunite, be in relationship, share our gifts, and the world will come naturally into balance. None of us wants our children or our children's children to live in a you-*or*-me world where they have to fight for survival. We want those children to be free, self-expressed, living in harmony and collaboration, with reverence for life and the resources we all share. All of us want a you-*and*-me world.

When we have the courage to let go of the dream we have now—the dream and drive and trance to accumulate more— then we have the space to envision and create the new dream, a dream that sees us engaged in respecting, preserving, honoring what we have. In that space of nourishment, in that vision of a new relationship with life, natural harmony and creativity abound.

What follows in the chapters ahead are ways to see and resee the world around you from the context of sufficiency. What follows are ways to redream and re-create the world, using money as the currency of love and conduit of commitment. What follows are distinctions of living life from sufficiency.

9

Taking a Stand

Give people a center and they stand fast.
—Manuel Elizalde, Jr., Pamamin, Philippines

More than two thousand years ago, the mathe-
matician Archimedes said, "Give me a place to
stand, and I will move the Earth." I like to say
that when we take a stand, we can move the *world*—the world of
ideas and people who act on them. Taking a stand is a way of living and being that draws on a place within yourself that is at the
very heart of who you are. When you take a stand, it gives you
authenticity, power, and clarity. You find your place in the universe, and you have the capacity to move the world.

Money is so intricately interwoven with every other aspect of
our lives that when we take a stand to make a difference with
our life, it has an organizing effect on our relationship with

money, and when we take a stand to make a difference with our money, it has an organizing effect on every other part of our life.

In an aggressive consumer culture like ours, where the financial worth of everyone and everything is the dominant theme, it takes some courage to stand for something different. The prevailing winds don't support a stand for values other than financial ones, for understanding and examining the distinction of enough, for waking up to the sufficiency and wholeness of the world around us, and seeing the value of what is there before us. That kind of stand takes a conscious effort, but once the stand is taken it unlocks new ways of seeing and being that lead to a surprising freedom and power with our money and our lives.

BREAKING THE SILENCE: FROM DHARMAPURI TO HOLLYWOOD

In 1986, in one forty-eight-hour period, I went from a startling encounter in a remote village in India to a lavish Beverly Hills dinner upon my return home. It woke me up to what it means to be powerless in the grip of destructive cultural traditions around money, what it takes to break that grip, no matter who or where you are, and the power of taking a stand.

In the state of Tamil Nadu, in the south of India, on a hunger initiative assignment, I and some of my colleagues were asked to meet with a group of women from a village in Dharmapuri, one of the poorest regions in India. There, gathered in a grove of subabil trees, we learned of the terrible secret and the burden of sorrow, shame, and guilt these women carried. In this region, female infanticide, or the killing of newborn girls, was commonplace. Females had little value in their society, and they lived hard lives of servitude. Making matters worse, the birth of a girl also carried the burden of a financial dowry that the girl's family had to provide when she married. This could and often did bankrupt poor families.

So, expectant mothers and fathers prayed for a boy. A woman who gave birth to a daughter was often beaten, and the baby girl killed, smothered, by the women themselves, immediately after birth. Women were shamed by their husbands if they produced girl babies, but also the belief among women was that life was so horrible for a girl, and she would become such a financial burden to the family, that it was cruel to let a girl child live, and more kind to kill her. The practice of killing baby girls was not openly spoken about, but it was accepted and silently endorsed by the men and most of the women of the village.

There were about sixteen women who gathered to meet with me and my four colleagues. Each one of them had killed at least one daughter herself, and had helped other women do the same. In this intimate and secret gathering these women talked for the first time about the horrendous experience of killing their newborn daughters, and about desperately wanting to heal themselves from that trauma. They wanted to save other mothers and babies from this horror. There with us—women from the other side of the world—they broke what had been an unbroken silence. They were able to grieve openly for the babies they had killed. They wailed and cried. They sobbed and we sobbed, then held each other. Witnessing their pain was almost unbearable.

Then they tearfully shared that they were banding together to create a commitment to the value of life and the value of girls. They committed to stop the horrid practice themselves and find the courage to help other women stop. They saw that taking the life of a daughter was much more costly than paying a dowry, and that that action had cost them their daughters' lives *and* their own.

The women began by promising they would draw the line that day in that moment and end the cycle forever. They would forgive themselves, ask forgiveness from God and the souls of their lost daughters, and never again assist another woman in killing a baby. Further, if they heard word of a planned infanticide, they would do what they could to talk the other women out of following through with it.

I was stunned by their confessions, torn by their grief, and moved by their courage. They would be the generation of women to break the silence in this region, to stand for their own value and the value of their daughters. They would be the generation to end this terrible tradition of killing.

Then they said something that affected me profoundly, though I didn't realize it until several days later. They said they couldn't have taken this courageous step without our "outside ears and eyes." They had wanted for some time to speak out, but they had felt helpless to do it from the inside of a culture that expected girl babies to disappear and women to remain silent. Now they felt the strength of their resolve. Our witnessing their resolution made it irreversible. They promised to tackle the crushing dowry system, a tradition that made female life a liability from birth. They vowed to begin the steps they knew would be most difficult—talking with the men.

Sitting with these women, immersed in their stories, I began to see how these killings had been tolerated, even made acceptable. In their souls they knew it was wrong. They now saw how the dowry system had twisted their perception of the value of life itself. By bringing the unquestioned tradition forward for conscious examination and reflection, they began the long journey toward freeing themselves from its grip.

After several days and many hours of intimate conversation, they asked me if there were things in my own culture that overwhelmed me. Looking from our common stand for the reverence and value of life, I shared with them that I was deeply upset by the violence displayed in the U.S. media at all levels and especially on television and in films. I said that we in the United States seem to recklessly generate the most obscene and gratuitous entertainment violence imaginable—all in the name of making money. These horrible scenes and messages are now exported all over the world, initiated by a very small number of powerful people in the New York and Hollywood entertainment industry. Probably fewer than a thousand people are really the creators of these violent programs and images, but the money that fuels that industry is overwhelming, and the addiction to the profits is matched by a growing appetite for imagery of violence and destruction in our whole society.

They told me that they understood, and that they would stand for my intention to speak of this in my own country and culture. They told me—looking right in my eyes—to remember that they would be there for me, to encourage me to speak out.

Within hours of my arrival home, my commitment was put to the test. I had hurried back to attend a dinner meeting in at an opulent home in Beverly Hills. There I was seated next to a man known as a talented director with a string of excellent movies to his name. As it happened, just before my trip to India, I had seen a preview of scenes from his upcoming movie, and it was terrible. It was a hideously violent film, not in keeping with the quality of films upon which he had built his respected career. We chatted a bit about our respective projects, and I finally asked him the question that was nagging at me. This violent movie was such a departure from his previous work, and so unbecoming his stature as a director. Why had he made it?

His reasons came down to easy money, he said. He wasn't proud of the movie, but the film had offered an unimaginable amount of money for a very brief investment of his time and talents. It was just too good a deal to pass up. It wasn't as if this rationale were a crime or even a surprise, especially in the Hollywood culture. In fact, in the Hollywood culture, it was business as usual. The question of irresponsible, demeaning, or degrading content and its effect in the world is simply not a topic for conversation in the movie business. Money so dominates the landscape there that it provides all the rationale anyone needs to do anything, even something that conflicts with their own integrity.

I was still thinking about the Indian women I had left just forty-eight hours before, and their comment that our conversation—my "outside ears and eyes"—had helped them connect with their own conscience and the courage to begin to live consistently with their deepest values. Now, back home, in the midst of this elegant dinner and the conversation about making bad movies for big money, I was confronted with the power of our own money culture to blind us to the compromises of conscience that it demands.

It's easy to see the insanity of another culture objectively. It's not so easy to see our own culture—our money culture—and our money behavior so objectively. We're surrounded by it, trapped in it, just as the Indian women were in theirs. In their environment and context they weren't considered insane to be killing their babies. They were being totally consistent with cultural beliefs that encompassed them, just as this fine director was totally in sync with the cultural beliefs that encompassed him as a film luminary who can earn millions of dollars for a few weeks of work on a violent, trashy film.

As we talked, I shared my story of the Indian women and encouraged him to see the possible parallel. I shared with him my awakened commitment now to question the unquestioned assumptions and attitudes about money in our culture that can lead to actions that demean and devalue life. I invited him to do the same. We had a thoughtful conversation about it. It was a start.

I can't know what that conversation meant to him, but for me it was a moment when the unchallenged silence around our toxic money culture became suddenly and painfully clear. I knew that for me to break that silence was the first step in breaking its grip in my own life, and perhaps for others.

BREAKING THE SILENCE, TAKING A STAND

The silent power of the money culture is the same for any of us. It is one of the most blind and intractable parts of our lives. We compromise ourselves, hurt ourselves, sometimes without pause, other times putting reservations aside, rationalizing our behavior as acceptable, even sensible. We complain, but we don't question. We groan and moan, but don't object or refuse. We feel trapped and unhappy, but we rarely take the steps that might make us free.

The Indian women of Dharmapuri faced a steep, uphill battle to halt the practice of infanticide and to challenge and dismantle the dowry system. It was a commitment certain to draw the ridicule of many other women, and harsh consequences from the men in the village. They acted with uncommon courage. Their stand for the life of their baby daughters was a stand for themselves. Their stand for themselves was a stand for the sanctity of all life, and for human dignity.

In my experience as a fund-raiser and in the field with those in need of money or resources to get a job done, I have seen time after time after time that an authentic stand, one grounded in the truth of sufficiency, is always trustworthy, always life affirming, always resonant and, hard as it may be to believe, always successful. When we take a stand that expresses our soul's commitment, it is empowered with the courage of the heart. A stand taker moves from "having a point of view" to discovering "the capacity to see" or the power of vision. When we take a stand, we gain access to deep and profound vision.

In Dharmapuri, the women's stand created a new field of clarity and truth telling in their lives, and this awakening spread through their families, their villages, their region, and their country. An authentic stand also reliably generates the resources to fulfill it and often does so in surprising, almost mysterious, ways. After taking their stand and becoming vocal about it, these women suddenly found allies everywhere.

One couple—the most famous male and female movie stars in India—heard about the campaign to stop female infanticide in the region and offered to help. They filmed a public-service announcement that played before every movie in the movie houses of Dharmapuri and throughout the state of Tamil Nadu, where the population was fifty-five million people, and movies have a tremendous reach. This short film skillfully told the story of the birth of their baby girl and the joy and reverence with which they received her into the world. It showed their excitement in having a baby girl in their lives, the thrill of ensuring that she had the best education possible, the achievements of their daughter as they raised and supported her. It depicted the gift that a daughter is in helping to provide for the needs of her parents as they begin to grow older and the absolute value of girls and women in the society of India. This film played over and over and over in movie theaters and tents, offering a new lens through which to view the value and contribution of females in their society.

Then a popular singer heard about the campaign, and she wrote and recorded a song that celebrated the value of daughters—how important they are to the future and well-being of the country, and how girls are the heart and soul of every family and every village. This recording became a hit and the song became so popular that everyone knew the words and would sing along whenever they heard it, reinforcing these new beliefs themselves with their own voices.

Journalists began reporting about this local campaign, and this new message began to take root in the media and in conversation on the street. Soon it was clear to everyone in that area that times were changing and that girls and women were being celebrated as valuable, important members of the society.

Today, the practice of having to put up a dowry for your daughter when she marries—the money practice that drove much of the fear of having a girl child—is no longer assumed. It is openly questioned and challenged, and there is an active, organized movement to abolish it. Girls are becoming significant wage earners, contributing to the family income and generating vital cottage industries for the family and for the society. Women are playing roles in governance and stepping up to leadership positions. The stand that a handful of women took more than twelve years ago in the subabil tree grove is changing the very fabric of life for everyone in the region.

That's just the way it is turned out to be a lie. Dowries and infanticide were only *the way it is* as long as people lived resigned to that myth. The women who mustered the courage to break the silence did something both brave and important that is available to each of us in our relationship with money. The conversation I had with the famous director was the beginning of breaking my own silence around the greed and abuses of our own money culture, in Hollywood and beyond.

MAKING OURSELVES HEARD WITH THE VOICE OF MONEY

In our own country, in our own communities, in our own families, our own marriages, and our own friendships, and even purely in our hearts and minds, we, too, can expect to be challenged by doubt and even disapproval for seeking a different way to be in our relationship with money.

There are many ways to break the silence and take action, but direct action with our money is one that is instantly available, personal, and powerful for each of us. Some of us may turn our attention to being more financially generous with organizations doing work that we want to support. Some of us may make a conscious effort to use our money more ethically, so we stop the flow of money toward those people and products that demean life. Some of us may devote ourselves to public service, or with our vote become advocates for socially responsible public spending by government on health, education, and safety.

However we choose, we express ourselves in the way we send our money into the world, and with every dollar goes the energy, the imprimatur, of our intention. The mind-set of scarcity and the longing for "more" lose their grip, and we begin to make different choices. Money becomes a conduit, a way to express our highest ideals. Money becomes the currency of love and commitment, expressing the best of who you are, rather than a currency of consumption driven by emptiness and lack and the allure of external messages.

One of the great dynamics of money is that it grounds us, and when we put money behind our commitments it grounds them, too, making them real in the world. We can wish for better schools, a clean environment, and world peace; we can even volunteer, but when we also put our money behind those intentions, we become really serious about them. Money is a great translator of intention to reality, vision to fulfillment.

When you live from a context of sufficiency and you take a stand for something, you open up your heart and the hearts of people in the world around you. And when you do that, you build the vision, create the reality, and grow it such that obstacles eventually fall away. Mahatma Gandhi, Martin Luther King, Jr., Elizabeth Cady Stanton, Mother Teresa—throughout history there have been people not elected or appointed or born to power who have altered the course of human events with the power of their stand—not only the visible leaders, but also those countless others who express their stand with their money through boycotts, contributions, or purposeful purchasing to support socially responsible causes.

Nobody thinks of Martin Luther King as a fund-raiser, but his stand for the rights of all people raised millions of dollars for civil rights work in this country. Mother Teresa raised tens of millions of dollars from people around the world who were moved by her to connect with their own longing to make a difference, and to make that statement with their money. This power is available to all of us: all people at all times in all sectors of society in all chapters of history. People with little or no money are just as capable of directing the flow of money and resources in meaningful ways as those with much more money. Purely in the act of taking a stand, they create the clearing and the context for conversation that invites others to step forward and be heard.

USING OUR CHOICES
TO ORGANIZE LIFE AND MONEY

I know that in my own life there have been times when I thought I didn't have enough of something to take even the first step toward making a difference in the grand scheme of things. Sometimes the "something" was money. Sometimes it was time, and sometimes it was the willingness to believe that I, myself, could have an effect.

When I was first engaging with the commitment to end hunger I thought I couldn't meaningfully participate because of my three children, my husband, and a whole host of practical obstacles. But when I really listened to my soul and allowed myself to feel the call of the world and what I had to contribute, I released myself into that, freed myself into that, and let it define my life. All my choices with money, from investment and contribution to spending and saving, flowed from that commitment. Everything was an expression of that defining commitment we had made. That is not to say there weren't moments of anxiety and challenge, but then, as now, when we returned to our soulful commitment and what we wanted to stand for, everything would flow, and we felt a sense of freedom.

Can you remember (before the rise of credit cards in your life) the joy of saving your money for something you really wanted? As a child, maybe it was a toy of your own choosing. Later, maybe it was your first car or your first house. Or perhaps it was a special gift for someone else. With that conscious commitment, every time you passed up the chance to spend your money on something else, any regret most likely was outweighed by the excitement of your commitment and the satisfaction of growing that much closer to achieving it.

Most of us think that freedom means to keep our options open, stay loose and available, and often that strategy does give you a little space temporarily. Eventually, though, keeping your options endlessly open becomes its own prison. You can never choose. You can never fall in love. You can never marry. You can never take the job. You can never really discover your destiny because you are afraid to commit fully.

If you look back on the experience of freedom in your life chances are that it wasn't when you were measuring the options against one another, or making sure you weren't getting stuck with a decision. It was when you were fully expressed, playing full out. It was when you chose fully and completely, when you knew you were in the place you were meant to be in, when perhaps you even felt a sense of destiny. That's when we're free and self-expressed, and joyful or at peace with circumstances—

when we choose them. We bring that freedom to our relationship with money when we center ourselves in sufficiency, choose to appreciate the resources that are there, feel their flow through our life, and use them to make a difference.

This experience of aligning our money and soul is available to us every day in even the smallest or most mundane transactions with money, or other choices we make in daily life that lessen money's grip on us. It was the awesome power of that stand taking with money and life that emerged one day in Beijing, at an international conference of the people who generally have the least money and little or no control of it in the world: women.

THE BEIJING WOMEN'S CONFERENCE: MONEY, SOUL, AND COURAGE

In 1995, I joined more than fifty thousand women from all over the world gathered in Beijing for the United Nations' Fourth World Conference on Women. The Beijing Women's Conference, as it came to be called, was a seminal event. I was awed by the ability of women from so many places to garner enough resources to get there, and to have used those resources in a way that would enable their voices to be heard globally. You could feel the energy of their commitment.

At the airport, in the sea of women arriving for the conference, I could tell from some of the clothing, the type of fabric and ethnic patterns, that many of the women were not from among the wealthy classes in their home countries. I knew from my experience in those countries that these were people who had very little money and yet had made a several-thousand-dollar journey to a gathering that must have meant the world to them. I knew these people couldn't afford it. This was two years' wages. And they were women from places where women are severely subjugated and underpaid, so how did they get there? How did they get there financially?

The answers came with each woman's story about the stand she had taken with her life. One of the most moving sessions was called the Human Rights Tribunal. It was a designated time for testimonies of human-rights abuses against women, and women went up on a witness stand, as they would in a court-room here, and shared their stories. The room could hold maybe five hundred people, and it was packed. I was lucky to get in. This crowd of vibrant, vocal women fell silent as woman after woman after woman went up to the witness stand, was sworn in, and reported what she had experienced.

The first woman who spoke was an indigenous Mayan farm woman from Guatemala. She was small, but not diminutive, wearing her beautiful and colorful Guatemalan clothing. The room was silent as she was helped to the witness stand by her Mayan sisters. She was injured in some way and seemed to be in pain. My eyes filled with tears before she even spoke. It was clear that something important was coming.

She shared in her soft voice, in Spanish that was translated into English, that she and her husband had eleven children. One day, the military came to her farm to find her husband and two oldest sons, who were part of the Indian insurgence. The three were in hiding, but she didn't know where, and she told the sol-diers she didn't know where they were. With that, the soldiers began a slow and meticulous torture, first by killing her animals one by one in front of her. She told them repeatedly, desperately, that she didn't know, didn't have the information. They refused to accept her answer. They killed her pigs, then her dogs, then her cows, her milk cows.

When they had slaughtered all her animals, they threatened to start killing her children. She screamed and cried that she didn't know the whereabouts of her husband and two sons—that they didn't tell her their hiding place precisely because they knew that if she tried to lie about it, the lying would place her and the family at even greater risk. She begged the soldiers to stop the killing. They did not. They killed each of her remaining children in front of her eyes. She was a nursing mother, and they tore her baby from her, cut off her breasts and then killed her baby. They killed every living thing on her farm. They left everything and everyone dead, except her, and they left her horribly mutilated.

In the audience, we listened in shocked silence and gasps as she recounted the savage attack. She had never seen her husband or sons again, she said. They remained among the disappeared. Traumatized, mutilated, and alone, she had begun the process of healing her body, but realized that healing her heart and her soul would take much more. From the depths of her pain and her grief, a new thought began to take shape, one that held a seed of hope. That thought was that women were the key to ending the violence: women like herself, women one by one and all together. She grew determined to have women hear her story, getting it out where it would have meaning and power.

She heard about the Beijing Women's Conference, the largest gathering of women in history, and she knew she had to be there. She still had her farm, so she sold it, sold all her possessions, all her cooking pots and extra clothing, everything. Then she took up a collection and borrowed money from her remaining extended family.

She pulled together just enough money for the airfare to

Beijing. Not enough to stay in a hotel or eat, or even to fly back; just enough to get there and testify. She told us all of this, fact by fact, took this horror and made it a contribution. She also shared that she had sold everything and had no funds, but that she knew that if she died now, her life would have been worthwhile because women with a commitment and passion would hear her story and use it in their work for peace, use it as a tool to help dismantle the forces of violence and oppression around the world. This roomful of five hundred women listened and wept.

The next woman was from Bosnia. In 1995 the war there was going full blast, and one of the systematic instruments of war was for men from opposing armies to rape the women and "impregnate them with the enemy." Only months before, this woman had been raped. Enemy soldiers had tied her to stakes in the ground, killed her husband and son, and then begun raping her. Over the course of the next ten days she had been raped about fifteen times. She described how it was, in all its frightening, and dehumanizing detail. She described man after man, all these violent, hate-filled men sexually assaulting her.

Now pregnant, she had withdrawn all the money she had to get to the conference and tell her story. She wanted to be heard, to make the violence known and witnessed in some way, and wanted to use the same forum to make a public vow. She promised the women there that she would raise this baby that was the son or daughter of the vicious enemy, with unconditional love. She promised that she would love this child who came to her through these most horrendous circumstances, and give it life outside of war, where the two of them could devote their lives to the work of peace and the end of war that justified this kind of savagery. By the end of her testimony, the audience was deeply moved. So many of us were in tears, some of us thought we couldn't take any more. But there was more.

The third woman was a bride-burning victim from India. She, too, needed help to make her way to the witness stand. Her face was so disfigured that until she spoke you could not tell where her mouth was. She had been set on fire in Delhi, several weeks before. Her husband and mother in-law had doused her with kerosene and tied her to a post, all over a dispute about the amount of the financial dowry. She had escaped and had found refuge with her family. They cared for her, but her burns were so extensive, it was clear she didn't have long to live. She began a legal process against her attackers, and then she heard about this conference in China. She knew this was where she belonged and had made this long journey to China to die at the conference. She told us that she had brought her charred, disfigured body to Beijing "because I knew if I died here my death would have meaning." And she did die there.

These women with so much pain, so many obstacles, and so little money had taken everything they had, every ounce of courage and strength, and every bit of money they could scrape together, to follow through on their commitment to the work of peace and the end of war and violence. At the end of these three testimonies, those of us in the audience took up a collection and created a funding future for all three of these women. For the woman from Guatemala, we found a place to stay, medical treatment for her wounds, and money to return home. For the woman from Bosnia, we created an education fund for her baby and a long-term fund for her and her child's well-being. The woman from India was burned so badly she was beyond medical help, but we provided her with the best possible care until she died in Beijing two weeks later.

These women had invested themselves completely and unselfishly, money and soul, in this commitment, and in return their needs were met and their mission accomplished. Their voices *were* heard. Their stories *were* told. Their contribution did have an effect on the thousands there at the Beijing conference, and thousands more around the world, as we have shared what we saw and heard that day. Beyond the power of the stories themselves, the women's courage and resourcefulness in garnering the resources to make themselves heard is a testament to the power we each have to honor our highest commitments and create opportunities for money to flow to us and through us to support that work. Their contribution of money, and ours, was not large in terms of amount, but it became powerful in service of our commitment.

In Beijing, I saw the financial power that becomes available to you when you take a stand. The stand garners the resources to fulfill itself, and you become an instrument of that stand. In the presence of these extraordinary women in Beijing, who came from places of great poverty and situations of the most routine and extreme subjugation, I saw that people like me and people everywhere and at all times have the same power to act in ways that honor our highest commitments, and in doing so create the opportunity for money to flow to us and through us to support that work.

CHANGE THE DREAM BY LEVERAGING VISION, MONEY, LIFE

Whether you are aware of it or not, you make an impact each day with your choices about how you live and how you allocate your resources. If "money talks" it is with our voice. Each financial choice you make is a powerful statement of who you are and what you care about. When you take a stand and have your money reflect that, it strengthens your sense of self.

You don't have to change careers, revolutionize your business, or pack up your family and move away from anything or to anything to take a stand. You express your stand in the way you earn money, choosing work consistent with your values. You express your stand in the way you use money to provide food, clothing, shelter, or education for your family. It can be in the money you use to support others in your community or beyond, through food depositories, or shelters for battered women, troubled children, or homeless people. It can be in the money you use to empower your own creativity and self-expression, or otherwise nurture yourself through classes, books, or music. It can be in the money you pay for the products you buy, supporting the companies that produce them. It may be money you contribute to local, national, and global causes that inspire you, and the opportunity you offer others to do the same. If you are an employer, it can be the money you invest in the resources to make your workplace an expression of integrity, where employees and management have what they need to express their excellence.

We each have the power to arrange life so that the stand we take with our money and our life with money is a right-now, every-day, every-week expression of our core values, not a some-day, next-year, or when-I-retire or when-I-have-enough expression of our core values. Every moment of every day there are chances to participate in expressing your individuality and creativity, in contributing to your vision for yourself, your family, your community, city, or world. When we bring this consciousness to our choices about money and use our resources—money, time, or talents—to take a stand for what we believe in, we come alive. We are flooded with a sense of purpose even in the smallest action, and a feeling of power and energy opens up in our life.

Whatever the nature of your own call to action, I invite you to take a stand. Separate yourself from the prevailing drift, and use the opportunity that we each have to deepen our values and become more determined to live by them and articulate them. We each can speak for sufficiency as a way of living and relating to money and to each other. Whether you do it with a dollar or a million dollars, whether you are a Guatemalan peasant or an African farmer, a person of inherited wealth or a laundress, a lawyer, a factory worker, a doctor, an artist, a clerk, a baker, or a banker, you have the power with your money to break the silence that protects a destructive, scarcity-driven money culture and take a stand for higher human values. Money carries the power and intention we give it. Endow it with your stand. Empower it to change the dream.

10

The Power of Conversation

Words do not label things already there. Words are like the
knife of a carver: They free the idea, the thing, from the general
formlessness of the outside. As a man speaks, not only is his
language in a state of birth, but also the very thing about which
he is talking.

—INUIT WISDOM

One day in 1987, the stock market plunged in a
crash that came to be known as "Black Monday."
Like many other people, Bill and I had invested
significantly in the stock market, and in a matter of hours, on
that one day, we lost what was for us frightening amounts of
money. As the television news teams shifted into continuous
coverage of this financial crisis, the fear in the air was palpable.
There was fear of another Great Depression like the one our
parents had survived in the 1930s. Now it was our turn to witness the loss of our financial security. It was terrifying for people
who had lost fortunes, and frightening for people who stood to
lose their jobs if companies failed or resorted to massive layoffs

to survive the economic crisis. Like so many others, Bill and I sat transfixed in front of the television and watched the news on all the channels all afternoon and evening, hearing interviews with people whose companies had gone under, people whose millions had vanished, and business, economic, and political leaders voicing their worst fears.

We were immersed in fear, and then something very different unfolded. We turned from the screen and began to talk about the effect this would have on our family. As we talked, we realized that the "money story" was part of the big conversation called the stock market, and it affected the amount of money we had in our lives. But that conversation had no effect on our experience of each other. We still loved each other. Our life was intact. Our children were unchanged, all three still beautiful, caring young people on their way to being great human beings. Our health was intact, and we felt great about our lives.

We saw that the public conversation was all about net worth going from high to low, and that this conversation could destroy our lives if we let it; we could engage in it, be upset by it, worry about it, or be afraid. We could go into that whole swirl, the swirl that was everywhere we were looking at that day, but we looked at each other and made a vow, a little deal, that we wouldn't do that. We would use the situation with the stock market as an opportunity to count our blessings and reconnect with the nonmaterial assets that were the foundation and core of our true wealth, our life, and our joy.

It wasn't that we weren't concerned about our financial future. We were. But the events in the stock market that day gave us exquisite access to a moment in which we were able to acknowledge and experience the beauty of our lives in a way we had not done in a long while. I remember how moved we were by our real prosperity being the heart, the sufficiency and fullness of our family, the bounty of our love. We reveled in that appreciation.

The crisis continued, however, and all around us, no matter whom you talked to and no matter what time of day or place, the conversation was about the fears, the anger, the money lost, and the dreams shattered. We decided that since our own shift in conversation and attention had created such a sustaining moment for us, we would share it with others around us and generate the conversation that might enable other people to do the same thing. With each friend who called, we talked through the anger and fear, and then on to the "other" conversation—the conversation about the value of the love and connections still there for us in our families and friendships, and our own inner resources that were not diminished—could not be diminished—by the fluctuations of the stock market. Of course, we remained concerned about the unsettling financial consequences, but we made a conscious choice to not panic and not obsess about it.

I was reminded of the written Chinese character that, depending on the context, defines "crisis" as "danger" or "opportunity." We realized that, although the stock market would do what it would do, when we let go of the conversation of fear and anxiety, and created a different conversation focused on the bounty of our lives—then our fear subsided. When we approached the circumstances without the noise of fear and high anxiety, the "crisis" lost its grip on us; the experience of "danger" did, indeed, transform into opportunity.

Over the next days and weeks, we, and some of our friends,

continued this deliberate practice of appreciative conversation, centering ourselves in appreciation of our assets of family, friends, and work, giving them our attention and working to make a difference with our lives each day. We never regained the money lost that day, but we quickly regained our sense of well-being and confidence about the future. We were able to think clearly and calmly as we navigated the challenging financial straits. Later, looking back, we realized that our recovery began the instant we shifted our conversation and then our attention from our losses to our remaining assets, financial and otherwise. For us, the experience of crisis associated with Black Monday lasted for just a few hours of one day. For those who remained stuck in the conversation of crisis—and some never left it—the experience of loss and fear continued, and over time depleted not only their financial reserves, but also their emotional, and for some, even their spiritual, resolve.

CONVERSATION CREATES THE CONTEXT OF LIFE

We think we live in the world. We think we live in a set of circumstances, but we don't. We live in our conversation about the world and our conversation about the circumstances. When we're in a conversation about fear and terror, about revenge and anger and retribution, jealousy and envy and comparison, then that is the world we inhabit. If we're in a conversation about possibility, a conversation about gratitude and appreciation for the things in front of us, then that's the world we inhabit. I used to think that the words we say simply represent our inner thoughts expressed. Experience has taught me that it is also true that the words we say create our thoughts and our experience, and even our world. The conversation we have with ourselves and with others—the thoughts that grip our attention—has enormous power over how we feel, what we experience, and how we see the world in that moment.

Scarcity speaks in terms of *never enough, emptiness, fear, mistrust, envy, greed, hoarding, competition, fragmentation, separateness, judgment, striving, entitlement, control, busy, survival, outer riches.* In the conversation for scarcity we judge, compare, and criticize; we label winners and losers. We celebrate increasing quantity and excess. We center ourselves in yearning, expectation, and dissatisfaction. We define ourselves as better-than or worse-than. We let money define us, rather than defining ourselves in a deeper way and expressing that quality through our money.

Sufficiency speaks in terms of *gratitude, fulfillment, love, trust, respect, contributing, faith, compassion, integration, wholeness, commitment, acceptance, partnership, responsibility, resilience, and inner riches.* In the conversation for sufficiency we acknowledge what is, appreciate its value, and envision how to make a difference with it. We recognize, affirm, and embrace. We celebrate quality over quantity. We center ourselves in integrity, possibility, and resourcefulness. We define our money with our energy and intention.

The difference between these two vocabularies and the power of their impact proved to be both an inspiring and disturbing aspect of the national response to the terrorist attacks of September 11, 2001. Immediately following the attacks on the World Trade Center, the Pentagon, and the fourth jet that crashed in Pennsylvania, in the midst of all the shock and the grief, the extraordinary generosity and compassion of people's responses filled the media and conversation all around us.

Day after day after day we heard the stories, not only of those who had died in the attacks or in heroic rescue efforts that day, but also of the hundreds and then thousands who continued to step forward in every possible way to express their caring in the form of letters, prayers, food, clothing, and money for families of the victims and for rescue workers. I remember going to the local blood bank near my home in San Francisco and finding a line around the block of people waiting to give their blood. As we waited in line, everyone talked to each other, sharing the shock and the desire to respond in some meaningful way. Everyone and every conversation was about how we all could help.

In those first weeks, it was as if we had all gone down to our own Ground Zero, the Ground Zero in our hearts and our souls. The public conversation expressed the most beautiful values and behavior in the inspiring examples of the rescue workers, the world's support and love for the American people, and every American's desire to help, give blood, or send money. People opened their hearts in so many ways. They openly expressed appreciation for their intact families as they wept for those who had lost loved ones. They laid down their religious differences and prayed together at interfaith gatherings. There was sudden compassion and concern for those in Afghanistan who had suffered under the oppressive rule of the religious extremists—especially the women and children whose lives had been so severely restricted. There were candlelight ceremonies and vigils, and we all felt and knew that we were connected by generosity and compassion.

Then after just a few weeks, when the collective state of shock and mourning started to show up as an economic downturn, specifically as a serious fall in retail sales, President George

W. Bush in a televised address called upon Americans to support the economy by getting back to business, the business of spending money. Shopping was portrayed as an expression of patriotism, a way to show the terrorists that they could not destroy our economy, our consumerism, the American spirit, or the American way of life.

I remember in the days just following the president's speech, at first there was an awkward, almost reluctant, halt in the public conversation of grief, generosity, and compassion. Then the conversation began to turn, with only a slight pause and a trace of squeamishness, to the new order of the day. Within just a few days the newspapers and television news crews were at the malls interviewing shoppers as if they were foot soldiers on the front lines of this new consumer patriotism. Retail sales figures were reported more prominently, with headlines that treated those figures in a way that suggested buying retail goods was a measure of the nation's emotional recovery from the terrorist assault. Stories about people and community events that suggested a reflective or spiritual response were replaced with stories about the economy and the weekend's top-grossing movies. Again and again, people interviewed at shopping malls became the media-appointed spokespeople for us all, describing their determination to shop and spend so as "not to live in fear."

Little if any attention was given to those whose thoughts went to deeper questions of our country's behavior in the international arena, and how to use our money and our might to promote partnership and peace with other countries. That conversation, which had just begun to be voiced before the president's talk, was suddenly moved off mike. As if on cue, the public's attention shifted from tragedy, sharing, and introspection to consumer spending and acquisition. A new defensive, defiant conversation had begun. And money was at the center of it.

The American flag now showed up in every conceivable marketable form, from cell phones, to underwear, to bumper stickers and food packaging. I was in Canada giving a talk, and returning to the United States, as I crossed over the border, I remember seeing a huge billboard of a flag, which usually gives me a sense of pride, but in this picture, the flag had little handles on it, like it was a giant shopping bag, and the words "America Open for Business."

This had become the new conversation, one in which American values shifted from qualities of citizenry and personal character to consumer spending and economics; from human values to consumer values. The timing of this promotion of consumerism as patriotism was particularly unseemly in the way it abruptly interrupted a nation in mourning. The crash sites were steaming rubble, nearly four thousand people were believed dead, their bodies not yet recovered, and our national conversation had turned to spending money as the way to save face, save the economy, and save the nation. It actually confirmed some of the "Ugly American" stereotypes of shallow, materialistic over-consumers that terrorists had used to justify their hatred.

I'm not opposed to buying things. I'm not opposed to people who run businesses or who are in retail. That's a very robust part of our lives, but it's not *who we are*. It's not what makes a person great or a nation great. It will not heal the nation from a vicious attack or the tragedy of the thousands of lives lost. It will not even save a self-destructive economy that relies on insatiable and unsustainable growth. And it will not garner respect from less consuming people and nations around the world.

If we were to look at that national conversation as a mirror for our relationship with money, we would see that in the moment of crisis, our natural response had been an expression of sufficiency. Suddenly we were all connected. We all had more than enough to share, money to contribute, blood to give. Our hearts were open. People came from everywhere to work together in collaboration. The country and the world stepped forward to help and to heal. The conversation generated a *you-and*-me world, which supported and expressed this kind of generous, generative relationship with money.

Then came the shift in the national conversation putting economic fears, spending, and acquisition at the center, and instantly we were gripped by the scarcity mentality. The ideas that *there's not enough, more is better,* and *that's just the way it is,* infused the public conversation. The you-*and*-me world vanished, replaced by the you-*or*-me world.

The fear of scarcity—not enough economic activity, not enough respect as a global superpower, not enough homeland security—became the rationale for using our money defensively, fearfully, even irrationally, as a conspicuous show of economic and military power and national political unity. This is the conversation that stoked support for an aggressive military response and shouted down those who sought to move more meaningfully through diplomatic and humanitarian partnerships. This is the conversation that defined our global neighbors as either "for us or against us," leaving no room for reasonable dissent, and which heightened fear and demands of vengeance against an ill-defined "axis of evil." This is the conversation that was designed to serve as a prelude to war.

Coming across the border from Canada, I remember seeing

that shopping bag flag and being so upset that I decided to write a commentary on it for publication when I got home. In the days that followed, as the shopping mania took over and consumer boosterism quickly replaced the deeper but quieter conversation of humanitarian values, I got so heartsick writing the article that I never finished it. The power of that scarcity-driven conversation stopped me in my tracks. The myth of *that's just the way it is* was the real clincher for me. I remember feeling hopeless to be heard. And I gave up.

About that time, I was scheduled to be in a meeting with twelve colleagues from a group called the Turning Tide Coalition, a dialogue group of respected activists who have led or are leading organizations and movements committed to creating a just, thriving, sustainable way of life. We had scheduled to meet together for two days and when we did, it was like a tonic for me and for all of us.

We acknowledged the discouraging shift in the national conversation from generosity and compassion to fear, uncertainty, anger, revenge, and war and decided to do what we could to help shift the conversation back to a more soulful center. Among our responses was this simple one: We began a series of e-mail communications inviting people to reconnect with those finer qualities in themselves and others, rather than feel lost in fear and misdirected consumerism. Some of the letters referred directly to the serious issues confronting the nation, and considerations that would generate more effective responses than a reflexive call to arms. With the December holidays approaching, we also shared that people we knew were participating in what could be called a great "gift shift." They were shifting from buying gifts to donating money or time, from spending money on presents to spending time with people, from making rote gestures to expressing deeper connections.

We sent the e-mails and letters to our personal and organizational lists of friends, colleagues, and others, and invited them to pass the letters along and add some of their own, to give these calmer, noncommercial and more considered sentiments a larger presence in the public conversation. We established a website where people could share their stories and gift-shift ideas.

In the very crafting of the messages we felt ourselves renewed. As the e-mails began to reach others, and we connected with first hundreds, then thousands of people, it was clear that many, many people were eager to rejoin a conversation for sufficiency, connection, and sharing that broadened and deepened with every voice.

Every message was evidence that, no matter what the circumstances or conversation, there is always an underlying yearning for connection and sufficiency. The astonishing speed and reach of the Internet letter campaign was a reminder of the presence of what has been called the "hidden mainstream" of people who think and see and speak from a context of sufficiency. They want to see their tax dollars, expenditures, and humanitarian-aid dollars invested in ways that promote sustainable living, global peace, and equity, and not in depletion, revenge, and military buildups. I was reminded again how vital it is that those of us in this hidden mainstream surface and speak up, to generate the conversation for sufficiency and invite others to do so.

This crucible event in history, and the war that followed, brought many things into sharp focus, including our relationship with money, as a nation and as individuals. The fear that we won't have enough oil drives much of our national policy and military strategy in the Middle East. As a nation, we appear more ready and willing to wage war over oil interests, even to the point of sacrificing innocent lives, than we are to move purposefully to scale back our use of fossil fuels and dependence on foreign oil. This insatiable appetite for more has dehumanized much of the world for America, and the consequences of that attitude are grave. The times call for honest conversation and self-examination as we see the true costs of our national consumer appetite and our reputation as arrogant, gluttonous consumers by so much of the global community. We can take a stand, change the dream, and shift the conversation to *enough*.

OWNING OUR LIFE WITH MONEY: LISTENING FOR GREATNESS, TELLING THE TRUTH

I spend most of my waking hours in conversation around money. Although the projects and budgets are often on a global scale, much of that conversation mirrors the kind of discussions we have around money every day—logistics—determining how much money is needed to get a job done, where it's going to come from, who will manage it, and how it will be used to accomplish the task. As mundane as they may seem, these questions and conversations can lead us to the deepest truths, fictions, and delicate deceptions we tell about money and our relationship with it.

During the 2003 stock market downturn, some of the wealthiest foundations in America began cutting back on grants to many agencies and organizations that perform vital work in programs supporting children and families, the environment, and public health, education, and safety. One week, in particular, my living room at home was like a revolving door as fund-raising and development staff from agency after agency—respected, well-run organizations—came to confer about their sudden and desperate funding crises.

In the philanthropic community, the foundations were understandably nervous about the economy and the drop in the return on their investment portfolios. However, in many instances, the foundations were financially strong, with millions, even hundreds of millions, of dollars or more, which continued to provide a solid foundation for operations and grants. They were cutting back on grants as a precautionary fiscal measure. Those cutbacks were having a devastating impact on the not-for-profit agencies and their ability to continue their important work here and around the world.

In the months that followed, the struggling agencies shifted their conversation to focus on ways to do more with less. At the same time, some foundations began to take a more considered look at the priorities served by the cutbacks. Was their highest commitment to ambitious financial goals, even if those goals required cutting back on grants for important work? Or at a time like this, was it more appropriate to support the work that represented the foundations' stated philanthropic missions, aligning their internal money-management decisions and expectations responsibly to honor that commitment? Those conversations led to still others about the nature of their investments and whether their portfolio was an accurate representation of their foundation's values. Was it appropriate to invest in and profit from the tobacco industry, for instance, when the foundation's mission was about public and community health?

The process of talking through these issues was, for people on both sides of the question, an opportunity for self-examination, an invitation to be honest and clear about motives, intentions, priorities, and commitments. It was a call to tune out the conversation for scarcity and the fears and protectionist reflexes it demands, and turn instead to a conversation for sufficiency, for knowing *there is enough* and we are enough to meet the challenge.

The conversation for sufficiency broke open the talk about money such that it was possible to bring the qualities of soul into play. It was in our purposeful efforts to listen not just to each other, but *for* each other's greatness, that greatness with money came forward. We can observe ourselves and listen to the way we frame our conversations and decisions about money. We can ask ourselves who we want to be in the moment and with our money; who we *need* to be to do the most good for the most people.

The conversation for sufficiency has been at the heart of every success story I have witnessed, whether it has been in a struggling village in Senegal or in the struggle or choices of people much closer to home. When the Magnificent Seven shifted the conversation in their village from defeat and departure to creative ideas for cultivating the land, the first thing to blossom was a sense of possibility and capability. From that grew strategies, determined action, and eventual success. Survivors of divorce or other personal and financial disasters who have gone on to build thriving lives often tell me that their turning point came when they were able to shift their attention and their conversations away from the hurt and loss of the moment, and begin to focus on their inner resources and talk seriously about the possibilities.

His Holiness the Dalai Lama, in his book *Ethics for the New Millennium*, shares the wisdom of the Indian scholar Shantideva who once observed that while "we have no hope of finding enough leather to cover the earth so that we never prick our feet on a thorn, actually we do not need to. Enough to cover the soles of our feet will suffice."

We can't always change the circumstances that surround us, but we can choose the conversation we generate about them. In a world of thorns, a culture where *there's not enough*, *more is better*, and *that's just the way it is* dominate the conversation, we have no choice but to walk in that world, but we can wrap our feet in leather, so to speak. Without denying or being blind to things that aren't working, we still can turn our attention to those aspects of life where we thrive and prosper, and make that conversation the context for our journey. We can choose our words and create new "life sentences" that true our relationship with money.

One of the most challenging things for me to uncover has been my own scarcity "life sentences" about money, phrases and constructs embedded in my belief system that I've accepted over the years without even knowing it, influencing my life with money. It has been a powerful exercise, and not always an easy one, to confront them, relook at their value, and rewrite them to be more truthful, often inviting profound change.

Money is a flashpoint for gender issues wherever you look. I was raised at a time and in a family where the expectations were that men make the money, and have that special power, and that women don't. In the 1950s, it was an exception when a woman was financially successful, and even though today it is more commonplace, for people of my generation it still shows up as a kind of exception and we're a little surprised by it.

Today's young women have a view informed by their own experience of the earning power of their peers and the women they know or see around them. They aren't such strangers to the idea of earning and managing money, but our culture still imposes a different standard in the conversation about money in men's lives and women's lives. The question arises, out loud or implied: What has the woman traded—marriage, family, children, responsible parenting, or basic integrity—to achieve her financial success? The questions might reasonably be asked of anyone regarding the choices he or she has made around money, but the fact that women come under that scrutiny more routinely than do men colors their relationship with money, and with men on the issue of money. The consequences play out in the details of everyday interactions.

In my own life, as a practical matter, I entrust my husband with the hands-on financial work and decisions in our family, and try to stay free of it myself. The question that arrangement presents is not about the financial wisdom my husband provides, but about the way I have excused myself from that interaction with money and interactions with him about money. I can rationalize by saying that he's just better at it than I am, or it's our way of job-sharing domestic duties, but if I'm honest about it, I know there are emotional dimensions of the arrangement that remain unspoken and unexamined.

The first monetary contribution I ever made, one that represented an eye-opening, conscious commitment, came as complete surprise to me. It was at a time when Bill was making money, and we were living comfortably enough. I wasn't very experienced at this fund-raising work yet, but was the coordinator for this small fund-raising strategy event for The Hunger Project. We had invited about forty people, and a respected businessman named Leonard led the meeting. After we had addressed the relevant issues of a fund-raising strategy, the moment came when I knew it was time to ask the participants for money, and I signaled Leonard. I was surprised when he asked me to sit down and join the group myself.

Leonard started passing out the pledge cards. I thought about the design work I'd done on them, and how well they'd turned out—no typos! Then the little basket of pencils came around, and there were all those pencils I'd sharpened, enough for everyone—things were going smoothly, and I felt great! Then Leonard personally handed me a pledge form, and I was a little bit stunned. After all, I was a young mother and I had this wonderful commitment to The Hunger Project, but I was being paid very little, and I didn't see myself as having any money.

At home, I had an allowance for groceries and household and nursery expenses, but basically, when it came to personal spending money, my piece of the family pie was rather small, and I felt I had no business making a pledge from that money. It was family money—not just mine—and I didn't feel free to make a commitment with it. But I felt moved from my soul to pledge $2,000, and as I wrote that figure down on the pledge card, I had this rush of feeling—yes, it would be a stretch, but it was also a real statement from me about my commitment, and I'd just have to do some rearranging of household and other money commitments to do that. So I felt this surprising sense of exhilaration and power when I signed the card with a $2,000 pledge and passed it in. It was the point at which I began to take a stand with money in the most personal way. I knew we could find a way to make good on that pledge.

I got in my car to go home and had barely pulled into traffic when I went into a total panic. What had I done?! I had no idea how I was going to get that kind of money. And how would I tell my husband? I felt I'd stepped out of line. How would I defend my choice to commit our money that way without checking with him first? I became acutely aware of my feelings of powerlessness—a kind of childlike deference to the man of the house—and of discomfort and worry around this subject of money and how I would explain myself to my husband, and how he would react. As it turned out, Bill came to support my fund-raising work and a deeper commitment of our family resources. But before I knew that, my worry was real.

This little incident seems so mundane, but our conversation about money at that time was loaded with life sentences for both of us, mine expressing a tradition of disengagement and dependence, his expressing a traditional assumption of management and control. The same gender power dynamic around money still plays out between women and men everywhere, all over the world, an unquestioned assumption, something we are reluctant to stir up or challenge because we fear the repercussions.

Around the world, women do enormous work: caring for children, cooking, feeding families, and managing homes, in addition to often having taxing and all-consuming careers. Especially in the less developed world, women's contribution is immeasurable, intense work that is never recognized as valid, never rewarded with money, and never even considered part of the economy. In Sub-Saharan Africa alone, 85 percent of the food farmers are women, but their work is unrecognized. It is given no monetary value.

In the more developed countries, the gender inequities that exist in the workplace show up starkly and shockingly around money. The same can be said for divorce settlements and attitudes toward traditional work performed by women, like nursing and teaching, how those are poorly rewarded despite the critical part they play in our culture. It plays out on a massive scale in the underfunding of organizations that care for people, while industrial and military activity is overfunded.

The gender and money distortion exists in dramatic proportions worldwide, but it starts right in our own homes, in our own families, in our own hearts, where helplessness or entitlement drive our feelings about money. Until those deeper issues around money are reconciled—between one woman and one man and between all women and all men—money will continue to be at times a blind spot and at other times a flash point in our relationship with money and with each other, from our most intimate relationships to the most public arenas of life, work, and public policy.

We all have life sentences embedded in our beliefs and our worldview. It is possible to rewrite them and consciously rescript our responses to include the inspiration we need to ground ourselves around money:

> *Money is like water. It can be a conduit for commitment, a currency of love.*
> *Money moving in the direction of our highest commitments nourishes our world and ourselves.*
> *What you appreciate appreciates.*

When you make a difference with what you have, it expands.

Collaboration creates prosperity.

True abundance flows from enough; never from more.

Money carries our intention. If we use it with integrity, then it carries integrity forward.

Know the flow—take responsibility for the way your money moves in the world.

Let your soul inform your money and your money express your soul.

Access your assets—not only money but also your own character and capabilities, your relationships and other nonmoney resources.

We each have the power to shift, change, and create the conversation that shapes our circumstances. The levers and dials of conversation are ours to use. When we listen, speak, and respond from the context of sufficiency, we access a new freedom and power in our relationship with money and life.

11

Creating a Legacy of Enough

The life you live is the legacy you leave.

My mother was dying. She was eighty-seven years old and had been diagnosed with terminal cancer in May. The doctors said she had only a few months to live, and she knew it was true. She decided to spend the time she had left living in the moment, appreciating her home, her garden, her family, and the familiar and beloved people and places of her life.

Her adult children, all four of us, lived varying distances from her home in Palm Springs and visited frequently. We all took turns staying with her, but as time went on, I eventually decided to come and stay with her for an extended period, to help usher in the end of her life. I saw approaching her death together as a unique opportunity for me and my mother, and our family, to seek access to a deeper relationship with one another than we had ever known. Many years before, the day before my thirteenth birthday, my father had died suddenly in his sleep of a heart attack. He hadn't been sick or ill, and he was young at fifty-one. But one night we all went to bed, and in the morning we all woke up and he didn't. It was a terrible shock and a traumatic loss for all of us.

So, to know openly that I could share in the final weeks and months of my mother's life was such a blessing. For me, it was an opportunity to deepen my own experience of the meaning of life itself, and of death not only as a sudden loss but also as an approaching endpoint that heightened and sharpened our experience of being alive.

In the days and weeks approaching her death, we talked for hours about life, and about her life. We reflected on how rich her life had been, and how important it was at the end of life to really take stock of the blessings and the gifts, and the pain, the suffering, the disappointments, the regrets, and the mistakes. Those painful memories and wounds always stay accessible it seems, no matter how many years intervene, and they're easy to recall without much effort. However, the blessings, the accomplishments, the achievements, the moments of grace, these were the things she really wanted to spend some time with. So we set aside a week to do just that, She wanted to complete her life by reaching into her memory and bringing to the fore so much of her experience that had been packed away as history in the busy activity of her living.

One day we turned our attention to her life with money. She was still able to sit up in a chair at that point and could still walk with a walker. We sat outside on her patio on a pleasant, sunny day, enjoying the hint of a breeze and the fresh smells of her garden and the flowers blooming there. At one point she began to talk about the fact that she had been an accomplished fund-raiser in her own lifetime, and she was proud that I had followed in her footsteps. She said that her fund-raising had been different than mine because it was a different era, a time of women's auxiliaries where women of substantial means get involved with charity almost out of an obligation. For some people, she said, it was a matter of status and social positioning for them to do this "charitable work." She acknowledged that those had been motivations for her, too, but that in retrospect, those opportunities to give of her time and herself to organize and raise money were some of the most beautiful and important experiences of her life.

She could still remember her first fund-raising project. She was a young wife and mother, in her thirties, living in Evanston, Illinois, when she took on a fund-raising goal for a local charity. The organization was a community agency that arranged for infant adoptions and provided a nursery for orphaned or abandoned babies and a place for prospective parents to visit with them.

Now, some fifty years later, she could recall as if it were yesterday how it felt when she committed to raise the $25,000 needed to expand the building that housed the orphanage and administrative office. It was a huge, nearly insurmountable goal for the organization at that time. My mother was very young and very green and had no idea how it would be done, but someone needed to take charge, and she did.

My mother and her team did every possible project to raise

this money. They organized bake sales, secondhand-clothing drives, and garden tours. They had a series of small fund-raising events that went on and on.

In those days people didn't often ask individuals for money as directly as is done today, but the funds raised from these events added up. As the campaign period neared its deadline, they were close to their goal, but still needed $5,000 to meet it. My mother said she felt it was her personal responsibility to find that last $5,000. She got her real introduction to fund-raising from the heart then, because she realized there were people everywhere who had adopted from this agency, who, if they only knew their money would make it possible for other couples to adopt, would gladly give it. With that insight, she got the list of parents and called them up, and asked to meet with them. One by one, she asked them to give money. And one by one, they did—$500 here and $250 there until it was done. She raised the last $5,000 herself this way and in the end she surpassed their goal and raised $26,133 in all.

She said that campaign had taught her that everybody everywhere wants to make a difference. Everyone wants a healthy and productive life for themselves and everyone else, and giving money or participating financially is one of the most extraordinary and powerful ways we can make that kind of difference. She said that those meetings with those families were each unforgettable, intimate interactions and she knew that her request of them had been a gift.

As we sat talking and thought about the families that were affected by that fund-raising drive, both the ones that gave the money and the families that later came to the new building to adopt the child of their dreams, were served for a lifetime. Then we realized that the babies that were adopted from that place at that time—those very babies, were now about fifty years old. They had been adopted and raised by families that loved them and wanted them. Those same babies were most likely parents themselves, and many of them grandparents by now, and a whole succession of families and love flowed from those now grown-up babies. We marveled that that $26,133 she raised was still at work in the lives of those people and their children and grandchildren. When you raise money for your highest commitments—in this case, my mom's commitment to have orphaned children loved and cared for—those financial resources continue to reap an unending harvest consistent with the intention of that money. We thought of all the babies who were adopted, after the fund-raising, from the new facility. She considered every baby adopted after that as part of this legacy she was able to help that agency leave. We were moved by that thought, and the power of money raised and given to make a difference.

In another conversation she recalled all the major fund-raising campaigns she had managed in her life: campaigns for the museum, a world adoption agency, the community symphony, the boys' club, the girls' club, a wellness program for Native Americans in the West where she lived now, a Braille institute, animal shelters, a literacy clinic, the nearby hospice center from which hospice professionals came now to care for her, a camp for ecological studies, a project returning portions of the desert to natural habitat, a camp that built wilderness trails through the mountains; and, as she listed project after project, organization after organization, she realized that she had probably raised millions of dollars that galvanized millions more and served still millions more people.

That money, though long ago spent, was in many ways still at work and even serving her. The trails were being walked by her great grandchildren, the hospice workers were now here serving her and her own family, the generosity and wealth that she had generated for her community were investments that were now returning to her. That money would be at work forever, not consumed and used up, but continuously returning value to everyone. It was a powerful realization and a poignant moment for both of us.

A few days later she said she wanted to acknowledge people who were important to her in her everyday life in the neighborhood, particularly the people who had been really good, really kind, to her. She saw these relationships as her abundant wealth and she wanted to let people know how much she treasured them. She got out the telephone book and turned to the Yellow Pages. She asked me to call the dry-cleaning shop. I called, then she took the phone and asked to speak to the manager. There was a pause while the clerk went to get the manager. Then my mother said:

"Ken, this is Mrs. Tenney. I'm dying and I will probably be gone by September and I'm speaking with my daughter about all the people who have made this final part of my life so special. You have been cleaning my clothes for the past twenty years, and I feel served and cared for by you and your people behind the counter. I appreciate you, and I want you to know that when a person gets old and can't do a lot for herself anymore, the people in the neighborhood who provide these needed services become the people who inhabit your life, the people who make your day. I'd like you to come to my funeral and I'd like you to sit right behind my family. I want you to give your address and phone number to my daughter so she can invite you to the funeral when it's time."

She talked to Marcy and Susan, who worked behind the counter there, and told them the same thing, going into quite some detail about how she appreciated them. Then she called the car-repair shop and talked to the man who took care of her car. We called the pharmacy, the delivery boy, the woman behind the cosmetic counter at her favorite store. We called her favorite restaurant, a little French restaurant, and she talked to the owners and her favorite waitress, Martine. She told them all how special it had been to know them and how well taken care of she felt. We called the hairdresser and the massage therapist and her manicurist. We called the people who delivered her groceries.

Each conversation was very moving. People were surprised. They weren't accustomed to hearing such appreciation for their work, especially from someone close to dying. I got everyone's names and addresses to invite them to her funeral when the time came.

Then we turned to the process of distributing some of what money there was left to all her eleven grandchildren and her three great-grandchildren. As modest as the dollar amounts were, she wanted to give them the money early enough so they could tell her how they wanted to use it, and she could share in that joy.

We lit votive candles and began. We gathered pictures from all over the house, and, one by one, sat with the picture of a particular grandchild in front of her as she spoke about their special qualities and life journey. Her eyes would fill with tears as she looked at the photos of her grandchildren and talked about how much she loved each one, how unique they were and how much she treasured them, reminiscing about what a gift they were to her life. Then she would write a note, write the check, and we would assemble the pieces in an envelope and prepare it for mailing. Each one took about a half hour; with eleven grandchildren and three great-grandchildren, it took us about three days. They were the richest of days. Her attention was so conscious, deliberate, and so heartful that it was nearly overwhelming for her, and she would need to rest before resuming the process the next day.

Eventually, with each member of the family remembered and acknowledged, she then turned to other memories, including more that reflected the quality of soul she had brought to her money life for all those years. She recalled the many charities and community-service agencies to which she had contributed, the times she had loaned people significant amounts of money even when she knew they would never pay her back. She felt that the money had been put to good use, and she didn't regret any of it. It made her feel fulfilled and blessed to have been able to do it, and pleased with her life. It was a life she felt had been well lived.

The next week we made sure that every bill and every cost that would be incurred by the next few months of care and the funeral itself was set up to be paid and taken care of without sacrifice on anyone else's part.

She didn't have much money left at the end of her life. In a way, she was proud that she didn't. George Bernard Shaw once said: "I want to be thoroughly used up when I die." My mother was the epitome of that thought. She remarked that she realized that she had used up her body and she had used up the financial resources she was blessed to have had, too. She was completely and totally drained, in the best possible way. Her life force and her material wealth were spent, and at the end, she had used every bit to celebrate, honor, and express her love for people.

Of course, my mother had horrible days, too; painful days and days when she was upset with everyone and expressed her anger. In the end, when she died, she was really done. Her life was complete and I remember thinking, my God, what a finish, what a life! And in those final weeks she left me clear about the lasting eternal power of blessed money, money that is directed with integrity, intention, and the eternal power of love. That was part of the great legacy she left.

I remember in the minutes after she died, I went into the room where her body was. I could feel that her spirit had left; her life force was no longer in that body. She wasn't inside there anymore, but there was a palpable feeling of her in the room, her stamina, her strength, her generosity, and her love. It was still present. I remember feeling so clearly in the moment that that is our legacy: the intentions we make real in the world through our actions, through our communications, through the conversations we generate, through the relationships we are blessed to have, and in the many ways we express our love. Through the wonderful tool of money we can speak who we are and touch the world.

When we gathered for the funeral, in addition to our family and close friends, all the people we had telephoned came—the dry cleaner, the mechanic, the chef and the waitress, the delivery boy, everyone came. These people were the vendors whose services she paid for, yet they, too, felt so intimately engaged with her life because she allowed them in.

She had showered them all with her appreciation and

acknowledgment, and I know it lasts to this day in their lives. Their lives were touched because my mom had the wherewithal, the grace, to make those simple telephone calls. Her grandchildren were blessed with the small financial gifts she had made to them while she was alive, and she reveled in the stories they told her about how they planned to use it. It has been years, now, since she died, and yet her money and her love are still at work and will still be at work for years to come.

My mother's legacy was, in part, a celebration of her way of being with money and the clear recognition of the sufficiency of life. From her fund-raising for and funding of those whose work she felt was important, to her parting bequests to family members, to her appreciation of the people in her life who knew her simply as a regular customer in the neighborhood, she impressed upon me the enormous difference one person can make in the lives of others. It was a reminder of the moments of connection through our money that are deeper perhaps than we imagine possible; and that when, in those moments, we act from the heart, then our money expresses that heart, which is our true wealth. She was not a rich matriarch; she was a passionate and generous participant in the lives and the work of others whom she nourished with her time, energy, and money, from the time she was a young woman until she died.

THE LEGACY OF MONEY CONSCIOUSNESS

Every one of us wants to leave a legacy of a healthy family, flourishing children, and an earth that is vibrant and supports life. We create our most lasting legacy not in what we leave behind, but in the way we live, and especially the way we live with money.

What kind of a legacy do you want to create? Whether you are a "dollar-aire" or billionaire, you do make a difference. You do leave a legacy. To make a difference with your money doesn't mean you have to have a lot of it, or be a public person, or be a lawmaker, or appear on *Oprah*, or leave an endowment to your favorite college. Every one of us creates a legacy in the way we live now. We create a legacy of sufficiency—or scarcity—in many ways, but especially in our relationship with money. We can deplete and take, accumulate and hold, or we can nourish, share, allocate, and spend consciously and contribute.

I had always thought growing up that having inherited money would be such a fabulous fate for someone—never to have to worry about money, or care about money or even *think* about money, except to know you had boatloads of it. The *more is better* myth is so strong it is difficult to believe that more could be problematic. But the truth tells a different story, and I have heard it and seen it again and again in my work with those who live that story.

At a recent conference, a young, fresh-faced blond woman of twenty-six shared with a small group of other inheritors, and me, that she had begged her father not to give her a pile of money, yet he had transferred $30 million to her that same week in trust. She felt crushed by the money, terrified by the responsibility, confused and burdened, and afraid that people would find out and hate her for it, or use her for it. The work he had done to earn the money had destroyed her family, dividing brothers and sisters, causing her parents' divorce and creating jealousies and envies she wanted no part of. She felt all that baggage, guilt, and bad feeling was passed on to her with the money and she could hardly bear it.

Most of us would be shocked to see the misery and sadness that more often than not accompanies that legacy of excess wealth. Of course there are exceptions and those exceptions are the people who work diligently to counter the effects of excess and entitlement, but contrary to what we imagine, great inherited wealth is not necessarily the lovely legacy it seems.

In countries and communities where money is scarce, but also in those lives in which money is overvalued, the most destructive aspect of that relationship with money is the legacy of an impoverished spirit that leads people to believe that money defines who they are and who they can choose to be in life. In the most resource-poor and resource-rich circumstances, we know that those who survive and thrive are those who draw from other and deeper resources to cultivate meaningful lives.

CREATING LEGACY: MODELING A LIFE OF ENOUGH

When Bill and I caught ourselves in what I called the siren song of success—when our children were little—we not only missed a great deal of the joy and nourishment available to us by being present to our children's sense of wonder and awe in the smallest, simplest things, but we also set a disturbing model for them. We were out and about earning, impressing others, acquiring symbols of so-called success, and putting our attention and even our trust in the unquestioned power of money, unwittingly sending them messages about what was important when you are a "grown-up."

If it hadn't been for Buckminster Fuller and later The Hunger Project, our lives might have continued in that unhealthy direction, but we were lucky. We were able to recenter ourselves in a whole other context and began to value making a difference more than making a fortune.

During this pivotal time Bucky was central to my life and work, and one night we were honored to have him come to dinner at our house. Our children were six, eight, and ten years old, and Bill and I, Bucky and our kids sat at our kitchen table. Bucky was often referred to as the "Grandfather of the Future" and it was so exciting—such a gift—seeing him there with our children sharing a simple, home-cooked meal. At one point, my eight-year-old daughter, Summer, said something that was profound in the way children do, speaking a deep truth with their innocent insight. Her remark was a kind of showstopper for the three adults at the table—Bill, Bucky, and me—and we looked at each other, touched by the wisdom of this child.

Then Bucky said something that changed my life and my relationship with my children forever. He said to Bill and me, "Remember, your children are your elders in universe time. They have come into a more complete, more evolved universe than you or I can know. We can only see that universe through their eyes."

Seeing my children as my "elders in universe time" was a surprising and inspiring thought. All the commanding events and technological advances of the day that gripped our attention now would be history for our children, the soil under their feet, from which their own dreams and greatest endeavors would grow in ways we could not even imagine. But our children could and did. What did it mean to inherit a world where high-speed computers, travel, and technology made the global community not an abstract notion or new frontier but a concrete reality?

What might it mean to grow up in a world where sufficiency was assumed, where generosity and collaboration were the prevailing human conditions?

I saw that they were stewarding us as much as we were stewarding them, though differently of course, and although I had always seen that we were learning a great deal from our children, I had never seen this profound truth about our relationship. It changed my perception of everything, and I began to draw on them—my universal elders—to see a uniquely futurist, yet accurate and evolved worldview.

To listen to them newly was to affirm their natural instincts and honor their natural knowing, appreciating it such that it could expand and contribute. It became clear to me that in the nourishment of our appreciation for them, they would deepen their natural wisdom and be less vulnerable to the myths of scarcity and the commercial and cultural hunger for more stuff and more money. The legacy they needed from us was not money itself but a way of being that would enable them to be creative, resilient, and fully expressed in the world with whatever money or other resources flowed through their lives.

In those early years of Hunger Project work our home became a haven for many people. It was a place to stay for friends visiting San Francisco, yes, but also a place to come and live and be nurtured after a difficult divorce, for one friend; a place to heal after a bout with cancer, for another. When training Hunger Project staff from other countries such as Ethiopia and India, colleagues would live with us for weeks at a time. I remember having our director from India, Lalita, staying in the den, her colleagues, Naji and Shalini in the guest room, while Hiroshi and Janet from Japan stayed in the basement game room, and Tunde Fafunwa from Nigeria slept in a sleeping bag under the piano. My children grew up with people from other cultures coming and going, sharing time, meals, and moments of joy with our family, knowing and expressing that we always had enough to share with whoever was there or coming next.

This call to share stretched their generosity at times, but also enabled them to experience the true wealth of sufficient resources for whoever needed to be with us. It greatly enriched all of our lives. What you share you strengthen and that which you share lasts forever as your true legacy.

This is the legacy we are at risk of losing—that our children are at risk of losing—in the commercial climate that surrounds them now from birth. In the advertising and marketing industry they call it "cradle to grave" marketing, a strategy calculated to engage children as consumers from the earliest moments of life, to plant the seeds of the scarcity lie and cultivate the myth of *more is better*.

The Center for a New American Dream, a respected social-action and consumer-education organization, writes that increasingly "today's children are exposed to TV commercials, banner ads, billboards, logos, and product placements ... advertisers are openly courting children on an unprecedented scale, rushing to create brand loyalties the minute a child is old enough to distinguish company logos or recite product jingles. Advertisers are targeting kids today because that's where the seeds of super-consumerism are planted."

It is difficult to raise children in this noisy 24/7 consumer commercial culture, to recognize the little-acknowledged distinction of *enough*, yet that is exactly what will give them the keys to a fulfilling and happy life. Children are naturally full of wonder and awe; the world is a place of joy and possibility for them. They thrive in love and acceptance and give us the gift of their joy, their playfulness, and their natural sense of possibility.

How do we guide our children to have an authentic relationship with money, when the consumer culture drives them to want and to buy things they don't need? How do we empower them to live with integrity in the face of that seduction? We can educate them about the inaccurate condition of scarcity and its myths, and demonstrate a context of sufficiency. The Center for New American Dream offers these practical suggestions:

> Help your child understand that every product is made from materials extracted from the Earth, and that material things don't just disappear when the garbage gets picked up.
>
> Teach your children about what happens to all that stuff. When we consume lots of plastic, heavily packaged goods, and products that easily break, we leave a heavy burden for future generations.
>
> Seek out sources of Earth-friendly products that are durable and made from biodegradable or recycled materials.
>
> Be a role model. Avoid impulse shopping. Limit your consumption of products that deplete the Earth.
>
> Introduce your child to books and other materials that reinforce these messages.
>
> (See a full list of resources for information in the Resource appendix.)

Let them know that this siren song of spending, going into debt, and accumulating and acquiring more is an unhealthy part of our culture and they don't need to fall prey to that. Let them know that there will be times when the call will be tempting, but they can be stronger than that pull.

Openly examine the way you're living with the money that flows through your life to see if your actions support a thriving, sustainable, just way of life for all people. Share the process of reflection, deliberation, and decision making around money issues, and invite your children to contribute their ideas.

More valuable and useful than any amount of money itself is to leave our children a relationship with money that is healthy. Leave them with an understanding that money flows in and out, that it should do that, and that it is a privilege to be able to direct the flow toward their highest commitments. Leave them with an understanding, evident in your life, that if you turn your appreciation to your inner resources, there is no lack of what you need to meet the challenge or opportunity presented by external circumstances. Leave them an experience of true wealth, the beauty and security of a life that values and honors our relatedness with each other, inspiring, sharing, and responsible stewardship rather than accumulation of cash or stuff.

A favorite Sufi poem, attributed to Hazrat Inayat Khan, offers a helpful perspective:

> *I asked for strength*
> *and God gave me difficulties to make me strong.*
> *I asked for wisdom*
> *and God gave me problems to learn to solve.*
> *I asked for prosperity*
> *and God gave me a brain and brawn to work.*
> *I asked for courage*
> *and God gave me dangers to overcome.*

I asked for love
and God gave me people to help.
I asked for favours
and God gave me opportunities.
I received nothing I wanted.
I received everything I needed.

The legacy we create begins at home and in family, whether we have children or not, but it also extends into the workplace and business environment. There we have the opportunity to replace the scarcity systems that drive the profit-at-all-costs mentality, with business, management, and economic philosophies built on principles and practices of sustainability.

At Fetzer Vineyards, Paul and his colleagues have created environmentally sustainable and earth-honoring practices that are also producing excellent wines. His wines win awards and his company is profitable and thriving, while creating a new model for commercial wine-making worldwide. His personal vision and action as a business leader is creating a legacy of sufficiency and prosperity for his own industry and for all who follow him.

Many other people in business and in their own individual approach to work are living these principles. Sustainability is ultimately a statement of ensuring sufficiency for everyone everywhere and for all future generations. The myths of scarcity have been the legacy for as far back as we can remember. Examples of making sustainable choices are part of leaving a legacy of enough in business, in parenting, in leadership, and that legacy is actively changing our world now.

What we buy, what we invest in, what we purchase for others, what we choose to finance and contribute to can make our world. The principles of sufficiency connect us with deep truths and soulful values that we can use to seed a future of satisfaction and freedom and selfhood in the face of a driving mythology of scarcity and lack.

The great futurist and scientist Willis Harman said, "Society gives legitimacy and society can take it away."

We can withdraw legitimacy from the myth of scarcity.

No matter how much or how little money we have flowing through our lives, we can use our money in a way that affirms life, instead of scrambling for more and obsessing about the movement of money up or down in our lives.

We can shift from scarcity to sufficiency, from complaint to commitment, from envy to gratitude.

We can, through the stand we take, through the power of conversation and through the conscious attention to our legacy, change the dream.

12

The Turning Tide

In the distance a hum, the soft sound of people waking up: waking up to what is possible for the earth at this sensitive juncture; waking up to the call that is coming from our ancestors and from future generations, a call to awaken.

—THE TURNING TIDE COALITION

The taxi from Verona darted through town traffic, past the old stone walls and out through the gates of the city. In a matter of minutes we had moved from the spicy bustle of Italian street life to the earthy sigh of the countryside, threading along steep, narrow, winding roads connecting exquisite Italian hill villages on our way to a retreat center in the tiny hill town of Cadine, nestled in the mountains two hours away. The sky was a cobalt blue. The mountains were crystal clear against the sky. I felt a sense of anticipation and excitement that something monumental was in store as I arrived and began to meet my new colleagues. We were there to sit and talk with His Holiness the Dalai Lama.

It was in the early summer of 2001, and I had been invited to something called the "Synthesis Dialogues," a gathering of thirty people, all global activists, religious leaders, or spiritual teachers. The purpose of the gathering was to engage with each other and with His Holiness about the state of the world.

The thirty participants were global and grassroots leaders from all parts of the world, each with a common commitment to human potential and spirituality. Each was at work on some aspect of the injustice, pain, and suffering that plagues the human family. These were people working in the trenches, confronting war, poverty, hunger, violence, and oppression that in some cases was massive in scale. Some of the participants had endured imprisonment and torture and yet had returned to the work, even more determined to catalyze change and transformation. Just being among them was humbling.

We met for several days with each other before His Holiness arrived. We shared our life stories and meditated together. We took walks in the mountains and we sang together. We connected deeply and earned each other's respect, grew to love each other, and were effectively at work and in dialogue by the time His Holiness the Dalai Lama joined us, accompanied by the Tibetan monks and scholars who travel with him.

The meeting had already been a potent and productive gathering for all of us even before he came. But when he joined us, when he brought his presence, his "holiness", everything moved to a different level. Somehow we each were able to separate ourselves from our own individual "story" or our own "life drama" and witness our world rather than grapple with its problems. In our conversation we did not skirt the problems of the world, but held them in clear view. His Holiness spoke of the tragic and cruel oppression of his people by the Chinese government, and the unbearable torture and atrocities being perpetrated on the remaining Tibetans inside Chinese Tibet. The story of his narrow escape from being killed by the Chinese as a teenager and now living in exile for decades was already well known in our circle. This is a man who is no stranger to hardship, oppression, injustice, and suffering.

Yet what emerged from our dialogues was indeed a synthesis, and a consensus, that the world is awakening, that the tide is turning. We saw and felt that even in the face of staggering statistics about the degradation of the environment, the escalation of violence and war, the rampant abuses of human rights, the sweeping epidemic of AIDS and other diseases, and the pain of widespread poverty, something fundamental is shifting at the core. Old inaccurate assumptions are dropping away, and an emergence, a spiritual power, a soulful surge and transformation is bubbling up everywhere and is more powerful, more steady, more unshakable than the challenges that confront us.

We all had different labels for it, but we knew we were talking about the same thing. For me, it was the beginning of the disintegration of scarcity and the you-*or*-me world it creates, especially destructive in our relationship with money, and its ultimate unworkability, its gross misreading of the real truth and integrity of life, and its unsustainable premise. We agreed that the vision emerging in its place was, and is now even more so, the you-*and*-me world that Buckminster Fuller predicted years before, a world where we live in the context and truth of sufficiency and respect for enough, exactly enough for everyone everywhere; a world that works for everyone, with no one and nothing left out; a world where solidarity replaces charity, and a world where the dream is a dream not for some at the expense of others, but a dream for all; a world where the intelligent and benevolent "force" of Nature is the force that we respect and align with; a world where the love of money is replaced by the use of money as an expression of love.

As we sat in a circle together, His Holiness listened to each of us, and spoke with us, reflecting on the nature of our respective commitments in the context of the whole. He described the universal desire people have to be happy and avoid suffering, and the way an ethical life becomes a fulfilling life. In our relationship with money, he said, when we bring the divine presence to this temple of plenty we create an authentic and ethical relationship with money that expands, enlarges, and magnifies its value.

In the dialogue with my colleagues there in the presence of His Holiness, I saw this as I had never seen it before. I felt it. It was visceral, physical, and deeply moving. I remembered a quote that I had heard years ago from Teilhard de Chardin: "We are not human beings having a spiritual experience, but spiritual beings having a human experience."

Sitting before the Dalai Llama, I experienced myself as a spiritual being, dealing in the realm of human experience. The retreat meeting, and the Dalai Lama himself, created the physical, intellectual, and spiritual space for clarity and reflection. From that synthesis emerged an even deeper, more exquisite experience of the truth and a renewal of commitment. The profound experience of those short days returns from time to time, and it is clear for me now as I think about the nature of this human experience of ours, and the fact that one of the most defining, demanding aspects of being engaged in the human experience is our struggle, our challenge, and our interactions with money. I saw again as I had seen many times before, but this time even more clearly, that money—an arena of life that so hooks and seduces us—can be our greatest ally in our own transformation and the transformation of the world in which we live.

Money travels everywhere, crosses all boundaries, languages, and cultures. Money, like water, ripples at some level through every life and place. It can carry our love or our fear. It can flood some of us such that we drown in a toxic sense of power over others. It can nourish and water the principles of freedom, community, and sharing. Money can affirm life or it can be used to demean, diminish, or destroy it. It is neither evil nor good; it is an instrument. We invented it, and it belongs squarely in the human experience, but it can be used by and merged with the longings and passions of our soul.

THE YOU-AND-ME WORLD ALREADY EXISTS

It was in the late 1970s when I heard Buckminster Fuller describe his vision of a you-*and*-me world, a world where we all know and live the truth that there is enough for everyone, with no one left out. At that time it was already a realistic expectation because, as he pointed out, there really was enough food in the world, enough resources, to take care of everyone. The challenge, he said, was that all our structures and systems—politics, government, health care, education, economics, and especially our money system—had been designed around scarcity, around the belief that there wasn't enough for everyone and that someone would be left out.

Bucky predicted it could take twenty-five to fifty years for those now inaccurate systems and structures built on the belief in scarcity—a you-*or*-me world paradigm—to crumble. He warned that it might be upsetting, confusing, even cataclysmic, but that when the transformation takes place, a new world will have been born: a world in which we treasure that there is enough, steward it wisely, and live in a context of sufficiency and prosperity for all—a paradigm of you-*and*-me.

It is a cataclysmic, scary time, and money is somewhere behind or under or running through virtually every conflict, disaster, and crisis around the world and every facet of our own lives. It is an especially tense and challenging time in our lives with money. We worry about losing our jobs and being unable to find new ones in a shrinking job market and a depressed economy. We worry whether we'll have enough money to be able to keep our homes, or feed, clothe, and educate our children as we would wish, whether we'll have enough money for retirement. We worry about our country investing lives and money in war. We worry about terrorism close to home, and at the same time about the spiraling costs of increased security measures at every turn, not necessarily feeling safer as a result.

In many ways it is worse than we want to think: terrorism, war, violence, revenge, and retribution plague our planet, species are going extinct at an unprecedented rate, burning of fossil fuels is destabilizing the world's climate; the apparent gap between those with affluent resources and those with little or none seems to be widening mercilessly; corruption and greed seem rampant and growing, even among those who already have inordinate amounts of money, resources, power, and privilege.

At the same time, it's better than we could hope. Hundreds

of millions of people are at work, awake to the challenges and tackling them at every level. Countless organizations and initiatives have sprung up throughout the world, addressing the basic needs of all humanity and all life. Civil society and citizens' action in every country on earth are more vibrant, emergent, and active than ever before in history. The Internet connects billions of us instantly, and we are experiencing our interconnectedness in potent and practical ways that make possible unprecedented cooperation and collaborations. The communications explosion has awakened our natural relatedness to one another and the awareness of the fact that we're interconnected. It has also facilitated a truly global conversation on important issues that affect us all. Ecological awareness and consciousness permeates every nation, village, institution, and population around the globe.

We are awakening to human rights and gender equity, and especially the power and the emergence of women and women's voices and leadership as resources in every aspect of society. More than two-thirds of the world's people live under some form of democratic government, giving an unprecedented percentage of the human race—including women and people of color—a voice in the determination of their future.

A surge of spirituality worldwide is bringing spirit more visibly into daily life, the workplace, the family, and the conversation for greater wisdom in nearly every setting where people are deeply grappling with how to live and be. More religious communities are recognizing the gift of diversity and teaching respect for other faiths. The Pachamama Alliance and other organizations and collaborators are effectively preserving primary rain forest lands and their inhabitants, and as a result, indigenous peoples have begun to emerge as a respected voice bringing ancient wisdom rooted in the laws of the natural world into conferences and councils of global decision makers.

Alternative and complementary medicine has surged in popularity and acceptance in the United States, opening the doors to newfound insights from traditions and practices in healing throughout the world. In many countries, alternative and complementary currencies, ranging from bartering to sophisticated economic exchanges of resources, are enabling people to share with one another outside the traditional money system.

The Hunger Project and its philosophy, which was ridiculed twenty-five years ago, has become the model for both enlightened philanthropy and programs that foster self-sufficiency and self-reliance and enable people to be the authors of their own development. The tragic hunger statistics of 1977—41,000 deaths a day—have been cut in half, to fewer than twenty thousand a day, and those numbers continue to go down steadily even as the world's population goes up. Progress is being made.

Large oil companies such as Shell and British Petroleum have renamed themselves "energy companies" and have targeted to be out of the fossil-fuel business and fully in the renewable-energy business within thirty years.

Young global activist organizations such as Free the Children and Youth for Environmental Sanity, Pioneers of Change, and hundreds of other organizations are inspiring and mobilizing young people worldwide to bring a new kind of thinking and leadership to the challenge we face.

As Paul Ray and Sherry Anderson say in their seminal book, *The Cultural Creatives: How Fifty Million People Can Change the World*, many millions of people "have taken on a whole new worldview ... a major development in our civilization. Changing a worldview literally means changing what you think is real . . . changes in values, your fundamental life priorities; changes in lifestyle, the way you spend your time and money; and changes in livelihood, how you make that money in the first place."

This is not a time of mere change. This is a time of transformation, and transformation comes not out of scarcity but out of the context of possibility, responsibility, and sufficiency. To quote the visionary ontological thinker Werner Erhard, "Transformation does not negate what has gone before; rather, it fulfills it. Creating the context of a world that works for everyone is not just another step forward in human history; it is the context out of which our history will begin to make sense."

In the Synthesis Dialogues with His Holiness the Dalai Lama, as we talked about the obstacles and challenges, opportunities and possibilities that present themselves in the different arenas in which we each worked, the nature of our work—the work of everybody everywhere—became clear to me. As a colleague of mine has said, the job of our time is to hospice the death of the old unsustainable systems and structures and to midwife the birth of new sustainable systems and new ways of being. To hospice those systems that have reached their limits and are unsustainable is not to kill them, but with some compassion and love, to witness their disintegration, and then to midwife with compassion and love the development and creation of new structures, systems, contexts, and constructs that support and empower sustainable ways of being. These ways are based in the reality and understanding of a world in which there is enough, in which we can all thrive, not each at the other's expense, but in collaboration and cooperation. Our relationship with money can be the place where this transformation begins for each of us. We can embrace money and soul in the same moment, and "actively coexist" with our money, as Alan Slifka, professional investor, philanthropist, and friend of mine puts it. "It's a matter of merging our tangible assets with our intangible assets. There's an opportunity to use money in a wholly different way if we have the courage to see the possibilities."

MY JOURNEY INTO MONEY AND SOUL

In service of a commitment bigger than any I ever thought I would make, my journey in fund-raising and activism has taken me far and wide culturally, but it has also taken me deep into my own relationship with life. This arena of my relationship with money, and with people who are dealing with their own relationship with money, has been a place where I have come to understand some of the universal truths about money. I am moved by the struggle we all have with money. I now see that this arena in which we brush up against the hard realities of life can be the place where we develop a kind of a spiritual practice in which we use the money that comes to us as an instrument of our intention and integrity.

When I made that first contribution to The Hunger Project it realigned my priorities. My financial life started to be more in alignment with my deep sense of self and soul. I began to have an experience of prosperity that was unrelated to any quantity of money or acquisitions. I could feel this alignment within myself, and I had done that through my use of money. That was the place where the tide turned in me. It was so surprising that money, this very thing I had used and seen others use to perpetuate accumulation, depletion, and making myself important with art and wine and stuff, ended up being *the same instrument* I eventually used to express my love for people and my affirmation of life, and to share my deepest dreams. Once that instrument, or vehicle called money, was in alignment with my soul, that was when the prosperity, joy, and sufficiency started to flourish. It wasn't in the money, but in its use as an instrument of soul.

That is possible for everyone: not only on a personal level, but also on a family level, a cultural level, society-wide. Lining money up with our soul, with our deepest dreams and highest aspirations, is the source of our prosperity, rather than simply having more of it to work with. Money used this way connects us to the whole of life, rather than money becoming an instrument that separates and fragments us from each other. That kind of prosperity is available to everyone, whether they are people with massive resources or people with moderate or fewer resources.

Using money as a direct expression of one's deepest sense of self is a powerful, miraculous thing. It is a practice, however, and I'm still working on it. I waste money. I buy products that are part of the problem rather than part of the solution. I get excited about money and disappointed about money and frustrated and conflicted over money issues. But I am also on a path, in a practice, that I'm sharing with you because I believe it is useful and important in our time. I'm seeing that more and more of us are awake to our higher commitments, concerned about how we're living, and this book is an offering to contribute to that process that is taking place all around us now.

The realization and sense of peace in the recognition that there is enough is not meant to disclaim the great needs of millions of people or of whole segments of our society. I work each day in that brutal realm. However, the fundamental understanding that there is enough has allowed me to approach not only those challenges and those problems, but also my own life, in a way that has opened up new relationships and new possibility at every turn.

So I offer this as an every-man-and-woman, every-day, possible way of engaging in this arena of money, this flow that runs through every relationship, whether it is with our mother or father, husband, wife, aunts, cousins, friends, employer, employee. Money is never really absent, and we can use it as a mirror for understanding who we are and what we stand for.

I also invite you to live a larger life—to see that when we really look at what we've got and let go of trying to accumulate more, we have the capacity for much greater lives than just "getting" and "having." Everyone wants more than the good life for just themselves. They want the good life for all, and when you realize there is enough, you get in touch with that possibility. It becomes the natural outcome of shifting your context. It worked that way for me, and I've seen it work that way for many others, around the world.

THE CATERPILLAR AND THE BUTTERFLY

Our struggle around money, and all the tension, fears, and excesses that go with it, has a parallel in nature. Evolutionary biologist Elisabet Sahtouris says that the caterpillar, at a certain point in its life cycle, becomes a voracious, overconsumptive glutton consuming everything in sight and within reach. At this point in its evolution it can eat hundreds of times its own weight, and the more it consumes the more fat and sluggish it gets. At that same moment of developmental excess, inside the caterpillar the *imaginal cells* begin to stir. Imaginal cells are specialized cells, and in the minority, but when they connect with each other they become the genetic directors of the metamorphosis of the caterpillar. At some point in the caterpillar's feeding-frenzy stage, the imaginal cells usher in the process in which the overconsumptive caterpillar becomes the "nutritive soup" out of which the imaginal cells create the miracle of the butterfly.

When I first heard this caterpillar-butterfly metaphor I loved it because it gave me a way to see the world the way it is, even its state of voracious greed, as a kind of evolutionary phase. It is such a fitting metaphor for our time. When I look at the inspired, devoted, and brilliant people at work in so many ways to repair and nourish the world, in families, communities, and sustainable enterprises everywhere on Earth, I see the imaginal cells of our own transformation. That's us, people like me and people like you, people whose stories I've shared in this book, and people appreciating them, people creating new ways, seeing new possibilities.

The fall of unsustainable structures in business, economics, politics, and government—the collapse of companies like WorldCom, Enron, and Tyco in recent years—and the unraveling of corporate corruption could be the beginning of the voracious caterpillar's becoming the nutritive soup from which will grow the miracle of the butterfly.

In this world of turmoil and conflict, violence and retribution, I believe there are millions of people taking responsibility not just for change, but also for transformation, for creating the miracle of the butterfly. We may be in the minority, but we are everywhere and we are connecting with one another in Senegal, in Ethiopia, in Ecuador and Afghanistan; in France, Sweden, Japan, and Germany; in Iowa, Michigan, New York, and California—even in Hollywood; in spectacular careers and in the workaday world that keeps it all going. We are the "hidden mainstream." We are the genetic directors of this living system. If we continue to connect with each other, we can create out of this gluttonous caterpillar the miracle of the butterfly.

I challenge you to use your money, every dollar, every penny, every purchase, every stock and every bond, to voice this transformation.

I challenge you to use the money that flows through your life—and it does flow through all of our lives—to express the truth and context of sufficiency.

I challenge you to move the resources that flow through your life toward your highest commitments and ideals, those things you stand for.

I challenge you to hold money as a common trust that we're all responsible for using in ways that nurture and empower us, and all life, our planet, and all future generations.

I challenge you to imbue your money with soul—your soul—and let it stand for who you are, your love, your heart, your word, and your humanity.

Dearest Reader,

Thank you so much for being part of this journey of *The Soul of Money* and leading a life of sufficiency, generosity, and prosperity.

To learn more, and for information about a gift I hope will help empower you in continuing this work, please visit me on my website at www.lynnetwist.com/freegift.*

I look forward to connecting with you.

Many blessings,
Lynne

*Offer and website are unaffiliated with W. W. Norton & Company Inc., which makes no guarantee of gift availability or accuracy, completeness, or fitness for any particular purpose of third-party website content.

RESOURCES

ORGANIZATIONS

(For nonprofit status, please check individual websites)

A Network for Grateful Living (ANGeL)
www.gratefulness.org

A global network of individuals, organizations, and communities exploring the transformative power of gratefulness in personal lives. Online and community-based educational programs and practices inspire and guide a commitment to grateful living, which supports social accountability by motivating a feeling of love, generosity, and respect toward one another, ourselves, and the earth. The network's online presence connects the global community and provides resources for those committed to grateful living.

The Abraham Fund Initiatives
www.abrahamfund.org

Promotes coexistence and equality among Israel's Jewish and Arab-Palestinian citizens. Works toward a prosperous, secure, and just society by promoting policies based on innovative social models, conducting large-scale initiatives, advocacy, and public education. Supports the vision of an Israel that is at once both the homeland of the Jewish people and a full, welcoming, and equal home for its Arab citizens, grounded in the belief that Israeli society must embrace the benefits of diversity in order to build a stable and secure democracy. Initiatives include teaching children the languages and cultures of their neighbors, improving police relations, narrowing the social and economic gaps between communities, and strengthening the foundation for a shared and equal society.

The Abraham Path Initiative
www.abrahampathinitiative.org

A nonprofit, nonreligious, and nonpolitical international organization cultivating the development of the Abraham Path along with local and international partner organizations. The mission of API is to support local partners in developing the Abraham Path as a catalyst for socioeconomic development and sustainable tourism; a place of connection between people from the Middle East and people around the world; and a creative space for stories that highlight the unique culture, heritage, and hospitality of the region.

Agape International Spiritual Center
www.agapelive.com

Teaches individuals about the transforming, healing power of prayer, meditation, and selfless service. Since its doors opened in 1986, Agape's active teaching and practice of the New Thought/ Ancient Wisdom tradition of spirituality has expanded into a transdenominational movement and community of 9,000 local members and 1,000,000 friends worldwide. Programs include the Rev. Dr. Michael Bernard Beckwith's weekly services, Agape's University of Transformational Studies and Leadership classes, ministries, and other outreach programs.

Amazon Watch
www.amazonwatch.org

A nonprofit organization founded in 1996 to protect the rainforest and advance the rights of indigenous peoples in the Amazon Basin. Amazon Watch partners with indigenous and environmental organizations in campaigns for human rights, corporate accountability, and the preservation of the Amazon's ecological systems. Amazon Watch also partners with communities, nongovernmental organizations, concerned shareholders, and citizens to persuade corporations, financial institutions, and governments to honor the rights of the indigenous people; strengthen the capacity of indigenous communities to advocate for their own rights; seek permanent protection for threatened areas and vulnerable populations; and educate corporate executives, shareholders, public officials, and the general public using media coverage, websites, publications, and documentary films.

Ashoka: Innovators for the Public
www.ashoka.org

Pioneered the field of social entrepreneurship over the past 35 years by finding, selecting, and supporting more than 3,000 of the world's leading social entrepreneurs in 89 countries. Provides financial support and other nonfinancial services to grow these enterprises and assist them in collaborating with like-minded peers around the world. Programs include learning and youth development, and environmental, health, and other initiatives to identify key principles and strategies, and then to disseminate them worldwide.

The Berkana Institute
www.berkana.org

A public foundation that creates strong and sustainable relationships by stewarding the earth's resources and building resilient communities. The institute connects trailblazing leaders and communities, and provides education, resources, and support to illuminate their stories as important examples of a better future taking place right now.

Bioneers/Collective Heritage Institute
www.bioneers.org

A nonprofit hub of social and scientific innovators with practical and visionary solutions for the world's most pressing environmental and social challenges. Provides a forum for education and uses media productions to leverage its content to millions of people around the world. Resources include an annual conference of social and scientific innovators; an award-winning radio series, *Bioneers: Revolution From the Heart of Nature*; an anthology book series; television programs; and an interactive website.

The Brande Foundation/The Coaching Project
www.thecoachingproject.org

Provides individual and group coaching to executives and their teams from national and international nonprofit organizations. The Coaching Project has evolved over 15 years through The Brande Foundation, which was started in 1987. Depending on criteria, partial and full scholarships may be available for this service. Other resources include books, online classes, CDs, and DVDs.

Buckminster Fuller Institute (BFI)
www.bfi.org

Dedicated to catalyzing transformative solutions to complex problems through design-thinking education. Programs combine unique insight into global trends and local needs with an approach to design that converges across the disciplines of art, science, and technology. BFI resources and programs include BFI.org, an extensive database of Fuller's life and work; the Fuller Challenge, its flagship program which offers an annual prize to support winning solutions; Open BFI, access to the materials that inform BFI's work; and mobile exhibitions, lectures, seminars, workshops, and hands-on training.

Caldera

www.calderaarts.org

Offers Oregon youth educational and economic resources otherwise unavailable to them. Mentoring programs are geared toward children, from sixth grade through graduation, and their families. Other programs include in-school residences, weekend intensives, and Camp Caldera.

The Center for a New American Dream

www.newdream.org

Provides consumer-education materials and works with individuals, institutions, communities, and businesses to conserve natural resources, counter the commercialization of American culture, and promote positive changes in the way goods are produced and consumed. Particular emphasis is on helping Americans consume responsibly to protect the environment, enhance quality of life, and promote social justice. The center's website provides visitors specific actions they can take to protect the environment and improve quality of life.

Center for Partnership Studies

www.centerforpartnership.org

Focuses on promoting human rights and nonviolence, gender and racial equity, childhood development, and new metrics that demonstrate the financial contribution of the work of caregiving. The Center for Partnership Studies works to catalyze movement toward partnership systems on all levels of society through research, education, grassroots empowerment, and policy initiatives. The center's work is based on the partnership model described by theorist Riane Eisler in her books *The Chalice and the Blade*, *Sacred Pleasure*, *Tomorrow's Children*, and *The Power of Partnership*. Resources include webinars, courses, and publications about partnership education, leadership, and more.

Citizens' Climate Lobby
www.citizensclimatelobby.org

A nonprofit, nonpartisan, grassroots advocacy organization focused on national policies to address climate change. The organization's approach to climate education is designed to create a broad, sustainable foundation for climate action across all geographic regions and political inclinations. Citizens' Climate Lobby volunteers are organized into hundreds of local chapters across the United States and around the world. Activities and actions include citizen-led meetings with Congress, letters to Congress, published media, and outreach events.

Community Environmental and Legal Defense Fund (CELDF)
www.celdf.org

Advances democratic, economic, social, and environmental rights from the grassroots to the state, federal, and international levels. Through grassroots organizing, public education and outreach, and legal assistance, nearly 200 municipalities across the

United States have enacted CELDF-drafted community rights laws that ban practices such as fracking, factory farming, sewage sludging of farmland, and water privatization, which violate the rights of people, communities, and nature.

Companion Arts
www.companionarts.org

Enhances the quality of life of family and professional caregivers by providing innovative and evidence-based services, products, and resources. Companion Arts has developed a number of customized programs for major healthcare institutions and audio resources for professional caregivers. The nonprofit has also explored how music and messages have a strong, positive effect on individual healing. Resources include "Care for the Journey," a series of CDs containing spoken word over music for professional caregivers created by educators, healthcare professionals, and wellness experts; as well as Heart of Healing, an audio resource for anybody on a healing path.

Conscious Elders Network
www.consciouselders.org

An educational, nonprofit organization fostering a budding movement of vital elders dedicated to growing in consciousness while actively addressing the demanding challenges facing our country. Conscious Elders Network works intergenerationally for social and economic justice, environmental stewardship, and sound governance. This network is committed to confronting the crises of the twenty-first century by committing their talents, resources, experience, and wisdom.

Days for Girls International
www.daysforgirls.org

Dedicated to creating a more dignified, free, and educated world through access to lasting feminine hygiene solutions. Days for Girls (DfG) accomplishes this through direct distribution with many nonprofits, by raising awareness, by helping other organizations start their own Days for Girls programs, and by helping ultra-low-resource communities start their own programs to supply DfG kits and training. Since 2008, DfG has created more than 300,000 kits and reached more than 100 countries.

Donella Meadows Institute
www.donellameadows.org

Works to bring economic, social, and environmental systems into closer harmony with the realities of the planet and the human race through systems thinking, system dynamics, and collaborative learning. The institute preserves Donella Meadows's legacy as a leader, scholar, writer, and teacher by using northern New England as a learning laboratory to test and apply tools and processes of systems thinking to move the world closer to sustainability.

Dream Music Puppetry Program
www.fin.here.org/programs/dream-music

Provides performance opportunities to puppet artists and encourages multidisciplinary collaboration to develop new puppetry techniques. This program was inaugurated with the premiere of Basil Twist's Obie-award winning *Symphonie Fantastique* in 1998. Under the artistic direction of Twist, and produced by HERE cofounder Barbara Busackino, the Dream Music aesthetic is geared toward puppet works that feature live music as a collaborative element.

Edgewalkers
www.edgewalkers.org

An international consulting and coaching organization with a focus on supporting individuals and organizations that feel called to be on the leading edge. Edgewalkers use all of their human potential and integrate their intellectual, emotional, physical, and spiritual energy in service to something greater than themselves. Services include assessments, coaching, workshops, retreats, and facilitator certification.

Educate Girls Globally
www.educategirls.org

Empowers major stakeholders to reform government schools and promote economic and social change even in the most traditional and tribal communities. Educate Girls Globally has developed a new strategy for educating and empowering girls in high-poverty areas where cultural and social traditions hold back women and girls from realizing their potential. By leveraging government investments already allocated to education, the program promotes systemic change, empowering girls to gain voice and choice, and become more actively engaged and productive citizens.

Feel Good
www.feelgood.org

A youth movement that works to end extreme poverty by mobilizing resources and public will. Since 2005, the movement has created 25 active chapters, helped more than 18,000 people out of poverty, and has raised more than $1.8 million to end poverty. Online resources include educational information, as well as information about starting and running a Feel Good chapter.

The Fetzer Institute
www.fetzer.org

Helps to build the spiritual foundation for a loving world. Its strategy is to help catalyze and support the emergence of a powerful global movement for spiritually grounded individual and societal transformation. While blessed with a significant endowment, the institute is not a funder, but rather works with program and funding partners to co-create and implement ambitious program initiatives in support of this global movement strategy.

Full Circle Fund
www.fullcirclefund.org

An active network of professionals who leverage their time, talent, and connections to help nonprofit organizations launch new initiatives, make a greater impact, and accelerate positive change in our community. Members explore key issues such as economic opportunity, housing, technology, health, and the environment.

Give US Your Poor: Homelessness & the United States
www.giveusyourpoor.org

A national initiative to end homelessness in the United States through public education about systemic root causes of homelessness, community action, and individual responses. Give US Your Poor began as a documentary film project looking at homelessness and has grown into a wider education campaign utilizing networks, media, public support, and the latest research on homelessness. Media resources include recorded music, video clips, documentary shorts, photography, and radio links.

Global Footprint Network
www.footprintnetwork.org

Provides tools to national governments, financial institutions, and international development agencies so that they can be more successful operating within nature's budget. The nonprofit was established to enable a sustainable future and does this by accelerating the use of the Ecological Footprint—a resource accounting tool that measures how much nature we have, how much we use, and who uses what. With the help of hundreds of individuals, leading businesses, scientists, NGOs, academics, and its more than 70 global partners, Global Footprint Network's presence spans six continents, 200 cities, and 23 nations.

Global Force for Healing
www.globalforceforhealing.org

Social profit organization that connects indigenous and remote birthing and health-related projects to each other and creates co-equal partnerships between groups of global citizens. Its mission is to co-create, connect, and communicate about global grassroots projects that demonstrate love as a primary force for healing, transformation, and sustainability. Current focuses include providing free consultation to grassroots health-related projects on organizational capacity building, educational initiatives, and relationship-based fund-raising, to empower all to be sustainable and thrive. Global Force for Healing currently works with 15 partner organizations in 12 countries.

The Global Fund for Women
www.globalfundforwomen.org

Makes grants to seed, support, and strengthen women's-rights groups working on critical issues such as sexual and reproductive health and rights, freedom from violence, and economic and political equality. Programs support women-led organizations that are fighting for justice in their own communities in order to create change at the root of the problem.

Global Security Institute (GSI)
www.gsinstitute.org

Dedicated to strengthening international cooperation and security, with a particular focus on nuclear arms control, nonproliferation, and disarmament. The Global Security Institute was founded by Senator Alan Cranston (1914–2000) who considered it unworthy of civilization to base security on terror. Programs include the Bipartisan Security Group, the Middle Powers Initiative, Parliamentarians for Nuclear Nonproliferation and Disarmament, and Disarmament and Peace Education.

Global Youth Action Network (GYAN)/TakingITGlobal
www.gyan.tigweb.org

A growing online collaborative among youth organizations from almost 200 countries. GYAN provides resources and recognition for positive youth action and facilitates intergenerational partnership in global decision-making. Programs include Global Youth Service Day (with Youth Service America), the largest annual celebration of young volunteers; and Global Youth in Action Awards.

TakingITGlobal is a resource for youth and organizations working to make a difference. A virtual community and expansive clearinghouse for today's youth movement, the site offers discussion boards, a database of thousands of organizations and events, opportunities, scholarships, internships, and more.

Greenheart International
www.greenheart.org

Creates global leaders through personal development, volunteer service, environmentalism, fair trade, and cultural exchange. Programs include Camp Greenheart, Greenheart Club, Greenheart Transforms, Greenheart Shop, CCI Greenheart, and Greenheart Travel. Each of these programs focuses on three key learning objectives: personal and professional development, environmental awareness, and cultural understanding.

Higher Ground for Humanity
www.highergroundhumanity.org

A supportive conduit for programs and organizations that promote humanitarian values and operate on the basis of higher principles. Promotes human excellence by pioneering collaborations for peace and generative prosperity for all people. Areas of emphasis include alternative health, environment, arts, youth issues, and developing the human spirit. The Holistic Health Initiative, dedicated to alternative health breakthroughs, is a key program.

HIVE
www.hive.org

A global community of leaders, innovators, and entrepreneurs who are working on creating a better world and are committed to something bigger than themselves. Members attend a 3-day leadership training program at the Innovation Hangar at the Palace of

Fine Arts in San Francisco. This provides the opportunity to work together with diverse peers from all over the world.

The Hoffman Institute
www.hoffmaninstitute.org

An educational organization dedicated to transformative adult education, spiritual growth, and the personal dimensions of leadership. The residential, week-long Hoffman Process improves quality of life, relationships, and careers. Participants learn how to transform counterproductive beliefs, perceptions, and emotional patterns that are limiting their lives. Participants are taught how to live from the positive dimensions of their beings, resulting in lives that are more free, open, loving, spontaneous, joyous, creative, balanced, and whole.

The Hunger Project (THP)
www.thp.org

A global, strategic organization committed to the sustainable end of world hunger. In 22 countries worldwide, THP's innovative, holistic approach empowers women and men living in rural villages to become agents of their own development and make sustainable progress in overcoming hunger and poverty. All of THP's programs are founded on three essential pillars: empowering women as key change agents, mobilizing entire communities into self-reliant action, and fostering effective partnerships to engage local government. The Vision, Commitment and Action workshop serves as a foundation for THP's work by awakening people to the new possibilities and empowering them to take action.

The Independent Sector
www.independentsector.org

A leadership network for nonprofits, foundations, and corporations committed to advancing the common good. Independent Sector's nonpartisan coalition networks collectively represent tens of thousands of organizations and individuals locally, nationally, and globally. Independent Sector's work is guided by the vision of engaged individuals, robust institutions, and vibrant communities working together to improve lives and the natural world, and strengthen democratic societies.

Inner Light Ministries
www.innerlightministries.com

An omnifaith outreach ministry dedicated to spiritual transformation. The ministry provides "Tools for Living"™ that encourage the practical application of universal spiritual principles to all of life's circumstances. Ongoing programs include Sunday services and the education ministry, which provides workshops and classes.

Inside Circle Foundation, Inc.
www.insidecircle.org

A not-for-profit organization dedicated to the inner personal growth of men in prison. The goal of the Inside Circle Foundation is to create environments in which prisoners can work and explore the issues in their lives that have prevented them from living up to their full potential as human beings. In these environments the foundation primarily utilizes self-help discussion groups and creative writing techniques such as journaling, autobiography, and poetry to achieve the inner development necessary to become healthy contributing members of society.

The Institute of Noetic Sciences (IONS)
www.noetic.org

A nonprofit organization dedicated to supporting individual and collective transformation through consciousness research and transformative learning, and engaging a global community in the realization of our human potential. IONS broadens the science of what connects us and creates real-world tools that empower people to apply conscious awareness in their personal lives, and in healthcare, education, and business. IONS's goal is to create a shift in consciousness worldwide to inspire people to take action as a collective whole to help humanity and the planet thrive.

Interfaith Youth Core (IFYC)
www.ifyc.org

A national movement designed to build religious pluralism, starting with college students and then spreading throughout society. IFYC believes American college students, supported by their campuses, can be the interfaith leaders needed to make religion a bridge and not a barrier.

International Youth Foundation (IYF)
www.iyfnet.org

One of the world's largest public foundations focused on children and youth. IYF works with over 220 businesses, governments, and civil society organizations to strengthen and expand opportunities for youth. Since 1990, IYF has mobilized $200 million in resources to fund programs and partnerships with more than 470 youth-serving organizations. Collaborations have helped millions of young people gain the skills, training, and opportunities critical for success. Together with its partners, IYF has built effective, sustainable, scalable initiatives in three thematic areas: education and employment, entrepreneurship, and social innovation.

Jean Houston
www.jeanhouston.com

A scholar, philosopher, and researcher in human capacities, Jean Houston is one of the foremost visionary thinkers and doers of our time. Dr. Houston is noted for her ability to combine a deep knowledge of history, culture, new science, spirituality, and human development into her teaching. Houston offers salon mentoring programs, as well as individual mentoring.

The Kudirat Initiative for Democracy (KIND)
www.kind.org

A not-for-profit organization with a mission to empower democracy and development in Africa by strengthening organizations and creating initiatives dedicated to the advancement of women. KIND's main focus and areas of intervention include leadership development; creating opportunities; and working collaboratively with other organizations, agencies, and individuals.

Landmark Education
www.landmarkeductation.com

An international training and development company offering innovative programs to empower participants to think and act beyond existing views and limits, and enhance personal productivity, organizational effectiveness, and communication. Delivers programs in 125 cities via 53 major offices worldwide. The Landmark Forum and other courses cover a wide range of interests and topics relevant to everyday life including quality of relationships, personal productivity, and enjoyment of life.

Mavericks 1000
www.maverick1000.com

An invitation-only global network of growth-oriented business leaders. Members share breakthrough ideas on the most critical issues facing twenty-first-century innovators and leaders. Programs include regional 3x Multiplier Retreats, Camp Maverick, and M3 Summits.

Mediators Foundation
www.mediatorsfoundation.org

Fosters global leadership for a peaceful, just, and sustainable world by identifying, supporting, and connecting visionary leaders working in the best interests of our small planet. Since its founding in 1987, Mediators Foundation has catalyzed civic and educational projects to address social issues of national and global importance, and worked for a better understanding of global cultures and values. Current projects include Living Room Conversations, The Bridge Alliance, and Wisdom Beyond Borders.

Mercy Corps
www.mercycorps.com

Since 1979, committed to alleviating suffering, poverty, and oppression by helping people build secure, productive, and just communities. This work is accomplished by listening closely to local partners to make sure that their voices, concerns, and suggestions are heard by key decision-makers. Initiatives include advancing food security, improving emergency response, building resilience, preventing and managing conflict, putting youth in the lead, and responding to crises in Syria and Iraq.

Millennium School
www.millenniumschool.org

An independent middle school in San Francisco built on the premise that middle school should have both stronger academics and a stronger focus on developing the habits and mindsets that lead to happy, meaningful, purposeful lives as adults. The nonprofit organization is guided by three essential elements for a healthy passage through middle school: a safe social environment, connection to the real world, and tools to understand oneself.

The Mind and Life Institute
www.mindandlife.org

Emerged to bridge the divide between science and introspective methods when investigating the nature of reality. Mind and Life has held 29 Dialogue events to bring together scientists and contemplatives on a wide range of critical subjects: addiction, ecology, ethics, attention, neuroplasticity, destructive emotions, altruism, economics, and more. In addition to the Dialogue events, the institute holds international symposiums, summer research institutes, think tanks, Call to Care programs, and Academy for Contemplative and Ethical Leadership programs. The institute also directly funds individual research via its grant and scholarship programs.

Move to Amend
www.movetoamend.org

A coalition of organizations and individuals committed to social and economic justice, ending corporate rule, and building a democracy that is accountable to the people, not corporate interests. Formed in 2009, Move to Amend is calling for an amendment to the U.S. Constitution to state that inalienable rights belong to human beings only, and that money is not a form of protected free speech under the First Amendment and, therefore, can be regulated in political campaigns. Online resources include the Take Action Toolkit, recommended readings, links, and documentaries.

The Natural Step
www.thenaturalstep.org

A global network of nonprofit organizations that seeks to accelerate the transition to a sustainable society by providing educational programs, advisory services, and transition labs to businesses and governments around the world. The Natural Step works with some of the largest resource users on the planet to create solutions, innovative models, and tools that will lead the transition to a sustainable future.

New Dimensions Foundation/New Dimensions Radio
www.newdimensions.org

Fosters global dialogue on social, political, scientific, ecological, health, and spiritual frontiers through worldwide radio broadcast interviews with the world's leading thinkers, social innovators, creative artists, scientists, and spiritual teachers. Programs reach more than 300 communities via public radio stations within the United States and more than 700 throughout the world. Founded in 1973, and listener funded.

NEXUS Global Youth Summit
www.nexusyouthsummit.org

A global movement to bridge communities of wealth and social entrepreneurship. With thousands of members from 70 countries, Nexus works to unite young investors, social entrepreneurs, philanthropists, and allies to catalyze new leadership and accelerate global solutions. Nexus has hosted over 20 summits across six continents to connect young people from diverse backgrounds and link communities that would otherwise never meet. Nexus also conducts research and provides thought leadership to facilitate collaboration and build a global culture of philanthropy.

The Nine Gates Mystery School
www.ninegates.org

Offers transformative learning experiences designed to challenge individuals to awaken their essential nature and truth while providing a sustained, supportive, ongoing community. The Nine Gates Mystery School includes two, 9-day residential programs for individual mentorship. The school delves deeply into the wisdom of the Celtic, African, Native American, spiritual psychology, Sufi, esoteric Christian, Hindu, sound healing, Kabbalah, and Buddhist traditions.

Nobel Women's Initiative
www.nobelwomensinitiative.org

Established in 2006 by Nobel Peace laureates Jody Williams, Shirin Ebadi, Wangari Maathai, Rigoberta Menchú Tum, Betty Williams, and Mairead Maguire to bring together their experiences in a united effort for peace with justice and equality. Fellow laureates Leymah Gbowee and Tawakkol Karman joined the initiative in 2012. The Nobel Women's Initiative seeks to use the visibility and prestige of the Nobel Prize to spotlight, amplify, and promote the work of grassroots women's organizations and movements around the world, to achieve nonviolent solutions to war, violence, and militarism.

The Pachamama Alliance
www.pachamama.org

Committed to empowering indigenous people to preserve their territories and way of life and thereby protect the natural world for the entire human family. Strategy includes supplying rainforest people with the tools, information, and resources necessary to support the continued strength and vitality of their communities and culture, and to contribute to the creation of a new global vision, equity, and sustainability for all. Global educational programs include the Awakening the Dreamer Symposium, a transformative educational program that explores the challenges facing humanity and the opportunities to create a new future; and the Game Changer Intensive, a 7-week online course designed to educate, inspire, and equip participants to be proactivist leaders in their community.

Pacific Primary School
www.pacificprimary.org

Founded in 1974 to foster a strong, diverse community; provide tuition assistance; support working parents; and emphasize the creative arts. The curriculum includes learning through hands-on exploration and play, expressive arts, and teacher- and child-inspired work. The staff guides the child's unique social, emotional, and intellectual growth with considerable attention being placed on the child's conflict resolution skills. The child's experience at Pacific Primary is the foundation for a life of learning, caring, and creating.

PeaceJam
www.peacejam.org

A nonprofit organization established in 1996 to connect youth with Nobel Peace Prize laureates. Programs include Compassion in Action, PeaceJam Juniors, PeaceJam Leaders, PeaceJam Ambassadors, Juvenile Justice, and PeaceJam Scholars. PeaceJam currently works with 13 Nobel Peace Prize recipients and in more than 39 countries.

Project Drawdown
www.drawdown.org

Facilitates a coalition of researchers, scientists, graduate students, PhDs, postdocs, policy makers, business leaders, and activists to assemble and present the best available information on climate solutions in order to describe their beneficial financial, social, and environmental impact over the next 30 years. Its main focuses are to reduce greenhouse gas emissions into the atmosphere through efficiency and resource productivity; replace existing energy sources with low carbon renewable energy; and bio-sequester carbon dioxide through innovative farming, grazing, and reforestation practices.

Rachel's Network
www.rachelsnetwork.org

A community of women at the intersection of environmental advocacy, philanthropy, and women's leadership with a mission to promote women as agents of change dedicated to the stewardship of the earth. Rachel's Network meets with cutting-edge thinkers, builds productive alliances, and connects like-minded women to strengthen its leadership and effectiveness. The network takes its name in honor of Rachel Carson, who challenged the long-held belief that humankind's needs justified the destruction of the environment.

Rainforest Action Network (RAN)
www.ran.org

Campaigns for the forests, their inhabitants, and the natural systems that sustain life by transforming the global marketplace through education, grassroots organizing, and nonviolent direct action. RAN's theory of change involves identifying the biggest problems, finding the right targets, and taking action. RAN pioneered the corporate campaigning model and has taken on big-name businesses such as the Home Depot, Citicorp, and Chevron.

Rainforest Connection (RFCx)
www.rfcx.org

Dedicated to safeguarding our planet's rainforests. RFCx repurposes cell phones into listening devices that are placed in rainforests to detect chainsaw activity in real-time; human monitors then transmit alerts. In this way, RFCx protects against illegal logging operations, as nearby agents are notified and dispatched in time to stop the destruction.

Rudolf Steiner Foundation (RSF)
www.rsfsocialfinance.org

A pioneering force in social finance. Founded in 1936, RSF provides socially responsible donors, entrepreneurs, and investors with innovative approaches to lending and donating money in fields such as food and agriculture, education and the arts, and ecological stewardship. RSF is committed to creating financial relationships that are direct, transparent, personal, and focused on long-term social, economic, and ecological benefit. Core offerings include the social investment fund and donor advised fund.

Seva Foundation
www.seva.org

Builds partnerships worldwide to create self-sustaining programs that preserve and restore sight. The Seva Foundation works worldwide to eliminate avoidable blindness through partnering with local hospitals and institutions, and by providing surgery, glasses, and medical treatment.

Shining Hope for Communities (SHOFCO)
www.shofco.org

Combats gender inequality and extreme poverty in urban slums by linking tuition-free schools for girls to accessible social services for all. SHOFCO's free schools become the center of holistic community services. This approach invites both genders to be part of the solution and builds a community invested in its own future. SHOFCO currently focuses its work in Kenya.

SOCAP
www.socialcapitalmarkets.net

A world-renowned conference series dedicated to increasing the flow of capital toward social good. SOCAP's annual flagship event in San Francisco is the leading gathering for impact investors and social entrepreneurs. Since its founding in 2008, SOCAP has brought together more than 12,000 global innovators, investors, foundations, governments, institutions, and social entrepreneurs.

Social Venture Network (SVN)
www.svn.org

Committed to building a just and sustainable world through business. Since 1987 SVN has supported diverse, innovative leaders who leverage business to serve the greater good. Through initiatives, information services, and forums, SVN strengthens community and empowers members to work together on behalf of a shared vision. Its Innovation Entrepreneurs program focuses on identifying women entrepreneurs, young entrepreneurs, and entrepreneurs of color.

The Soul of Money Institute
www.soulofmoney.org

Founded by Lynne Twist and based on the principles shared in this book. The institute's mission is to empower those in the private sector, the social profit sector, and the public benefit sector to be inspired, authentic, and effective in fund-raising, philanthropy, and the financial fulfillment of their vision. Programs and resources include speaking, workshops, consulting, and coaching by Lynne Twist and others. Twist's topics include the Soul of Money, Fundraising from the Heart, enlightened philanthropy, corporate giving programs, the empowerment of women, global citizenship, hunger and poverty, sustainability, indigenous people, youth, and socially responsible business.

Spark
www.sparksf.org

A learning community that educates its peers on issues impacting women around the world and best practices in global philanthropy. Spark engages in a process in which members identify potential issues and grantees, secure monetary and in-kind donations, and evaluate outcomes. Spark aims to increase the overall investment in women's organizations around the world, as well as to increase the number of young people who give to women's causes.

Tipping Point Community
www.tippingpoint.org

Working to break the cycle of poverty in the San Francisco Bay area. Tipping Point screens nonprofits rigorously to find, fund, and partner with the most promising groups working to educate, employ, house, and support those in need. The website contains a complete list of grantees.

Water for People
www.waterforpeople.org

Helping communities break free from the cycle of poverty and spend time growing, learning, and thriving, instead of walking for water and fighting off illness. Water for People has already helped 4 million people and currently works in nine countries: Honduras, Guatemala, Nicaragua, Bolivia, Peru, Malawi, Rwanda, Uganda, and India.

Wisdom 2.0
www.wisdom2conference.com

Focuses on living connected to one another through technology in ways that are beneficial to well-being, effective to work, and useful to the world. Wisdom 2.0 addresses this challenge through its series of conferences, meetups, and workshops. Its flagship event is an annual conference that gathers 2,000 people from all over the world for a series of mainstage sessions, breakout rooms, yoga classes, participant-led hosted conversations, and more.

Women's Capital Collaborative—at RSF Foundation
www.rsfsocialfinance.org/give/give-to-rsf-projects/womens-capital-collaborative

Supports the diverse needs of women-led social enterprises in the United States. Women's Capital Collaborative is the first source of holistic, integrated capital to support women-led organizations with a social mission. Utilizing gift money, Women's Capital Collaborative provides critical capital in the form of loans, grants, and investments to social enterprises.

Women Donors Network
www.womendonors.org

A network of progressive women donors who connect, learn, and take action through grant-making, investing, and advocacy. The network's programs are designed to ignite change, provide donors with opportunities to support progressive movement-building, take action in partnership with allies, and engage in nimble and strategic grant-making. Major programs include an annual conference and an On-the-Hill DC lobby trip, network-wide strategic initiatives, member-led donor circles, and regional events and trainings. Through individual and collective philanthropy, members give away more than $150 million a year.

Women's Earth Alliance
www.womensearthalliance.org

Designs capacity-building trainings where women access skills and tools in appropriate technology, entrepreneurship, and advocacy. The alliance secures seed funding, mentorship, and a global alliance to equip women with the skills and tools they need to protect our earth and strengthen communities from the inside out. With these resources in hand, members go on to launch their own environmental projects and teach others to do the same. More than 5,000 women have accessed these trainings, reaching an additional 750,000 people in 18 countries with their environmental innovations.

Women's Earth and Climate Action Network (WECAN)
www.wecaninternational.org

A climate-justice-based initiative established to unite women worldwide as powerful stakeholders in sustainability solutions, policy advocacy, and worldwide movement building for social and ecological justice. Engages female grassroots activists, indigenous and business leaders, scientists, policy makers, farmers, academics, and culture-shapers with the goal of stopping the escalation of climate change and environmental and community degradation, while accelerating the implementation of just climate solutions. WECAN achieves this mission through women's empowerment; advocacy at international policy forums; trainings; on-the-ground projects; advocacy campaigns; and political, economic, social, and environmental action.

Women's Learning Partnership for Rights, Development, and Peace (WLP)
www.learningpartnership.org

An international nongovernmental organization that works to empower women and girls in the Global South, particularly in Muslim-majority societies, to reimagine and restructure their roles in their families, communities, and societies. WLP uses the programmatic strategies of leadership and advocacy curriculum development; training at the grassroots, national, and regional levels; strengthening civil society; and women's human rights advocacy and movement building. WLP works throughout Africa, the Americas, Asia, and the Middle East.

Women Moving Millions
www.womenmovingmillions.org

A philanthropic community of people committed to large-scale investment in women and girls, with the goal of ending gender inequality. Since its founding in 2007, Women Moving Millions has inspired over 230 members to pledge over $600 million to organizations and initiatives that share its commitment to advancing women and girls around the world. Women Moving Millions also offers a number of programs, including the Circles Program, the Speaker Series, and the Writers Program.

Youth for Environmental Sanity (YES!)
www.yesworld.org

Committed to connecting, inspiring, and collaborating with young and intergenerational changemakers. Focused on restoring balance and sustainability; means-to-end consistency; partnership across historic divides; and international space for the role of love and spirit. YES! brings these core elements into social change movements worldwide by convening transformational gatherings called Jams and building partnerships with diverse social entrepreneurs. YES! was founded in 1990 by Ocean Robbins (then age sixteen) and Ryan Eliason (then age eighteen), and has held more than 100 weeklong gatherings for visionary young leaders from more than 65 nations.

Youth Speaks
www.youthspeaks.org

Through the intersection of arts education and youth development practices, civic engagement strategies, and high-quality artistic presentation, creates safe spaces that challenge young people to find, develop, publicly present, and apply their voices as creators of societal change. Youth Speaks produces local and national youth poetry slams, festivals, and reading series, alongside a comprehensive slate of arts-in-education programs during the school day, after school, and on weekends. In addition, it creates internationally recognized theater and digital programming, and has helped launch a national network of over 70 programs.

Youth Venture
www.youthventure.org

A national organization that helps teams of young people create new ventures (nonprofits, socially oriented businesses, or clubs) to address issues of concern in their communities and the world. The Dream It, Do It Challenge is a program composed of four 6-hour sessions anchored by a set of core activities that support participants in each distinct phase of venture implementation, from the genesis of the original idea to execution to initial financing, and then to implementation. Youth Venture has launched 10,000 youth-led ventures.

BOOKS

Axelrod, Terry. *Raising More Money: A Step-by-Step Guide to Building Lifelong Donors.* To order, go to www.raisingmoremoney.com.

Chopra, Deepak. *Creating Affluence: Wealth Consciousness in the Field of All Possibilities.* Novato, Calif.: New World Library, October 1993.

Cooperrider, David L., Peter F. Sorensen, Jr., Diana Whitney, and Therese F. Yaeger, eds. *Appreciative Inquiry: Rethinking Human Organization Toward a Positive Theory of Change.* Champaign, Ill.: Stipes Publishing, September 1999.

Eisler, Riane. *The Chalice & the Blade: Our History, Our Future.* Harper San Francisco, October 1988.

————. *The Power of Partnership: The Seven Relationships That Will Change Your Life.* Novato, Calif.: New World Library, March 2002.

————. *Tomorrow's Children: A Blueprint for Partnership Education for the 21st Century.* Boulder, Colo.: Westview Press, August 2001.

Gary, Tracy, and Melissa Kohner. *Inspired Philanthropy: Your Step-by-Step Guide to Creating a Giving Plan, 2nd Edition.* San Francisco: Jossey-Bass, August 2002.

Hyde, Lewis. *The Gift: Imagination and the Erotic Life of Property.* New York: Vintage, March 1983.

Inspired Philanthropy: Creating a Giving Plan: A Workbook. San Francisco: (Kim Klein's Chardon Press) Jossey-Bass, September 1998.

Kinder, George. *The Seven Stages of Money Maturity: Understanding the Spirit and Value of Money in Your Life.* New York: Delacorte, April 2000.

Kiyosaki, Robert, and Sharon Lechter. *Rich Dad, Poor Dad: What the Rich Teach Their Kids About Money That the Poor and Middle Class Do Not!* New York: Warner, April 2000.

Lawson, Douglas M. *Give to Live: How Giving Can Change Your Life.* Alti Publishing, September 1991.

Lietaer, Bernard. *Community Currencies: A New Tool for the 21st Century.*

————. *The Future of Money: Beyond Greed and Scarcity.* January 2001.

————, and Richard Douthwaite. *The Ecology of Money.* Resurgence Books, February 2000.

Meadows, Donella. *Global Citizen.* Island Press, May 1991.

————. *Limits to Growth: A Report for the Club of Rome's Project on the Predicament of Mankind.* New American Library, reissue edition, October 1977.

————, et al. *Beyond the Limits: Confronting Global Collapse, Envision-ing a Sustainable Future.* White River Junction, Vt.: Chelsea Green, August 1993.

Needleman, Jacob. *Money and the Meaning of Life.* New York: Dou-bleday, October 1991.

————, and Michael Toms. *Money, Money, Money: The Search for Wealth and the Pursuit of Happiness.* Carlsbad, Calif.: Hay House, June 1998 (book and audiotape).

Nemeth, Maria, Ph.D. *The Energy of Money: A Guide to Financial and Personal Fulfillment.* Ballantine Wellspring, April 2000.

————. *You & Money: A Guide to Personal Integrity and Financial Abundance.* Tzedakah Publications, April 1996.

————. *You and Money: Would It Be All Right with You If Life Got Eas-ier?* Vildehiya, 1997.

O'Neil, Jesse. *The Golden Ghetto: The Psychology of Business.* Center City, Minn.: Hazelden, The Affluenza Project, December 1997.

Orman, Suze. *Courage to Be Rich: Creating a Life of Material and Spir-itual Abundance.* New York: Riverhead (book and audiotape), March 1999.

————. *The 9 Steps to Financial Freedom: Practical and Spiritual Steps So You Can Stop Worrying.* New York: Crown (book and audio-tape), December 2000.

Rich, Harvey L., M.D. *In the Moment: Celebrating the Everyday.* New York: Morrow/HarperCollins, November 2002.

Robin, Vicki, and Joe Dominguez. *Your Money or Your Life: Trans-forming Your Relationship with Money and Achieving Financial Inde-pendence.* New York: Penguin, September 1999.

Rosenberg, Claude. *Wealthy and Wise: How You and America Can Get the Most Out of Your Giving.* Boston: Little, Brown, September 1994.

Sahtouris, Elisabet. *A Walk Through Time: From Stardust to Us: The Evolution of Life on Earth*. Foundation for Global Community, John Wiley & Sons, October 1998.

Shore, William H. *The Cathedral Within: Transforming Your Life by Giving Something Back*. New York: Random House, November 2001.

Traband, Les. *Obtaining Your Financial Black Belt: Power and Control Over Your Money*. Buy Books, 2000.